ENGLAND IN THE AGE OF
AUSTEN

ENGLAND IN THE AGE OF AUSTEN

—ᴟ—

Jeremy Black

INDIANA UNIVERSITY PRESS

This book is a publication of

Indiana University Press
Office of Scholarly Publishing
Herman B Wells Library 350
1320 East 10th Street
Bloomington, Indiana 47405 USA

iupress.org

Manufactured in the United States of America

First printing 2021

Cataloging information is available from the Library of Congress.

ISBN 978-0-253-05192-9 (hardback)
ISBN 978-0-253-05193-6 (paperback)
ISBN 978-0-253-05194-3 (ebook)

For Celia and Ambrose in friendship

CONTENTS

PREFACE

> Only some work in which the greatest powers of
> the mind are displayed, in which the most thorough
> knowledge of human nature, the happiest delineation of
> its varieties, the liveliest effusions of wit and humour are
> conveyed to the world in the best chosen language.
>
> —Jane Austen on novels, *Northanger Abbey*

IT IS A TRUTH UNIVERSALLY acknowledged that Jane Austen ignored the world in which she lived in order to focus on the deeper level of personal relations. Where, after all, are the Industrial Revolution, the American Revolution, the long and difficult wars with France, and the contentious politics of these years, all of which were urgent during her lifetime, 1775–1817, and would have been prominent in the newspapers she and others read? These are not discussed in her works, and references to all except the wars with France are limited.

Less surprisingly, there is no echo of the radicalism reproduced in the film *Peterloo* (2018) reflecting a major episode two years after she died, nor that adopted by the pseudonymous "Vox Populi" in the letter he (presumably) published on January 9, 1779, in the recently launched, Southampton-based *Hampshire*

Chronicle, a newspaper that circulated in the area where Austen lived. This letter proposed to substitute taxes on hunting, hunting horses, coach horses, racehorses, and Jews for those on the necessaries of life, urged a prohibition on the wearing of jewelry, and called both for the abolition of salaries for major posts and for financial contributions from the peerage. That argument was eccentric to the political debate in 1779, but radicalism, in a range of forms, including millenarianism, was far less so from the 1790s.

Yet these exclusions scarcely mean that Austen lived separated from the wider world or that her novels ignore this world. Far from it. Indeed, a host of references, admittedly albeit often brief ones, have been ably elicited in scholarly editions and literature. Austen is only apparently uninterested in the broad sweep of history. In fact, through her novels she gives an unparalleled sense of the flavor of life for people of her class in her time. There is, of course, much in the England of her time that she does not write about, but it is part of the backdrop to her work. Her novels, therefore, serve as a kind of gateway into that England: both the England she writes about and the one she does not write about. This book displays some of the many points at which her novels open up to the history of the time and helps bring Austen's England to life, weaving together incidents and discussions in the novels, aspects of Austen's own life, and events from the lives of some of her contemporaries to illustrate that history. So certain key figures, like George III and Fanny Burney, crop up repeatedly. Rather like Austen's characters, they can provide a focus for the discussion of historical changes and continuities.

Austen's own views on her world are hard to pin down, despite excellent biographies and supplementary scholarship. The detailed evidence for the entire course of her life is sometimes elusive. Although she was far from being a somewhat prebiographical figure, like all too many eighteenth-century individuals, Austen is very much located in her novels, both because they are superb and because she left relatively little evidence of her own views and experiences. Austen was not a Boswell, a Johnson, or a George III, all of whom are far easier to approach. There are no surviving diaries and relatively few surviving letters.

This was not simply because she died at forty-one, but it is also the case of letters per year. In a common pattern for the age, some letters may have been deliberately destroyed. Thus, her sister Cassandra both long survived Austen and, according to a remark by an aged niece of Austen's whose recollections could well be faulty, made an effort to destroy letters written by Austen that she regarded as inappropriate. Presumably these would have been those seen as intimate and/or indiscreet—for example, in discussing health issues. As a result, as with most authors, it is necessary to explain Austen's world without always being able to draw direct connections between it and her opinions or to establish whether those connections are intended as causative or just indicative.

England in Austen's lifetime was certainly a world that was changing. In 1775, the year in which she was born, Britain's most populous colonies in North America began a long fight for independence. Their success by 1783, and the eventual establishment of the United States of America, would totally destroy the unity of the British Empire and assert a set of principles, seen with the Declaration of Independence in 1776, that suggested a radically different political system and culture.

The American Revolution was not the sole evidence of change. The world's first iron bridge, designed in 1775, was erected at Coalbrookdale in Shropshire in 1777–79. It had a 120-foot span and carried the road on arched ribs springing from the bases of two vertical iron uprights. The construction details were worked out by experienced iron founders. Wrought iron had long been a valued decorative material, but replacing charcoal with coke smelting meant that reliable and precise cast iron had become available. So many people came to see Coalbrookdale that a new hotel was built for them.

Heroic paintings were produced in praise of scientific discovery and technological advance—for example, by Joseph Wright of Derby. The side not shown was the hardship and insecurity produced by economic transformation. This came to the fore with violent disturbances in the 1810s, notably by the Luddites, that broadened out from their origins in concerns about labor-saving machinery that contributed to unemployment.

The year after Austen's birth, 1776, saw not only the American Declaration of Independence but also the publication of Adam Smith's *The Wealth of Nations*. This provided the basis for modern economic theory and argued the case for the free trade that was to become the ideology of the nineteenth-century British state and the context for economic transformation. That year also saw the first volumes of Edward Gibbon's *Decline and Fall of the Roman Empire*, finished in 1788, which suggested that progress was possible and that it was not inevitable that a fresh wave of "barbarians" would destroy modern Europe as had occurred in imperial Rome.

However, instead of coming from without, the "barbarians" were to come from within in the shape of the French Revolution. Beginning in 1789, this uprising demonstrated its revolutionary character not only by executing the king in 1793, for England had done likewise in 1649 with Charles I (much to the regret of Austen), but by abandoning Christianity and replacing the Christian calendar. These developments took place in France, which is closer to Hampshire than Highland Scotland, which she also had not visited but mentions in her juvenilia.

Nevertheless, these developments were not the theme and topic of Austen's work, and they did not set its tone. Instead, as she pointed out, she essentially wrote on the women in a small number of country families: "3 or 4 Families in a Country Village," as she told her niece Anna in a letter of September 1814. This was the period when she was writing *Emma*. That novel, in part, deals with the claustrophobia of such a village and the disproportionate significance of new arrivals, whether permanent, such as (through marriage) Augusta Elton, or temporary, as with Frank Churchill. So also with the other novels, bar *Northanger Abbey*, as they are essentially set where their respective heroines live, rather than focusing, as with Catherine Morland in Bath and Northanger Abbey, on a journey of personal discovery that owes much to new societies that are encountered and, crucially, the people in them, and not the places themselves.

Austen's focus on a small number of families offered a reality different from that of England's comprehensive history in the period but still one with multiple aspects and contexts, including those of this history. Moreover, although the contrasts of tone in Austen's novels are understandably not those in England as a whole, there is correspondence at least in antithesis as well as holding together differing tendencies and characters.

That holding together captures Austen's sense of community. This is related to her Anglican piety, which is discussed in chapter 5; her patriotism, notably her naval interests, discussed in chapter 10; and her commitment to the countryside, rather than the town, which is discussed in chapter 2 and chapter 12.

England's communities were far more varied than those discussed by Austen, but in them was, as in her novels, a similarity of tension and combination. Indeed, there was a common structure in the response to the challenges posed by change to customary attitudes. Change combined anxiety with the fluidity produced by money and concern about its ability to rerank society as well as underline existing rankings. The monetary values of matrimonial options presented this element most succinctly and are particularly striking to modern readers. They accorded, however, with the values of the age. Ultimately, Austen's focus on the personalized psychological aspects of this relationship of tension and combination offers something very different to that provided by the historian. However, there is a common grounding in the need to reconcile contrasts in order to provide explanation as well as to give life to a narrative.

At the same time, Austen and, more particularly, her novels and their assemblage of apparently familiar characters become points of reference and departure across a host of genres, some of them surprising. In the film *Pride and Prejudice and Zombies* (2016), the Bennet sisters learn Chinese martial arts in order to fight off zombies while Darcy is the leading zombie hunter.

This book has excited more social interest than anything else I have recently written. Discussing Austen has kept me on my mettle at many tables, notably that in the kitchen at home, but also more widely, which is a testimony to the intellectual vigor as well as social energy of many friends. I thank them here. Jennika Baines has been a most encouraging editor and is always a pleasure to work with. I am most grateful to Leopold Auer, Troy Bickham, Lesley Castens, Jonathan Clark, Eileen Cox, Marjorie Dawson, Grayson Ditchfield, Bill Gibson, Will Hay, John Avery Jones, Augusta Kyte, Penny Pulver, Jane Spencer, and two anonymous readers for commenting on all or part of an earlier draft of this study. I am grateful for advice on particular points from Edward Day, Mike Duffy, Sue Parrill, Bill Robison, Neville Thompson, and Richard Wendorf. They are not responsible for the errors and flaws that doubtless remain. I have benefited from the opportunity to give papers for a University of Virginia Summer School at Oxford and at Millfield School. It is a great pleasure to dedicate this work to Celia and Ambrose Miller, two friends of true charm.

ABBREVIATIONS

Add	Additional Manuscripts
BL	London, British Library

Jane Austen's novels, by year of publication

Sense	*Sense and Sensibility* (1811)
PP	*Pride and Prejudice* (1813)
MP	*Mansfield Park* (1814)
Emma	*Emma* (1815)
Persuasion	*Persuasion* (1817)
Northanger	*Northanger Abbey* (1817)
Sanditon	*Sanditon* (1817)
Susan	*Lady Susan* (1871)
Later Manuscripts	The 2008 Cambridge edition is employed here
Juvenilia	The 2006 Cambridge edition is employed here
Letters	Deirdre Le Faye, ed., *Jane Austen's Letters* (3rd ed., 1995)

All books are published in London, unless otherwise stated.

Northanger II, 6 means *Northanger Abbey,* volume two, chapter six. For *Sanditon* there are only chapters, while *Lady Susan* is a sequence of letters.

ENGLAND IN THE AGE OF
AUSTEN

ONE

THE RISE OF THE NOVEL

Though totally without accomplishment,
she is by no means as ignorant as one might expect
to find her, being fond of books and spending
the chief of her time in reading.

—Description of eighteen-year-old Frederica, *Lady Susan*

"OUR FAMILY, WHO ARE GREAT novel-readers and not ashamed of being so." Writing in December 1798, Austen was in no doubt of her knowledge of the genre. She read, and reread, novels with great attention, and her own novels appeared against the background of the development of the form—notably so in the late eighteenth century. Moreover, the names of her characters sometimes reflected her detailed knowledge of novels, as with *Catherine*, which, when she revised it in 1809, has a reference to Hannah More's novel *Coelebs in Search of a Wife* (1808).[1] Austen's active rereading and copious memory combined with her undoubted pleasure in making such references.[2]

Austen's love of novels is shown not only in her reading of them but also in her fondness for burlesque works. In addition to her own, notably in her juvenilia and also brilliantly in *Northanger Abbey*, came her delight in such novels by others. Thus, in March

1814, she recorded her pleasure with Eaton Stannard Barrett's *The Heroine*. Her relationship with the novel genre was not only with the burlesque. Austen also wrote in response to the conventions she discerned, resisting both hidden biases and more overt assumptions. In doing so, she often deployed her characters, as they could be limited by these very conventions in their perception of reality, as with Emma, Harriet Smith, and Catherine Morland. Thus, a reading of novels could lead to a failure to understand people, as some of the characters in Austen's novels revealed, but crucially not the novels themselves. Instead, the ability of her novels to deal with this failure was an aspect of their very success, both in characterization and in narrative. Reading Austen's novels revealed the failings of other readers in the person of some of her characters.

Austen's novels are understandably widely seen as the apogee of a tradition of novel writing, one that, in turn, was to be superseded first by the greater personal emotional engagement of romanticism and, subsequently, by a different tradition of social realism in the novels that followed during the nineteenth century. Responding to those novels that came before, Austen and her readers were guided by the standard themes of the genre. Within that context, she offered the emotional engagement and social realism that appeared reasonable.

Far from conforming to a common tone, form, or intention, novels in her lifetime varied greatly in content and approach, a trend encouraged by the size and diversity of the reading public, as well as by the absence of anything as tidy as the smooth development of the literary review genre.[3] There has since been a multiplicity of theoretical reflections on the rise of the novel both before and during her life.[4] Initially, this rise was discussed in terms of the works of Daniel Defoe, Samuel Richardson, and Henry Fielding, but this focus neglected what was a far greater range of early novels, many written by women, and, in doing so, misleadingly simplified the origins of the genre. Although English writers played the key role in its eighteenth-century development, there were important seventeenth-century precursors—including, in Spain, Miguel de Cervantes's *Don Quixote* (1605–15)—and, indeed, a range of literary types the novel looked to, notably picaresque tales, travel books, and romances.

Romances were particularly important in England in the early eighteenth century, and a novel of that time could be a short story of romantic love—for example, Eliza Haywood's successful *Love in Excess* (1719–20). A common feature of the early novels of these decades was their claim to realism. Indeed, Austen noted in *Northanger Abbey* that novels offered "knowledge of human nature."[5]

This commitment to realism can be seen in Daniel Defoe's *Robinson Crusoe* (1719), *Colonel Jack* (1721), *Moll Flanders* (1722), *A Journal of the Plague Year* (1722), and *Roxana* (1724). Their subjects were very different, and they looked back to varied influences—*Robinson Crusoe* to travel literature and spiritual autobiography and *Colonel Jack, Moll Flanders,* and *Roxana* to picaresque tales—but the common theme in these alleged autobiographies was authenticity, and they had affinities with criminal biographies, a very popular genre. The romantic tales, such as those of Haywood, also claimed to be accounts of real life and manners, while the most distinctive novelistic account, Jonathan Swift's *Gulliver's Travels* (1726), was presented as a true account and was believed to be so by some readers. When she visited Lyme Regis in 1804, Austen lent a manservant a copy of *Robinson Crusoe*.

Swift's combination of traveler's tale, picaresque novella, and satire in *Gulliver's Travels* proved inimitable. Samuel Richardson's first novel, *Pamela* (1740), was somewhat different. A very popular book on the prudence of virtue and the virtue of prudence, the title continued: *or Virtue Rewarded.* The appeal of this novel reflected in part its ability to span sustained sexual frisson with clear morality, to move from page-turning sexual perils for

Pamela to a happy ending, and to employ the form of letters in order to provide the direct and sympathetic insight of the heroine and focus the readers' attention on her. Pamela, a young maidservant, resists the lascivious advances of Mr. B, in part thwarting attempted rapes by fainting at opportune moments. In the end, a realization and appreciation of Pamela's virtues leads him to propose marriage, thus fulfilling the fantasy of social aspiration: Pamela marries her employer, although many of the revisions to *Pamela* sought to make the servant more of a lady and thus the work less radical. The importance of writings to the structure and form of *Pamela* was seen not only with the letters but also because the theft of Pamela's journal leads Mr. B to this appreciation.

Pamela's content and success invited well-deserved skits and parody, especially Henry Fielding's satirical *An Apology for the Life of Mrs Shamela Andrews* (1741) and his *Joseph Andrews* (1742), which sold 6,500 copies that year, as well as James Dance's comedy *Pamela* (1742). John Cleland employed the epistolary style of *Pamela* in his pornographic novel *Memoirs of a Woman of Pleasure* (1749), otherwise known as *Fanny Hill*. There is an epistolary character to Austen's novels, as in *Pride and Prejudice* in the very long letter Darcy hands to Elizabeth, the letters from Mr. Collins, and the letters that bring news of Lydia's elopement with Wickham and the subsequent trajectory of events.[6] This epistolary character is an accurate reflection of the role of correspondence in personal relations in this period. A stray recollection by Cassandra Austen and much critical conjecture leads to the conclusion that *Sense and Sensibility* may have been composed in letter form first, as possibly was *Pride and Prejudice*. The unfinished *Lady Susan* survives in this form. Other novelists, both male and female, also used the epistolary form, as with Sir Walter Scott in the early sections of *Redgauntlet* (1824).

The novels of the 1740s displayed considerable diversity in content. A common theme, however, was psychological accuracy, appropriately so given the influence of Lockean philosophy and its reading of the molding by, and of, experience.[7] Richardson's narratives were composed of letters, which allowed him to vary the tone by using different styles for his writers and helped give *Pamela* an impetus and an urgency matching the plot of virtue vying with seduction. Fielding insisted that his novels were "true histories" in that they revealed the truth of behavior. This approach was especially suited to the ironic voice he successfully adopted as narrator, comparable to that in his plays, such as *Tom Thumb* (1730), and in his journalism. Thus, in the last chapter of *Joseph Andrews*, "this true history is brought to a happy conclusion." History indeed frequently appeared in the title of novels, as in James Ridley's *The History of James Lovegrove, Esquire* (1761).

In novels there was an emphasis on individual free will, and hence moral responsibility, rather than determinism. In short, novels offered a world that was best understood in moral terms and where there was no sense of changing moral standards or even moral relativism. Austen herself particularly liked Richardson's novel *The History of Sir Charles Grandison* (1753–54), which she frequently reread, as does Mrs. Morland in *Northanger Abbey*. At the same time, the "heroism of sentiment" to which Austen refers entailed implausible self-sacrifice.[8] As such, it was a counterpoint, in a very different context, to religious tales.

The different methods, styles, and tone of Richardson and Fielding, all of which influenced Austen, helped energize novel-writing as they encouraged debate as to best practice, while both had their imitators. There were similarities with landscape gardening, on which see chapter 2. With his emphasis on the female plight and perspective, and his stress on appropriate gentlemanly behavior, Richardson looked ahead to the sentimental novel. The novel as the true depiction of life was taken a stage further in Laurence Sterne's very popular *The Life and Opinions of Tristram Shandy, Gentleman* (1760–67). As the first-person narrator, he presented the confusion of perception in a fashion that extended to the appearance of the book. Volume 9, chapter 25 of this is as follows:

> When we have got to the end of this chapter (but not before) we must all turn back to the two blank chapters, on the account of which my honour has lain bleeding this half hour—I stop it, by pulling off one of my yellow slippers and throwing it with all my violence to the opposite side of my room, with a declaration at the heel of it—
>
> That whatever resemblance it may bear to half the chapters which are written in the world, or for aught I know may be now writing in it—that it was as casual as the foam of Zeuxis his horse: besides, I look upon a chapter which has, *only nothing in it*, with respect; and considering what worse things there are in the world—That it is no way a proper substitute for satire.
>
> —Why then was it left so? And here without staying for my reply, shall I be called as many blockheads, numskulls, doddypoles, dunderheads, ninnyhammers, goosecaps, jolt-heads, nincom-poops, sh-t-a-beds—and other unsavoury appellations, as ever the cake-bakers of Lerné, cast in the teeth of King Gargantua's shepherds—And I'll let them do it, as Bridget said, as much as they please; for how was it possible they should foresee the necessity I was under of writing the 25th chapter of my book, before the 18th, etc?
>
> —So I don't take it amiss—All I wish is, that it may be a lesson to the world *to let people tell their stories their own way.*

The freedom of writing in this novel was arresting, but so was another source of uncertainty: the abandonment of the omni-scient narrator with panoptic vision, apparently able to manipu-late events and characters as he or she chose. Instead, in *Tristram Shandy*, Sterne presents the story as if the novelist has only an uncertain grip on events, characters, and, indeed, perception. Clearly delineated episodes are tossed hither and thither in a sea of whimsical chaos. The Yorick sermons consciously added to the identity confusion of the novel. Sterne's arresting approach was much imitated, at least up to the 1790s.

Austen drew on the method of speaking to the readers that was successfully seen with Fielding and Sterne. Thus, in *Northanger*

Abbey, as she wraps the story up, she explains the reasons for General Tilney's hostility to Catherine Morland, ending that passage: "I leave it to my reader's sagacity to determine how much of all this it was possible for Henry to communicate at this time to Catherine, how much of it he could have learnt from his father, in what points his own conjectures might assist him, and what portion must yet remain to be told in a letter from James. I have united for their ease what they must divide for mine."[9] This style was similar to that of Fielding. Subsequently, in the rush to the end that is characteristic of Austen's novels, attention is drawn to the physical nature of that particular novel and, with it, of all novels: "The anxiety, which in this state of attachment must be the portion of Henry and Catherine, and of all who loved either, as to its final event, can hardly extend, I fear, to the bosom of my readers, who will see in the tell-tale compression of the pages before them, that we are all hastening together to perfect felicity."[10] Novelists were fully self-aware. Austen commented on the style and content in her own work, as at the close of *Sense and Sensibility*.

Northanger Abbey also provides an amusing sense of confusion due to the variety of perspectives offered, notably those of Catherine Morland, Henry Tilney, and the narrator; indeed, Catherine is unreliable on the significance of what she sees and how it relates to her more lurid imagination, one greatly fed by gothic novels.

Tristram Shandy contained sentimental scenes, but the sentimental novel was a more fully fledged type. It was particularly influential in the 1760s and 1770s only to reach an impasse in the 1780s and be assailed in the 1790s by different voices, tones, and subjects.[11] Sentimental novels, and the sensibility they reflected, on which Austen was raised as a young woman, were far more than simply literary themes and tropes or, indeed, related guides to the development of acceptable polite behavior and its link to emotionalism and, separately, to romance, both false and true. There was also an interest in emotion as the basis for a community of feeling, with shared experiences created in terms of a "sympathy" that was not limited to the individual who expressed it.[12] This last was a characteristic of writers as well as of their characters.

Female novelists were very important in the development of the genre, which itself engaged at length with the issues and perspectives of women and therefore on the female parts of social relationships. The gender dimension is clear. Sentimental novels were especially designed for women, as was noted in an advertisement in the April 25, 1776, issue of *Swinney's Birmingham and Stafford Chronicle* for *Isabella: or The Rewards of Good-Nature. A Sentimental Novel.* Intended in part to convey acceptable sentiments in a narrative format, these novels provided amusements and instruction to the fair sex but also left the depiction of men problematic unless in response to the female sentiment on offer. Love intrigues played a major, but also exhortatory, role in sentimental novels such as Frances Brooke's *The History of Emily Montague* (1769). Her use of the term *history*, which to contemporaries meant narrative, seen also in her *The History of Julia Mandeville* (1763), remained typical in the presentation of the genre, while Brooke looked back in adopting the epistolary style and forward in focusing on the possibilities women faced and in setting a novel in Canada.[13]

Sentimentality and history joined novels to another important, but underrated, art form of the period: gossip. Indeed, especially with the epistolary novels, there was a note of appropriate, if not exemplary, gossip in their themes and tone. History, novels, and gossip all offered accounts of individuals and thus focused on how best to understand and represent individuality, not least with reference to social norms.[14] Circumstances were part of the interplay, and they provided an opportunity for both individuality and social norms. Gossip was also internalized in the plot and revelations of motivation in Austen's novels, as is repeatedly the case in *Emma*.

Sentimental novels required a commitment from narrator and reader that was very different in tone and consequences from the ironic authorial distancing of Fielding or the undercutting shifting of perspective of Smollett. At the same time, located by their genre, such novels were easy to understand, not least as plot-driven entertainments with clear moral guidelines. Genre helped encourage the mimicry of successful novels.[15] A misunderstanding overcome was a frequent theme in sentimental novels, which rested on a certainty that true value existed and that a combination of emotion and reason would reveal it. Sudden, much-merited fortune was the result for those characters who responded well.

Austen's work drew on this practice, but also played with it. In a work better known for its humor at the expense of the gothic novel, Austen's overt undermining of the conventions of sentimental novels was seen with Catherine Morland's return home from Northanger Abbey:

> A heroine returning, at the close of her career, to her native village, in all the triumph of recovered reputation, and all the dignity of a countess, with a long train of noble relations in their several phaetons, and three waiting-maids in a travelling chaise and four, behind her, is an event on which the pen of the contriver may well delight to dwell; it gives credit to every conclusion, and the author must share in the glory she so liberally bestows.—but my affair is widely different; I bring back my heroine to her home in solitude and disgrace; and no sweet elation of spirits can lead me into minuteness. A heroine in a hack post-chaise is such a blow upon sentiment, as no attempt at grandeur or pathos can withstand. . . .
>
> But, whatever might be the distress of Catherine's mind, as she thus advanced towards the Parsonage, and whatever the humiliation of her biographer in relating it, she was preparing enjoyment of no every-day nature to those to whom she went.[16]

The confidence of the sentimental novel contrasted with what has been discerned in some of the literature of the period as a less certain self. A form of uncertainty influenced some of the writing about experience,[17] but a certainty of values was more often apparent.

Many, including King George III, Samuel Johnson, and Charles, First Earl of Liverpool, were unenthusiastic about novels, although Richardson could be admired as he offered an exemplary morality. Both George III and Johnson preferred religious works to novels and were wary of the different emotions aroused by fiction. George III favored works on theology, history, jurisprudence, science, the arts, and the classical inheritance.[18] He did not really take to novels until he became blind, when one of his daughters read them to him nightly.[19]

By the end of the eighteenth century, alongside the large number of novels then rejected, including Austen's "First Impressions" (later *Pride and Prejudice*) in 1797, about 150 novels, 90 of them new, were being published annually, and a large proportion appeared in serial form. Indeed, in his piece on "Modern Novels" in the *Annual Register* of 1797, George Colman the Younger referred to the "small fry of scribblers" wriggling "through the mud in shoals" (vol. 39, 448). Many of the novels themselves were multivolume: Jenny Warton's *Peggy and Patty: or The Sisters of Ashdale* offered four volumes of sentimentality.

The extent of the market was indicated by the frequency with which the financially embarrassed Charlotte Smith published novels. Having translated Prévost's *Manon Lescaut* (1785), from 1788 she published a series of sentimental novels reflecting the love of nature. The success of her first, the four-volume *Emmeline: or The Orphan of the Castle* (1788), led her to write the five-volume *Ethelinde: or The Recluse of the Lake* (1790), the four-volume *Celestina* (1792), the three-volume *Desmond* (1793), the four-volume *Old Manor House* (1793), and the four-volume *The Banished Man* (1794). Her other novels included *The Young Philosopher* (1798) and *The Solitary Wanderer* (1799): the former contained, among its notes of pathos, scenes of losing a daughter in London and losing another to madness, the latter a frequent theme of such novels.

Women were crucial to the advance of the novel as writers, readers, and subjects.[20] Women engaged as writers because of the inherent interest of the task and the possibility of earning money, as Austen eventually did, but also due to the closure of the public sphere, which ensured that energy and attention were devoted to the personal world. In *Persuasion*, Anne Elliot rebuts Captain Harville's criticism of women's fickleness in novels, poetry, songs, and proverbs on the grounds that they were written by men: "If you please, no reference to examples in books. Men have had every advantage of us in telling their own story. Education has been theirs in so much higher a degree; the pen has been in their hands. I will not allow books to prove any thing."[21]

Many of the topics tackled by novels were inherently political in the broadest sense; notably, those that dealt with courtship and family life brought up issues of obedience, identity, and self-protection, the first of which were frequently patriarchal issues. Indeed, as a result of such considerations, novels very much addressed particular circumstances, both those of the sociohistorical moment and the specific experience of the authors.[22] Thus, Mary Hays (1759–1843) made use of her own experiences, notoriously so in her *Memoirs of Emma Courtney* (1796), a novel in which she drew on her love letters in an unsuccessful romance and her offer to live together without marriage.

Novelists could employ language to challenge conventional plot assumptions. This is in part political, but a key element is also comic. From the outset of her writings, there is a comic element in Austen's work. While parody, its major form in her early writings, can sometimes be political, it is essentially comic. This is an aspect of Austen's personality also highlighted in the correspondence. As with other writers—for example, Fanny Burney and Emily Brontë—there was a contrast between her novels and her private writings,[23] a contrast that throws light on cultural and social norms and therefore on the conformity that was involved.

Johnson claimed over dinner on April 29, 1778, that "all our ladies read now,"[24] although, in *Sense and Sensibility*, Lady Middleton's dislike of Elinor and Marianne Dashwood in part comes because "they were fond of reading."[25] In *Pride and Prejudice*, Mary Bennet asked Mr. Bingley for the use of the library at Netherfield,[26] the form of sociability with which she was most comfortable. Reading linked the home to public places. In the home, the idea and language of taste left much space for women, including for their reading.[27] This home environment drew on a public sphere in which women readers favored subscription and circulating libraries. These libraries tended to form a readership that responded to books as instances of genres rather than as necessarily distinct texts. Austen herself subscribed to a library in Basingstoke in 1798. The scale of such institutions could be considerable. Liverpool Library, a subscription library whose members owned shares, had over four hundred members by 1799, and between 1758 and 1800, the library acquired an average of almost two hundred books annually. A subscription library was established in Portsmouth in 1805, and the fictional Fanny Price became a subscriber to pursue "the biography and poetry which she delighted in."[28] There were one thousand circulating libraries by the end of the century, including nine in Bath and others in the coastal resorts of Sidmouth, Dawlish, Exmouth, and Teignmouth.[29]

Female writers were dependent on female readers as a reliable market for their writing, and women could be important in subscription lists. At the same time, Austen presents many male readers, including John Thorpe and Henry Tilney in *Northanger Abbey* and Captain Benwick in *Persuasion*, the last a keen reader of poetry, including Byron and Scott. Indeed, news of his engagement to Louisa Musgrove leads to the assumption that she would learn to be an enthusiast of both.[30] In *Pride and Prejudice*, two of the officers often go to the local library,[31] and in *Love and Freindship*, when Edward Lindsay is upbraided by his father for refusing to marry in accordance with his wishes, the father says: "Where Edward in the name of wonder did you pick up this unmeaning gibberish? You have been studying novels I suspect." In contrast,

Charles Musgrove is "without benefit from books," and Mr. Rushworth is "ignorant . . . in books."[32]

In *Sanditon*, Sir Edward Denham, an unattractive character,
had "read more sentimental novels than agreed with him."[33] He
is critical of many novels and uses that as a way to praise himself:

> The mere trash of the common circulating library, I hold in the high-
> est contempt. You will never hear me advocating those puerile ema-
> nations which detail nothing but discordant principles incapable of
> amalgamation, or those vapid tissues of ordinary occurrences from
> which no useful deductions can be drawn. . . . The novels which I
> approve are such as display human nature with grandeur—such as
> show her in the sublimities of intense feeling—such as exhibit the
> progress of strong passion from the first germ of incipient suscepti-
> bility to the utmost energies of reason half-dethroned—where we
> see the strong spark of woman's captivations elicit such fire in the
> soul of man as leads him—(though at the risk of some aberration
> from the strict line of primitive obligations)—to hazard all, dare all,
> achieve all, to obtain her. . . . They hold forth the most splendid por-
> traitures of high conceptions, unbounded views, illimitable ardour,
> indomitable decision . . . the potent, pervading here of the story . . .
> our hearts are paralyzed. . . . These are the novels which enlarge the
> primitive capabilities of the heart.[34]

A far more meritorious course of reading, one in which judgment is encouraged, is suggested by what Edmund Bertram offers
Fanny Price in *Mansfield Park*, and this also provides an opportunity to appreciate Austen's views: "He knew her to be clever, to
have a quick apprehension as well as good sense, and a fondness
for reading, which properly directed, must be an education in
itself . . . he recommended the books which charmed her leisure
hours, he encouraged her taste, and corrected her judgment;
he made reading useful by talking to her of what she read, and
heightened its attraction by judicious praise."[35] As such, Fanny
is able to choose books from the library.[36] The pictorial appeal
of reading was seen in Sanditon village, where "two females
in elegant white were actually to be seen with their books and

campstools." The resort has a library.[37] In *Sense and Sensibility*, Marianne Dashwood has "the knack of finding her way in every house to the library" and, when depressed and back at home, proposes to "divide every moment between music and reading. . . . Our own library is too well known to me. . . . But there are many works well worth reading at the Park. . . . By reading only six hours a day, I shall gain in the course of a twelvemonth a great deal of instruction."[38]

The image of libraries dominated by the works of women for female readers increased. So did the presentation of the female reader as an icon. Elizabeth Bennet prefers reading to cards,[39] as does Darcy. Cards are inherently about conversation, while reading is private. Describing truly accomplished women, Darcy adds to the usual list that "she must yet add something more substantial, in the improvement of her mind by extensive reading."[40] So with Charlotte Heywood in *Sanditon*, who enjoyed reading novels but is not misled by them.[41]

Austen criticizes young women who do not read, as in *Catherine, or the Bower* (1792), in the character of Camilla Stanley, the daughter of a wealthy MP: "Those years which ought to have been spent in the attainment of useful knowledge and Mental Improvement, had been all bestowed in learning Drawing, Italian and Music, more especially the latter, and she now united to these Accomplishments, an Understanding unimproved by reading and a Mind totally devoid either of taste or judgment. . . . She professed a love of Books without Reading."[42]

Kitty discusses books with Camilla. Although Kitty "was well read in modern history" herself, and able to debate Richard III with Edward Spencer (as Austen would have been with anyone), she chose rather to speak first of books of a lighter kind, of books universally read and admired, and begins with Charlotte Smith's novels, with which Austen was familiar. Austen has Camilla and Kitty discuss whether the five-volume *Ethelinde: or the Recluse of the Lake* (1789) is too long.[43] Camilla, in contrast, cannot discuss politics and is ignorant of geography, but she is proud of her family and her connections and thereby is condescending and heartless to Kitty.[44]

Women's reading appears to have troubled some male commentators. Female novel reading certainly provided female writers a way to address their anxieties about literary authority and a means to establish their rights to such authority.[45] In her preface to *Evelina*, Burney commented: "Perhaps were it possible to effect the total extirpation of novels, our young ladies in general, and boarding-school damsels in particular, might profit from their annihilation: but since the distemper they have spread seems incurable, since their contagion bids defiance to the medicine of advice or reprehension . . . all attempts to contribute to the number of those which may be read . . . without injury, ought to be encouraged."

The gender dimension is to the fore when judging a book from the outside: "For every thing announced it to be from a circulating library," Mr. Collins "protested that he never read novels." This response led to surprise from Kitty and Lydia Bennet.[46] However, Collins's response matched his reading aloud from James Fordyce's frequently reprinted *Sermons to Young Women* (1766), which was very critical of novels.

In practice, Austen was not the only novelist in her family or, indeed, the only novelist with a close connection to the clergy. Cassandra Cooke, who was the first cousin of Austen's mother; the wife of Austen's godfather, the Reverend Samuel Cooke; and Austen's hostess on several occasions at Great Bookham, Surrey, wrote one novel, *Battleridge: an Historical Tale, Founded on Facts. In Two Volumes, by a Lady of Quality* (1799). In fact, 48 of the 1,058 subscribers to Fanny Burney's *Camilla* (1796) were members of the clergy.[47]

Nevertheless, Mr. Collins was not alone in his doubts. Imaginative literature was regarded as potentially exacerbating the female imagination. Fiction and philosophy especially were often banned for women and girls. Women were thought especially vulnerable to new philosophical ideas. The danger of women reading radical texts was repeatedly imagined in fictional works, such as novels, in terms of sexual transgression leading to illness, breakdown, and death. This convention is mocked in Sheridan's play *The Rivals*, in which Lydia, fearful of being found out, urges the hiding of such works, including Smollett's novels.

Austen offers a very different criticism of novels as implausible and therefore misleading. This is to the fore in the account of romance. Austen's criticism was shared by other writers—for example, by Maria Edgeworth in her novel *Belinda* (1801), a work that indicates the moral and social utility of the novel as well as the misleading character of most novels. Indeed, *Belinda* satirically cuts the gothic novel as well as its romantic counterpart.[48]

Despite, and at times because of, the varied strictures offered, many women enjoyed reading and explicitly commented on its pleasurableness. This reading was far from confined to novels. According to Edward Gibbon, the first volume of his *Decline and Fall*, which was published in 1776, was read by "fine-feathered ladies." Among other issues, reading permitted critical engagement with concerns over authority, which was seen with both novels and history, although that engagement could accentuate the anxiety provoked by reading. Sentiment could combine with a critical approach to social practices in Austen's work, as when Fanny Price rejects Henry Crawford, trusting that she has done right and hoping that her uncle's displeasure would abate "as he considered the matter with more impartiality, and felt, as a good man must feel, how wretched, and how unpardonable, how hopeless and how wicked it was, to marry without affection."[49] By looking at how others constructed an account of the self,[50] it was possible to offer one's own and, therefore, develop individuality—for character, writer, and reader. At the same time, the situation was made more complex, as in Austen's work, by the self being handled, as it were, from outside, an approach that offered the prospect of an ironic stance by author, readers, and other characters in the novel. Austen manages to combine the internal and external presentations of character. Thus, in a fashion at once instructive and skillful, we understand events from Emma's point of view but, at the same time, are guided to be critical of her perspective.[51]

Austen's authorial perspective was significant in her comments on the substance and style of other novels. Thus, one way for her to handle the close of *Northanger Abbey*, and to guide reader expectations, was to comment on the contrast between the romance of Catherine Morland and Henry Tilney and the clichés of sentimental novels: "I must confess that his affection originated in nothing better than gratitude, or, in other words, that a persuasion of her partiality for him had been the only cause of giving her a serious thought. It is a new circumstance in romance, I acknowledge, and dreadfully derogatory of an heroine's dignity; but if it be as new in common life, the credit of a wild imagination will at least be all my own."[52] She concluded that novel with a question, inviting the reader to determine "whether the tendency of this work be altogether to recommend paternal tyranny, or reward filial disobedience."[53]

So also with the last stages of *Sense and Sensibility*. There is a droll placement of the characters that cuts across cliché and undermines pretension. Marianne Dashwood, "instead of falling a sacrifice to an irresistible passion," in the shape of Willoughby, finds love "in time" with Colonel Brandon, whom "she had considered too old to be married,—and who still sought the constitutional safe-guard of a flannel waistcoat!" As for Willoughby: "That he was for ever inconsolable, that he fled from society, or contracted an habitual gloom of temper, or died of a broken heart, must not be depended on—for he did neither. He lived to exert, and frequently to enjoy himself. His wife was not always out of humour, nor his home always uncomfortable."[54] There is also an undercutting of social language. Thus, in Austen's description of

Robert and Lucy Ferrars, they "were on the best terms imaginable with the Dashwoods; and setting aside the jealousies and ill-will continually subsisting between Fanny and Lucy, in which their husbands of course took a part, as well as the frequent domestic disagreements between Robert and Lucy themselves, nothing could exceed the harmony in which they all lived together."[55]

The contrast with reality comes at the very close of the book. In place of the poor relationship of the Ferrars, with the nasty mother, the selfish daughter, and the son Robert, who was "proud of tricking Edward," came "strong family affection . . . among the merits of Elinor and Marianne, let it not be ranked as the least considerable, that though sisters, and living almost within sight of each other, they could live without disagreement between themselves, or producing coolness between their husbands."[56] The ironic tone of the word *though* sits alongside the clear advocacy of sisterly harmony. The latter looks to Austen's own family experience and is a theme in her novels.

NOTES

1. S. Derry, "Jane Austen's Reference to Hannah More in *Catherine*," *Notes and Queries* 235, no. 1 (March 1990): 20.

2. J. Harris, *Jane Austen's Art of Memory* (Cambridge, 1990).

3. P. Gael, "The Origins of the Book Review in England, 1663–1749," *Library*, 7th ser., 13 (2012): 84.

4. M. McKeon, ed., *The Theory of the Novel: A Historical Approach* (Baltimore, MD, 2000).

5. *Northanger* I, 5.

6. *PP* II, 12; III, 4, 5, 6, 8, 10.

7. E. Tavor, *Scepticism, Society and the Eighteenth-Century Novel* (New York, 1987).

8. *Emma* III, 13.

9. *Northanger* II, 15.

10. *Northanger* II, 16.

11. J. Todd, *Sensibility: An Introduction* (London, 1986).

12. A. Pinch, *Strange Fits of Passion: Epistemologies of Emotion, Hume to Austen* (Stanford, CA, 1996).

13. L. McMullen, *An Odd Attempt in a Woman: The Literary Life of Frances Brooke* (Vancouver, Canada, 1983).

14. J. Richetti, *The English Novel in History, 1700–1780* (London, 1998).

15. W. L. Oakley, *A Culture of Mimicry: Laurence Sterne, His Readers and the Art of Bodysnatching* (London, 2010).

16. *Northanger* II, 14.

17. F. V. Bogel, *Literature and Insubstantiality in Later Eighteenth-Century England* (Princeton, NJ, 1984).

18. J. Boswell, *Life of Johnson* (Oxford, 1980), 157.

19. F. Bickley, ed., *The Diaries of Sylvester Douglas, Lord Glenbervie* (London, 1928), 2:76.

20. E. J. Clery, *The Feminisation Debate in Eighteenth-Century England: Literature, Commerce and Luxury* (Basingstoke, UK, 2004).

21. *Persuasion* II, 11.

22. J. Spencer, *The Rise of the Woman Novelist: From Aphra Behn to Jane Austen* (Oxford, 1986).

23. J. Simons, *Fanny Burney* (Totowa, NJ, 1987).

24. James Boswell, *Dr. Johnson's Table-talk: Containing Aphorisms on Literature*, 2 vols. (London, 1807), 2:199.

25. *Sense* II, 14.

26. *PP* III, 13.

27. A. Vickery, *Behind Closed Doors: At Home in Georgian England* (New Haven, CT, 2009).

28. *MP* III, 9.

29. H. M. Hamlyn, "Eighteenth-Century Circulating Libraries in England," *Library*, 5th ser., 1 (1947): 197–222; P. Kaufman, "The Community Library: A Chapter in English Social History," *Transactions of the American Philosophical Society*, n.s., 57, no. 7 (October 1967): 1–67; V. Berch, "Notes on Some Unrecorded Circulating Libraries of Eighteenth Century London," *Factotum* 6 (October 1979): 15–19.

30. *Persuasion* I, 11; II, 180.

31. *PP* I, 7.

32. *Juvenilia*, 108; *Persuasion* I, 6; *MP* II, 3.

33. *Sanditon* 8.

34. *Sanditon* 8.

35. *MP* I, 2.

36. *MP* I, 3.

37. *Sanditon* 4, 6.

38. *Sense* III, 6, 10.

39. *PP* I, 8.

40. *PP* I, 8.

41. *Sanditon* 6.

42. *Juvenilia*, 248.

43. *Juvenilia*, 249, 286.

44. *Juvenilia*, 252, 278.

45. J. Pearson, *Women's Reading in Britain, 1750–1835: A Dangerous Recreation* (Cambridge, 1999).

46. *PP* I, 14.

47. Spencer, *The Rise of the Woman Novelist*; C. Turner, *Living by the Pen: Women Writers in the 18th Century* (London, 1992); J. Batchelor, *Women's Work: Labour, Gender, Authorship, 1750–1830* (Manchester, UK, 2010).

48. D. Thame, "Madness and Therapy in Maria Edgeworth's *Belinda*: Deceived by Appearances," *British Journal for Eighteenth-Century Studies* 26 (2003): 271–88.

49. *MP* III, 1.

50. J. Baker, M. Leclair, and A. Ingram, eds., *Writing and Constructing the Self in Great Britain in the Long Eighteenth Century* (Manchester, UK, 2018).

51. M. Mudrick, *Jane Austen: Irony as Defense and Discovery* (Princeton, NJ, 1952).

52. *Northanger* II, 15.

53. *Northanger* II, 16.

54. *Sense* III, 14.

55. *Sense* III, 14.

56. *Sense* III, 14.

TWO

RURAL ENGLAND

The Epicenter of Austen's World

Several respectable correspondents have favoured us with
answers to the enquiry in our last by R.P. respecting the
most effectual cure for the bite of this noxious animal
[the viper], all of which concur in recommending the
oil of olives, or common salad oil, warmed and rubbed
into the wound, as infallible. The fat of vipers, extracted
by frying it, is also said to be a cure equally certain.

—*Salisbury and Winchester Journal,* January 5, 1789

RURAL ENGLAND WAS THE EPICENTER of Austen's
world—both the life she experienced and the lives she portrayed.[1] This landscape was worked for agricultural purposes,
and the cultivation of centuries had molded the landscape and
been molded by it. Set in this landscape, the society of rural
England, the structure, norms, and practices she knew, was what
she presented. The aspirations of her characters were rural. This
contributes to her current appeal as there is a degree of nostalgia today for the ruralism depicted and its apparent values and
pace of life. Indeed, that nostalgia and ruralism link the representation of the early nineteenth century to that of more recent
decades.

Austen's rural society, however, was defined by a demographic structure very different from those of today. Indeed, Austen, who died at the age of forty-one, very much experienced the harsh population statistics of the past, although they play an indirect rather than a major role in her writing. Many characters die, but these deaths happen off narrative in the sense of the attention of author and reader. Deathbed scenes are not to the fore. Instead, the deaths are instrumental to the plot.

Austen's death, possibly of Addison's disease or of Hodgkin's lymphoma, after a very painful illness, a death which she attributed to bile and rheumatism, and from conditions which probably could be cured today, ensured that her corpus was unfinished. Only twelve chapters of her novel *Sanditon* were completed; the future development of this novel invites speculation. Her parents, George Austen (1731–1805) and Cassandra Leigh (1739–1827), were long-lived by the standards of the age, but not her grandfather William Austen (1701–37), or her eldest brother, James (1765–1819), or her cousin Eliza (Elizabeth, 1761–1813). So, it is to these unpredictable and apparently arbitrary facts of life and death that we turn first.

It is easy to treat the eighteenth century as a unit: to use a modern concept, the "long eighteenth century," generally seen as 1689–1815. However, this period was not static or uniform. Instead, the situation when Austen was born was changing rapidly, as contemporaries were well aware. Indeed, Thomas Malthus, a cleric from a clerical background, addressed population issues, publishing *An Essay on the Principle of Population* in 1798. This warning about the problems stemming from population growth is one perspective on the five Bennet children and the Heywoods' fourteen, which greatly affected their living standards.[2] Malthus's arguments are echoed in the more unpleasant and personal reflections of the childless Mrs. Norris on the nine children of her impoverished sister Frances, Mrs. Price. Her wealthier sister, Maria, Lady Bertram, is not the target of such criticism, but she also has fewer children.

Whereas England averaged an annual population increase of 0.3 percent in 1700–55, between 1755 and 1801 the increase was 0.8 percent. As a result, the population of England and Wales rose from 6.20 million in 1751 to 8.89 million in 1801. It went on to grow to 10.16 million in 1811 and 12 million in 1821, a rapid rate of increase. This increase was particularly visible in the expansion of cities, including the largest, London.

Rural England was both hierarchical and changeable—like its urban counterpart but differently so. The economic transformation of rural England is addressed in part in the next chapter, but change was not only a matter of the agricultural revolution and its limits. The social imprint of this change was of most interest to novelists. Social patterns were the product of dynamic relationships, especially the daily reaffirmation of status; the continuous interaction between, and within, groups; and the multiple links of friendship, kinship, and patronage. In England, there was no fixed, caste-like rigidity, which would have left scant room for social mobility. Instead, there was an active land market, as well as the impact of agrarian fortune or failure.

Alongside such shifts, the weight of the past was apparent in the distribution of wealth, status, and power, which were all factors to the fore in Austen's world, not least in the matrimonial stakes. During her lifetime, there was scant change in the ways individuals could determine or change their social position. Certainly, in comparison with the following two centuries, the rate of social change was low. However, that does not imply there was little social change. In addition, although it cannot be measured with precision, social mobility was greater than on the Continent, as was the interaction of social groups.

Status and power were linked to wealth, although they were not identical with it. This situation was repeatedly probed by writers, including Austen in her major works and especially in *Sanditon*, a late work of the postwar period that is particularly sensitive to the issue. This linkage of status, power, and wealth was generally regarded as appropriate in English society. However, at the same time, there was a long-standing degree of tension over the terms of this linkage, as well as the definition of acceptable wealth, and notably of land as opposed to other forms. Related to this, the traditional vocabulary of social "orders" appeared less relevant. The legitimacy of money, which many saw as disruptive, as opposed to landed wealth, was a continuing matter of controversy. Certainly it was disruptive as far as the matrimonial stakes were concerned.

The relationship between capital and income greatly favored the former. Indeed, the ability to create income without capital was limited, which helped increase the tendency to borrow and thus the role of credit. Nevertheless, despite the role of inherited capital, opportunities for self-advancement from imperial expansion or industrialization existed. Men who had earned their money in India and the West Indies made their mark, creating positions back in English society, as in *Mansfield Park*. In *Sanditon*, Miss Lambe, an heiress from the West Indies, is one of the young women whose education is being finished under the care of Mrs. Griffiths: "She was about seventeen, half mulatto, chilly and tender."[3] The *chilly* is best explained as a reference to the cold of Britain after the West Indies.

Although the Bertrams of Mansfield Park are not criticized, certainly not explicitly, for earning their money in part from a plantation in Antigua, a British island colony in the West Indies where sugar was cultivated, those who had earned their money abroad could in fact arouse suspicion. Samuel Foote's play *The Nabob* illustrated the disdain with which people treated new money made in the empire, as was the case with Warren Hastings, an empire builder in India who was tried for corruption in one of the great political spectaculars of the age. Fanny Burney, who attended the trial, was very sympathetic toward Hastings. As was known within the family, Hastings may have been the true father of Austen's cousin Eliza, although this claim was much disputed. Eliza certainly was a product of women being sent to the colonies to find a husband, as discussed by Austen.

Self-advancement also came from trade, which was an issue as a source of money and social uncertainty. Austen sometimes was positive about those who had made money through trade. The Coles in *Emma* and, far more, the Gardiners in *Pride and Prejudice* fall into this category. In contrast, in *Emma* the Sucklings, the family of Mr. Elton's wife, are mercilessly caricatured for their concern (at least as expressed through Mrs. Elton) with material goods and status. At the same time, in a multilayered response, Mrs. Elton's concern is in part a matter of her almost painful uncertainty about her social and personal position. Money gained through trade and other means can be honorable, but valuing people only in terms of their wealth is very much not, according to Austen: John Dashwood eyed Colonel Brandon "with a curiosity which seemed to say, that he only wanted to know him to be rich, to be equally civil to him."[4]

Many former London merchants had moved out of the capital—for example, the Heathcote family of Horsley. The care taken by the newly affluent to buy status helped ensure they did not undermine notions of social hierarchy. Indeed, the very existence of social distinctions was seen as obvious and arising from the natural inequality of talents and energies. Egalitarianism found favor with few writers on social topics, and social control by the elite was a fact. These assumptions pervaded society, encouraging the ranking by birth and snobbery that features so prominently in Austen's novels and through which characters establish their personality and the plot advances.

The desire to preserve family status and wealth in part lay behind Hardwicke's Marriage Act of 1753, which increased the power of parents by outlawing clandestine marriages in England, a crucial challenge to the marriage market and the related social assumptions. This act encouraged couples to elope to Gretna

Green just into Scotland, where Lydia Bennet is (wrongly) feared to have gone in *Pride and Prejudice*. In 1774, Robert Nugent, an opportunist in all things including his marriages, attacked the act in the House of Commons as "tending to prevent an union of willing hearts, and to hinder young girls from giving their hands to such hearty young men as they could like and love, in order that miserly parents might couple youth with age, beauty with deformity, health with disease." Certainly, the power of fathers over the marriage of children, particularly daughters, emerges repeatedly in Austen's novels. Far less so for sons, but it is still a factor.

The desire to preserve family status and wealth by controlling marriage, as seen in Hardwicke's Marriage Act, was also crucial to the system of entail (a limitation of the inheritance of property) that threatened the future of the Bennet women in *Pride and Prejudice*. Under this system, the entire estate would be inherited by the next male relative—in their case, a cousin, the egregious Mr. Collins. This arrangement, which Mr. Bennet regrets, explains Mrs. Bennet's eagerness for Mr. Collins to marry Elizabeth and thereby keep access to the property and her somewhat extreme anger when Elizabeth turns him down. Somewhat differently, the death of George Austen in January 1805 left his wife and unmarried daughters in a difficult position, rather like that of the clergyman in *The Watsons*.

Social differentiation, or at least an awareness of distinctions of rank and status, may have become more acute in this period in response to social mobility and the pressures of commodification that commercialism created, although neither element was new. This concern about mobility owed much to the degree to which heredity and stability were regarded as intertwined. Yet Lady Catherine de Bourgh and Sir Walter Elliot are scarcely presented by Austen as exemplars of hereditary rank, although neither, interestingly, was at the height of society, unlike Darcy or, to a lesser extent, Fitzwilliam.

Concern to keep land within families, or, more particularly, their male line, is seen with the role of the entail, not only for the Bennets in *Pride and Prejudice* and the Dashwoods in *Sense and Sensibility* but also for Sir Walter Elliot in *Persuasion*: "He had condescended to mortgage as far as he had the power, but he would never condescend to sell. No; he would never disgrace his name so far."[5] Sir Walter repeatedly emerges in a very poor light, and even more because the book was published at a time of postwar economic problems and of concern with the related tensions. His wartime attitudes are clearly unacceptable. He thought Frederick Wentworth, a naval hero, "a very degrading alliance" for his daughter Anne. A man without a "fortune," the hero had "no connexions" to secure even his farther rise in that profession.

The obsession with rank and the practice of condescension seen with Sir Walter affect other relatives; faults were corrosive and generally operated through condescension, as with Lady Catherine and the Bingley sisters, Caroline and Louisa. The baronet's married daughter, Mary, expects precedence over her mother-in-law because of her inherited rank. Yet, as with many writers, criticism of an individual was not criticism of an entire order but rather a call for good behavior by its members.

Austen's mother was proud of the aristocratic connections of her family, the Leighs, although the most distinguished—James, first Duke of Chandos (Austen's great-grandfather married one of his sisters)—was a connection that was shadowed by the financial problems of Henry, the second duke, which led, in 1747, to the demolition sale of the family seat, Cannons in Middlesex. That was not an Austen-like plot. A more attractive (and recent) experience was provided by Austen's brother Edward, who was adopted by a wealthy, childless, distant cousin, Thomas Knight. Edward married well in 1791 and changed his name in 1812 to inherit the Knight family estates, but he did not cut himself off from the Austens. Indeed, far from it.

Austen was well aware of the peerage and used current names for some of her characters.[6] She also captured the gradations of expectation in the social elite very well in a conversation between Colonel Fitzwilliam and Elizabeth Bennet. The former contrasts himself with his cousin Darcy: "He is rich, and many others are poor. I speak feelingly. A younger son, you know, must be inured to self-denial and dependence." This earns the rejoinder: "In my opinion, the younger son of an Earl can know very little of either. Now, seriously, what have you ever known of self-denial and dependence? When have you been prevented by want of money from going wherever you chose or procuring any thing you had a fancy for?" In turn, Colonel Fitzwilliam correctly notes: "Younger sons cannot marry where they like."[7] This rules out Elizabeth for him, which represents his loss. Austen presents this problem more generally and for women as well as men.

Social status is clearly understood as finely graded, but that can also be made inappropriate, at least to a degree, as with the discussion of Lady Russell's attitude toward Sir Walter Elliot: "She was as desirous of saving Sir Walter's feelings, as solicitous for the credit of the family, as aristocratic in her ideas of what was due to them. . . . She had prejudices on the side of ancestry; she had a value for rank and consequence, which blinded her a little to the faults of those who possessed them. Herself, the widow of only a knight, she gave the dignity of a baronet all its due."[8]

At the same time as the emphasis on lineage, there was a growing sense that status, instead, should be a matter of conduct. In contrast, indeed, Austen links "pride and ill nature" in the case of Mrs. Ferrars.[9] The stress on civil as much as social virtue contributed to the importance of conduct judged polite and reflected it. Yet, if morality was increasingly prescribed, and indulgence proscribed, this process represented not a middle-class reaction against noble culture but a shift in sensibility common to both. For every decadent aristocrat depicted on the stage in the second half of the eighteenth century, there were several royal or aristocratic heroes. Thus, rather than seeing the commercialization of leisure as a triumph for middle-class culture, the role of the middle class was largely one of patronizing both new and traditional artistic forms and emulating the aristocracy, rather than developing or demanding styles that were distinctive, consciously or otherwise. Indeed, George III played a key role in exemplifying a moral purposefulness that fitted with Austen's values.

From a different perspective, the expansion and profitability of the commercial and industrial sectors of the economy led to a growth in the middling orders, who were increasingly difficult to locate in terms of a social differentiation based on rural society and inherited position. Moreover, thanks to an active land market, status could be readily acquired by the wealthy. By 1790, about one-fifth of the membership of the House of Commons came from backgrounds outside the landed elite. This mobility strengthened, rather than weakened, the social hierarchy,[10] whatever Sir Walter might have thought. At the same time, social flux led some to emphasize social distinctions. This represents the range of responses that can be described as Tory, one of the two major political traditions of the century.

Social differentiation was reflected in a range of activities and spheres, such as sport and dress, and, more generally, in conversation and socializing—for example, visiting and receiving visitors. Hunting, a key aspect of socializing, was restricted to the affluent by the laws that entrenched this differentiation. These laws were maintained by gamekeepers and mantraps, and both the legislation and its defense helped make clear the nature of hierarchy and power in the rural community. Hunting was restricted by legislation, and, keeping horses, especially hunting horses, was expensive. Mr. Bingley returns to Netherfield for the shooting, another very expensive process redolent of status. This point is discussed further in the next chapter.

The seating arrangements in churches, and the treatment of the dying and their corpses, also reflected social status and differences, as did the provision of health care: only the wealthy could afford church pews, indoor tombs, and fashionable doctors. Patterns and practices of crime and punishment, credit and debt, also reflected social distinctions. Aristocratic debtors escaped the imprisonment for debt that was a frequent consequence of the role of credit in society.

Power and wealth were concentrated. The hierarchical nature of society and of the political system, the predominantly agrarian nature of the economy, the generally slow rate of change in social and economic affairs, the unwillingness of governments composed of the social elite to challenge fundamentally the interests of their social group or govern without their cooperation, and the inegalitarian assumptions of the period all combined to ensure that the concentration of power and wealth remained reasonably constant. The old order could be "insolent and disagreeable,"[11] as in the person of Lady Catherine de Bourgh. This arrogance was particularly directed against those seen as challenging the instrumental assumptions of the elite about others, as with Lady Catherine's consistently harsh and condescending response to Elizabeth Bennet.

Across Europe, those who enjoyed power and wealth tended to be nobles/aristocrats by birth or creation. In Britain, accordingly, the peerage dominated government, politics, and the military. All adult, male, non-Catholic English peers were members of the House of Lords, and only they were eligible for membership. The sole male peers were heads of families and thus the current chiefs of respective lineages. The peers were influential collectively, as well as often individually. In 1782–1820, fifty-seven of the sixty-five ministers were peers or the sons of peers. Moreover, most new peers were relations of existing ones.[12] There were 189 male peers in 1780 but, due to many creations, 220 by 1790.

The size of the English peerage was far smaller than that on the Continent because the ownership of a significant amount of land was not itself an indication or cause of noble rank. However, the (nonaristocratic) gentry who had such land enjoyed considerable social status.

There was an active land market, and, by European standards, land and status could be readily acquired. Nevertheless, marriage and inheritance, rather than purchase, remained the crucial means by which land was transferred. Moreover, surname substitution, a frequent practice, helped strengthen a sense of continuity in land ownership while the pattern of estates itself did not alter.[13] The socially prominent who were wealthy, famously the "single man in possession of a good fortune,"[14] were the prime catches in the marriage market and thus best able to preserve and increase their wealth by marriage. Lady Catherine de Bourgh was simply stating the obvious about the pattern of social endogamy when she haughtily informed Elizabeth Bennet in a truly dramatic clash of values (and personalities) where Austen's opinion is clear: "My daughter and my nephew [Darcy] are formed for each other. They are descended on the maternal side, from the same noble line; and, on the father's, from respectable, honourable, and ancient, though untitled families. Their fortune on both sides is splendid. They are destined for each other by the voice of every member of their respective houses; and what is to divide them? The upstart pretensions of a young woman without family, connections, or fortune."

Elizabeth's first retort is that she is "a gentleman's daughter." Lady Catherine crushes this by asking: "But who was your mother? Who are your uncles and aunts?" After thus being told she is a nobody, Elizabeth responds with the more pointed and radical response: "Whatever my connections may be, if your nephew [Darcy] does not object to them, they can be nothing to *you*."[15]

This response is a determined statement in favor of individualism, youth, and personal attraction over caste and age. This statement is also significant for the dynamics of female relationships, including between the generations. These dynamics are easily as significant in Austen's books as male-female relations.

At the same time as Elizabeth's robust response, Elizabeth's mother, Mrs. Bennet, jealously maintained downward social distinctions, as with her determination to differentiate the accomplishments of her daughters from the occupations of her servants: "*I* always keep servants that can do their own work; *my* daughters are brought up differently"[16] and "assured him with some asperity that they were very well able to keep a good cook, and that her daughters had nothing to do in the kitchen."[17]

In Austen's novels, social condescension in the sense of patronizing is very much associated with the existence and maintenance of rank, and women are part of this process. John Dashwood, an appalling snob, throws light on the attitude of his wife, Fanny: "Mrs Jennings too, an exceedingly well-behaved woman, though not so elegant as her daughter. Your sister need not have any scruple even of visiting her, which, to say the truth, has been a little the case, and very naturally; for we only knew that Mrs Jennings was the widow of a man who had got all his money in a low way; and Fanny and Mrs Ferrars were both strongly prepossessed, that neither she nor her daughters were such kind of women as Fanny would like to associate with."[18]

Mrs. Bennet complains that "great ladies in general" are patronizing, and Lady Catherine de Bourgh, who is described otherwise by Mr. Collins in a form of guilt by association (for both), in fact is example of this.[19] Moreover, Miss Bingley's snobbery is amply on display with reference to George Wickham. Referring to his "guilt," she adds, "Really considering his descent, one could not expect much better."[20] So also with Emma's harsh judgment on Mr. Elton, the vicar: "He must know that the Woodhouses had been settled for several generations at Hartfield, the younger branch of a very ancient family—and that the Eltons were nobody. . . . The Woodhouses had long held a high place in the consideration of the neighbourhood which Mr Elton had first entered two years ago, to make his way as he could, without any alliances but in trade, or anything to recommend him to notice but his situation and his civility."[21]A lack of breeding is discerned: "She had often, especially of late, thought his manners to herself unnecessarily gallant; but it had passed as his way, as a mere error of judgment, of knowledge, of taste, as one proof among others that he had not always lived in the best society, that with all the gentleness of his address, true elegance was sometimes wanting."[22]

A different perspective, and therefore possible critique, was offered by Elizabeth Bennet: "What praise is more valuable than the praise of an intelligent servant? As a brother, a landlord, a master, she considered how many people's happiness were in his guardianship!—How much of pleasure or pain it was in his power to bestow!—How much of good or evil must be done by him!"[23] Nevertheless, servants' perspectives are not offered in Austen's works. There is no equivalent to Pamela. However, the perspective of being a dependent is very much presented, although the course of action followed varies, as in the case of Jane Fairfax, who is far from being a passive respondent to her status.

The consciousness of different ranks, which ensures that the unpleasant General Tilney never loved his daughter Eleanor "so well . . . as when he first hailed her, 'Your Ladyship,'" on her marriage to a viscount, underlines the complexities of social relations, not least due to the complications of the matrimonial resetting of familial links in this period. Snobbery, an eighteenth-century constant, was a consequence of a society that was at once "emulative" and keen to limit the consequences. A viscount was a rank considerably above an ordinary lord, let alone a knight, but the wives of both were called ladies. However, although Eleanor was now a viscountess, it was not a normal form of address, and it certainly was not used between family members unless they were reserved and lacking in affection.

Alongside the awareness of social difference between nobility and gentry, the absence of serious tension between them was an important feature of landed society and a crucial aspect of stability. This was very much part of the world depicted by Austen, although she was aware of tensions, real and possible. The nobility and gentry formed a homogeneous group that was often educated together and then intermarried and socialized together—a situation that was helped by the inheritance of noble status only by the eldest son. His brothers, therefore, were gentry. This group, however, was not a social class, as the later sense of class identity was weak and was overlaid by other elements of social identity.

Although not part of this group, the middling orders generally cooperated with the landed elite in order to achieve their objectives. This wide-ranging alliance was important to a sense of national superiority and was seen as of broader significance in British society. Confronting the challenge of the French Revolution, John Trevor, British envoy to Savoy-Piedmont, accurately reported from Turin in 1792: "The misfortune is that in this country [Savoy-Piedmont] the whole society is divided into two classes, the *Court and Nobility,* and *the Bourgeoisie,* and the line drawn between them is so rude and marked that the two parties have long been jealous and might too easily become hostile; there are none of those intermediate shades which blend the whole together into one harmonious mass as in our happy country."[24]

Elite dominance was not free from tension and challenge. It could be qualified by strong traditions of popular independence, especially in the major towns; by activism from part of the propertied "middling orders," including the impact of moral reform on elite practices; by the porosity of social boundaries and the related constant renewal of power structures; and by the existence and complexities of divisions within the elite. These divisions were such that, except in the revolutionary crisis of the 1790s, the elite did not feel compelled to unite in politics in order to fend off a challenge from below. At the same time, reciprocal assumptions of paternalism and subordination were significant and helped maintain elite dominance and the alliance on which, in part, it rested.

Command of local government—indeed, total command in many respects—by the elite reflected their position in local society. Justices of the peace (JPs), such as Mr. Knightley in *Emma* and Austen's brother Edward, were the crucial figures in local government and in the maintenance of law and order, and the bench of JPs, all male, was dominated by the gentry, as well as by the Anglican clergy toward the end of the century. Knowledge of the activities of JPs, both family members and those of the locality, ensured that Austen was in a position to write about them. At the Coles' party in *Emma*, Frank Churchill notes "that his father, Mr Knightley, Mr Cox, and Mr Cole, were left very busy over parish business." Subsequently, news of the presence of a gypsy group is sent to Mr. Knightley, for, as reported, their activity should lead to arrest and imprisonment, while Mr. Knightley hears of the engagement of Jane Fairfax and Frank Churchill at the end of "a few lines on parish business from Mr Weston."[25] Other local officials, notably poor law guardians and churchwardens, looked to the JPs.

As commissioners, the gentry were also the crucial figures in the local allocation of the Land Tax, which was paid by all landowners, including peers, unlike the considerable tax immunities of much of the Continental nobility. More generally, Austen is careful to provide details of capital wealth and, even more, incomes, and that information helps offer a moral point as it indicates an individual's capacity to do good, as well as throws light on other aspects of his or her character.[26]

Those who can be variously termed the middling orders or ranks, or the middle class, are (and were) difficult to define, but they tended to emphasize values of professionalization, specialism, and competence that helped define their social function and presence. At the same time, these groups could be concerned with hierarchy and background, an aspiration to gentry status, and snobbery. The wealthy Bingley sisters "were in the habit of spending more than they ought, and of associating with people of rank; and were, therefore, in every respect entitled to think well of themselves and meanly of others. They were of a respectable family in the north of England—a circumstance more deeply impressed on their memories than that their brother's fortune and their own had been acquired by trade."[27] Thus, their social origin was not grand, as was that of Darcy and Fitzwilliam, the latter a name redolent of connection. They came from the landed aristocracy, even if both are cadets in the shape of a younger son of an earl (Fitzwilliam) and his wealthier cousin, Darcy, who was not a victim of primogeniture, as was Fitzwilliam. The sisters wanted their brother to purchase an estate, rather than being only a tenant who was wealthy enough to purchase one.[28] Miss Bingley is particularly harsh in conversation with Darcy, attacking local society as represented by Sir William Lucas's party: "The insipidity and yet the noise; the nothingness and yet the self-importance of all these people!"[29] Mr. Weston might be happy to "marry a woman as portionless even as Miss Taylor,"[30] but others were more sensitive to these issues.

The expansion and growing profitability of the economy led to growth in the middling orders, and some rose in status, as with Sir William Lucas in *Pride and Prejudice*. However, at the individual level, there was also much fragility, as well as ambition, in status and position, as Sir William shows with his obsessive reference to having been received at court, which would have been by George III. This period did not have the protection offered today by insurance and pensions. More generally, attempts to associate together in order to provide a measure of security could offer only limited protection.

It has been argued that there were signs of a new ethos in literature, in contrast to supposedly aristocratic habits of self-indulgence. However, it is important not to exaggerate the significance of such ideas. They were neither new nor politically pointed and significant, and much of the landed elite would have accepted these ideas.

Marriage was a key means not only to the acquisition of status but also the inheritance of property. Indeed, marriage brought landed society at all levels into play and extended to the royal family, which helped lead to the 1772 Royal Marriages Act. The Regency crisis under George III in 1788–89, and the subsequent establishment of George, Prince of Wales, as the prince regent in 1811, drove the question of unworthy heirs to the fore. This element played out very differently in the two crises, but each was significant to the politics of Austen's life and also focused attention on issues of succession, their unpredictably, and the suitability of heirs. These issues were repeatedly important to her novels.

Primogeniture—inheritance by the eldest son, a key ethos and practice in landed society—created an important distinction within the apparent monolith of the old order. As matrimonial options, eldest sons, the heirs, were very different from "the spares." Thus, Charles Musgrove differs from his wife on the suitability of Charles Hayter as a connection, their difference reflecting factors that could play a role. His wife was decided in her opinion:

> "Nothing but a country curate. A most improper match for Miss Musgrove, of Uppercross."
>
> Her husband, however, would not agree with her here; for besides having a regard for his cousin, Charles Hayter was an eldest son, and he saw things as an eldest son himself. . . . "He is the eldest son; whenever my uncle dies, he steps into a very pretty property."[31]

With his characteristic distortion of natural responses, John Dashwood asks, "Can any thing be more galling to the spirit of a man . . . than to see his younger brother in possession of an estate which might have been his own?"[32] Edward Ferrars, the elder son in question, has acted appropriately, of course, and was certainly not a prodigal son.

Austen provides a highly unsympathetic account of the situation of heirs in her discussion of the Bertrams of Mansfield Park. The great extravagance of the feckless heir, Tom, ensured that one of the two livings destined for his younger brother, Edmund, has to be sold for the lifetime of the next incumbent: "The younger brother must help to pay for the pleasures of the elder." Austen has Tom respond with "cheerful selfishness . . . that he had not been half so much in debt as some of his friends."[33] This is not a positive account of the social elite. Indeed, Sir Thomas takes Tom with him when he goes to attend to the problems of the family plantation on Antigua "in the hope of detaching him from some bad connections at home"[34]—a criticism of the elite.

The general situation obliged younger sons to define and support their own position and made the disposal of wealth acquired outside this constraint more significant. Younger sons went into the military (as with the likeable and observant Colonel Fitzwilliam in Pride and Prejudice), the Church (meaning the Church of England), and "trade." The marital choices of younger sons were affected by their social position as members of the elite.

The marriage of the sons of land with the daughters of commerce was a standard way to obtain wealth, particularly for younger sons. However, eldest sons could do the same, and were bigger prizes, especially as they offered a title that would enhance the woman in question as well as her family. Mary Crawford thinks that "Lord Edmund or Sir Edmund sound delightfully; but sink it under the chill, the annihilation of a Mr.—and Mr. Edmund is no more than Mr. John or Mr. Thomas." She later adds, "A poor honourable is no catch."[35]

Less frequently, the daughters of land married the sons of commerce. This practice cost less in dowries than the daughters of commerce marrying the sons of land. However, assumptions are not necessarily fulfilled. William Elliot does not marry Elizabeth Elliot as she wishes. Instead he "purchased independence by uniting himself to a rich woman of inferior birth," the daughter of a rich grazier, which is taken as a snub to the Elliot blood.[36] Years afterward, when his wife is dead, the prospect of Anne Elliot marrying him apparently arises. This would have restored the family home to Kellynch and the title of Lady Elliot to the family. However, this prospect only exists in Lady Russell's imagination.

Marital conventions were less exclusive than on the Continent but still existed and were expressed in, and greatly compounded by, snobbery. At the same time, there were serious concerns about the system that could be expressed in fiction by the authors and experienced by the readers. In Charlotte Smith's first novel, *Emmeline, The Orphan of the Castle* (1788), the eldest daughter of Lord Montreville is secretly married to the younger son of the villainous Croft family, who, as lawyers, are lower in status but seek her fortune.

Despite snobbish disdain for "trade," a disdain that affected the acceptability of figures such as Samuel Whitbread in real life and Mrs. Jennings in *Sense and Sensibility*,[37] the sons of land were allowed to marry the daughters of commerce. In Eliza Parson's novel *The History of Lord Clayton and Miss Meredith* (1790), the miserly Earl of Bromley decides to marry his son to the daughter of the wealthy Mr. Jarvis, who has made his fortune in the East Indies, in other words, for the British, India, not Indonesia.

In Austen's essentially conservative novels, it is not so much the sons of commerce and the daughters of land, but rather the sons of land who marry "beneath them," which was the alliance that was most acceptable to social norms, both in terms of traditional pejorative ideas of gaining the money of commerce and with reference to more recent sentimental concepts. Moreover, Austen shows, with Darcy and Elizabeth Bennet, that the idea of marrying "beneath" a rank, at least at this level, is of only limited value as it is. It is clear that a happy future for the couple is anticipated, and the entire story is of social distinctions and mental rigidities overcome. In her *History of England*, Austen has Frederic Delamere, the hero of Charlotte Smith's *Emmeline*, as one of her three "first of Men." The heir of Lord Montreville, he proposes to the heroine, his possibly illegitimate cousin and thus a woman far below him in status; goes through much in his quest for her; and eventually dies in a duel. The last is an instance of their more general convenience as a plot device.

Tory distrust of commerce is indicated in Austen's work, as in Emma's disdain for what she knows and imagines about the antecedents of Augusta Hawkins, Mr. Elton's intended: "She brought no name, no blood, no alliance . . . the youngest of the two daughters of a Bristol—merchant of course, he must be called."[38] The last suggested distrust of any background in commerce. Emma is a terrible snob, but the novel shows that she is correct to dislike Augusta.

From a different direction to that of Toryism, William Godwin, a radical writer, claimed in 1805 that money had taken over: "I saw that the public character of England . . . was gone. I perceived that we were grown a commercial and arithmetical nation. . . . Contractors, directors, and upstarts,—men fattened on the vitals of their fellow-citizens—have taken the place which was once filled by the Wentworths, the Seldens, and the Pyms."[39] Thomas Carlyle (1795–1881) was to make a similar observation from a more conservative perspective. He focused on the significance of what he termed in *Chartism* (1839) "cash payment . . . the universal sole nexus of man to man."[40]

The social order was most conspicuously displayed in the stately homes and parks (or grounds) of the social elite. Many of both survive; they provide the setting for film and television versions of Austen's novels and thus subliminally have affected, and continue to affect, assumptions about both the novels and Austen's world. Saltram in Devon was extensively used for the film of *Sense and Sensibility* while Lyme Park in Cheshire appeared as Pemberley in the 1995 BBC version of *Pride and Prejudice*. Other locations include Chatsworth (Pemberley in the 2005 film), Lacock Abbey, Belton House (Rosings in the 1995 version), Renishaw

Hall, Stourhead, Burghley House (Rosings in the 2005 film), Groombridge Place (the Bennets' house in the 2005 film), and Basildon Park. Thus, the last was used as the location for Netherfield Park both in the 2005 film version and the 2016 film *Pride and Prejudice and Zombies*. There was also the setting not offered, that of the empire as a means to regenerate the elite, including the aristocracy, by means of wealth, position, and role, thus enabling them to live in the idyllic countryside. In turn, aristocratic forms of sociability were introduced into colonial governance.[41]

Another form of conspicuous display was that aristocrats were accompanied by servants. Moreover, the latter wore distinctive uniforms in the shape of livery, such as those worn by the servants of Darcy and his sister when they called on Elizabeth Bennet at Lambton.[42] The use of livery and the ownership of particular carriages assisted those who liked to note the movements of the prominent, as did Mr. Collins.

The environments landowners created and sustained helped mold the imaginative world of their contemporaries. Novels, plays, and paintings used mansions, which are generally referred to as stately homes, as well as their parks for their settings and, notably, their values. These locations were attractive and also represented much more, especially what was bound up in continuity of ownership. This continuity represented social stability and status and, to many, the honorable conduct that differed from the commercialism and crassness of new money.

Stately homes not only dominated the landscape visually and socially, but they were a testimony to wealth, confidence, the income generated by rising demand for crops, the profits stemming from agricultural improvement (on which see chap. 3), the benefits of mineral rights such as coal, and greater political and social stability. War with Revolutionary and then Napoleonic France from 1793, and, in the context of continued population rise, its detrimental impact on food imports, brought yet further profits from rising agricultural rental income, encouraging both the enclosure of agricultural land and the building of stately homes. Thus, Frederick, fourth Earl of Bristol (also bishop of Derry in Ireland), the only earl-bishop in British history,[43] began work at Ickworth, with its dramatic oval rotunda, in 1795. Costs nevertheless were high, and the expense of building could be ruinous, contributing to the serious debts affecting many landowners. The converse of rising rental income was the high food prices that contributed to misery and discontent in the late 1790s and the Corn Laws from 1815 that kept prices high to the benefit of the landed elite.

The stately homes were frequently new to a degree not appreciated today. In *Pride and Prejudice*, Lady Catherine's seat, Rosings, is "a handsome modern building, well situated on rising ground,"[44] which makes the 2005 film setting of sixteenth-century Burghley House inappropriate despite eighteenth-century remodelings of many interiors and of the park. Mansfield Park is a "spacious modern-built house," "modern, airy, and well situated," and contrasts with Sotherton Court, which "was built in Elizabeth's time, and is a large, regular brick building—heavy, but respectably looking, and has many good rooms. It is ill placed. It stands in one of the lowest spots of the park; in that respect, unfavourable for improvement. But the woods are fine, and there is a stream, which, I dare say, might be made a good deal of. Mr Rushworth is quite right I think, in meaning to give it a modern dress."[45] The visit to Sotherton reveals furnishings "in the taste of fifty years back,"[46] which for most people was not intended as praise. Austen herself, however, sympathizes with the continuity of honest old places.

Although the houses proclaimed hierarchy, longevity, and status, they also reflected a concern with being up-to-date. The latter, indeed, was an affirmation of the currency of their status. A rejection of the past, in at least one form, was dramatized when older mansions were replaced or rebuilt, which happened frequently. Thus, while landed estates might indicate continuity, stately houses, like the new enclosures on the estates that were designed to increase agricultural effectiveness, reflected change. Whether new or rebuilt, the model for stately homes was a harmonious unity, which generally required large-scale building, and not the incoherence of a tacked-on extension. Prominence was proclaimed through such work, and competition between families was important to this process.

Meanwhile, lesser houses reflected the motifs and styles of greater works. Their families looked to those in the greater houses on the pattern shown by Austen. These houses were also frequently new, as with Mr. Suckling's Maple Grove near Bristol in *Emma*. In *Sanditon*, Mr. Parker abandons "the house of my forefathers . . . an honest old place" for the new Trafalgar House, built on "a beautiful spot.—Our ancestors, you know always built in a hole.—Here we are [the old house], pent down in this little contracted nook, without air or view, only one mile and three quarters from the noblest expanse of ocean between the South Foreland and the Land's End, and without the smallest advantage from it." Mrs. Parker regrets the loss of the "very comfortable house," which is not as exposed to the wind as the new one, and the shady garden of the old house. Her pompous and foolish husband, in contrast, welcomes "the grandeur of the storm." Trafalgar House "on the most elevated spot on the down was a light elegant building."[47]

Stately homes presented and proclaimed a redefinition of taste and style. A long-standing theme that reflected a concern to be up-to-date, this was seen in this period with the interpretation of classical themes for modern architecture and landscape design, and their incorporation accordingly. Proportion was a key aspect of a number of styles. Such an impression captured inherent harmonies that were regarded as natural and culturally significant, with balance acting as a means, as well as symbol, for an appropriate politics. The tightly controlled symmetry of Palladianism was an architectural language that worked at a number of scales, and outer symmetry lent itself to the symmetry of interior layout and rooms. The standard Palladian repertoire was of a central block with a great portico and colonnades and loggias on either side. The Palladian style was disseminated by emulation and through publications, such as William Pain's *The British Palladio: or Builder's General Assistant* (1785). Darcy's Pemberley is described as "a large, handsome, stone building."[48]

There was also a developing interest in the gothic style, which, in the late eighteenth century, became more fashionable and intellectually respectable as a reaction against Italian-inspired classicism. The gothic, however, was largely used for rebuilding. New gothic houses were unusual. Horace Walpole's suburban villa at Twickenham, Strawberry Hill, was the gothicizing rebuilding of a seventeenth-century house. An extension to Sherborne Castle built in 1787 was given three pointed gothic arches in the center to make it seem historic. Two years later, it received the accolade of a visit by George III. The gothic was also seen in interior details such as bookcases. It was not regarded as a style equal to classicism until the work of architects such as James Wyatt at the close of the century. In 1794–96, he added a large gothic apsidal-ended music room to Powderham.[49] Aside from gothic, there was also the Elizabethan revival of the new west front at Montacute in 1786–87. Like Sherborne Castle, this was relatively close to Austen's father's rectory.

With his fancy for a cottage, the arrogant Robert Ferrers in *Sense and Sensibility* tells Elinor Dashwood: "My friend Lord Courtland came to me the other day on purpose to ask my advice, and laid before me three different plans of Bonomi's. I was to decide on the best of them. 'My dear Courtland,' said I, immediately throwing them all into the fire, 'do not adopt either of them, but by all means build a cottage.'"[50]

Joseph Bonomi (1739–1808), a well-known neoclassical architect, moved to London in 1767 and was a successful designer of country houses from 1784, including alterations to Hatchlands Park.

The neoclassical style was particularly appropriate for the smaller and more compact houses increasingly in favor with patrons in the closing decades of the eighteenth century. Very few large houses were built in the period, in part because the major landowning families were already well catered for. There was new wealth, some of it ennobled, but the general preference was now not for the great show houses, whether baroque or Palladian in style, of earlier in the century, the Blenheims or Wentworth Woodhouses. Instead, the preference was for less grandiose houses that were decorated to very high standards and comfortable.

In this respect, these neoclassical houses were strongly redolent of the decorative ethos of Robert Adam, and the emphasis was on private elegance, not public show. The latter was more clearly the characteristic of buildings in towns, such as the Pantheon in London, that served public functions. In 1807, Austen visited the Lances, who lived at Chessel House near Southampton: "Their house is one of those which are to be seen almost anywhere among the woods on the other side of the [River] Itchen. It is a handsome building, stands high, and in a very beautiful situation."[51] Standing high was significant: it provided views but also ensured the house was part of the view for both travelers and arriving visitors. Combined with the beauty of the situation, this provided a setting for a house that, in turn, was enhanced by the house as a handsome building. Both features could be captured in illustrations.

Not all new country houses, however, were small. Attingham Park, with its massive entrance front, the portico having particularly high Ionic columns, designed by George Steuart in 1782, was an appropriate tribute to the wealth of the Hill family and matched and furthered the social ambition that led to their obtaining a peerage.[52]

The new houses had to be decorated and furnished. The superficial but fashionable Mary Crawford feels that Mansfield Park has to be "completely new furnished."[53] The stylistic shift was away from baroque decoration toward a subtler neoclassicism with an arresting elegance. A less ornate tone for furniture was developed by Thomas Chippendale (1718–79), and a lighter, less ornamental, and simpler style followed with George Hepplewhite (c. 1727–86) and Thomas Sheraton (1751–1806). Stockton-born Sheraton established himself in London in about 1790 and began publication of a series of manuals on furniture design. Thanks to such design books, fixtures, fittings, and furniture became more standardized, and London fashion had a national scope. Thus, Northanger Abbey has furniture with "all the profusion and elegance of modern taste. The fire-place, where she had expected the ample width and ponderous carving of former times was contracted to a Rumford [a new design], with slabs of plain though handsome marble, and ornaments over it of the prettiest English china."[54]

The new houses required large numbers of books for the libraries that became an established feature, which helps explain the numerous book subscriptions by members of the elite. The development of the country house library made the stately home a repository of classical culture in the midst of the country. However, in Persuasion, the snobbish Sir Walter Elliot "never took up any book but the Baronetcy,"[55] the list of the baronets and their genealogies. For him, the library was a male room, as it was for Mr. Bennet in Pride and Prejudice: women had to be invited to enter. Pride in lineage was indicated not only by Walter Elliot's reading, if that term could be used for the referencing, particularly self-referencing, involved in his taking up that book, but also by the armorial devices employed on bookcases and in book plates, as well as on crockery and cutlery. The importance of display was also reflected in the showy silver and china receptacles used for punch, tea, and other purposes.

Numerous portraits were also needed for the large spaces created in the public rooms. In the sitting room of Sanditon

House, "the whole-length portrait of a stately gentleman, which, placed over the mantelpiece, caught the eye immediately, was the picture of Sir Harry Denham."[56] At Sotherton Court: "Of pictures there were abundance, and some few good, but the larger part were family portraits, no longer any thing to any body but Mrs Rushworth."[57]

Many members of the elite were keen collectors of paintings. Aristocratic recreations, notably horses and hunting, were an important theme, as in the works of George Stubbs (1724–1806). Unsurprisingly, he and others presented patrons with attractive images of appropriate and socially enhancing behavior, rather than the far grittier reality of the confusion of hunting and sporting occasions. Indeed, aside from serving as a form of portraiture, which in this period was stylized in its depiction of appropriate poses, hunting scenes were outdoor conversation pieces that showed their subjects in the right company, with servants as deferential attendants. There were also echoes of the depiction of classical scenes. Dogs and horses, moreover, were frequently painted, and there was a substantial literature on hunting.

It was common to display paintings of houses and grounds. These works of art reflected pride of ownership, as well as the enjoyment offered by viewing such works. Both these and portraits provided an exemplary background for socializing and an equivalent to the crests and other motifs seen on furniture, porcelain, and decorations.

Taste was displayed through patronage in both design and collecting. The need to show paintings led to particular requirements in interior design. This was even more the case with collections of marble statuary, which were acquired to be seen and thus to display the connoisseurship of the owner. Thomas, second Lord Berwick, had Attingham Park rebuilt to display the paintings and statues he acquired on his grand tour of Italy in 1792–94. The Outer Library, also called the Museum, housed part of his impressive sculpture collection, and the giant pilasters struck a clear classical theme.

It was important to create spaces within which refined socializing could occur, as that socializing indicated taste and supported status. At Pemberley, "the rooms were lofty and handsome, and their furniture suitable to the fortune of their proprietor; but Elizabeth saw, with admiration of his taste, that it was neither gaudy nor uselessly fine; with less of splendour, and more real elegance, than the furniture of Rosings . . . the dining parlour . . . a large, well-proportioned room, handsomely fitted up . . . a very pretty sitting-room, lately fitted up with greater elegance and lightness than the apartments below."[58] Sanditon House is described as "large and handsome . . . everything had a suitable air of property and order . . . Lady Denham valued herself upon her liberal establishment, and had great enjoyment in the order and the importance of her style of living.—They were shown into the usual sitting room, well-proportioned and well-furnished;—though it was furniture rather originally good and extremely well kept, than new and showy."[59] At a different level, but one of social aspiration and the refracted taste of Lady Catherine's Rosings, Mr. Collins points out "the good proportion" of the rooms in his rectory, which he receives as part of his clerical living, as well as its aspect.

It was necessary to find spaces for dining, dancing, music, and cards, and this was accompanied by differentiation by room, a process that had gathered pace over the previous century. Closets were intended for private reflection, anterooms for gatherings before meals, and so on. Corridors enabled functions and people to be kept separate and were also an aspect of the segregation of servants, as were back staircases. An understanding of these points is important to appreciating the novels of the period.

Differentiation also created particular decorative requirements. In his influential *Works in Architecture* (1778), Robert

Adam described dining rooms as "apartments of conversation in which we are to pass a great deal of our time. This renders it desirable to have them fitted up with elegance and splendour, but in a style different from that of other apartments. Instead of being hung with damask, tapestry etc they are always finished with stucco, and adorned with statues and paintings, that they may not retain the smell of the victuals." Still-life pictures were hung in the dining room to remind people of food. In *Persuasion*, Austen refers to the cost of decoration, with Elizabeth proposing "to refrain from new furnishing the drawing-room."[60]

Music was a major requirement, and many stately homes sported music rooms. Music making, both communal and private, was an important activity in these households. So also were amateur theatricals, such as that planned in *Mansfield Park* only to be abruptly ended by the return of the critical Sir Thomas Bertram. For the Austen family, both were popular. Like many girls, including those in her novels, Austen was taught to play the piano. These major aspects of socializing were central to genteel living, both in town and in the country.

In a plot worthy of Austen, Edward Nares, a fellow of Merton College, Oxford, took an active part in the private theatricals at Blenheim (which had a long lineage), but he pushed his connection too far, for George, fourth Duke of Marlborough, refused to allow him to marry his third daughter, Lady Charlotte Spencer, and in 1797 Nares eloped with her. This was one of the more dramatic backgrounds for a country living, in his case Biddenden in Kent from 1798. Eventually, a friend from the days of the Blenheim theatricals, Robert Jenkinson, later second Earl of Liverpool, was to become prime minister, and, in 1813, he appointed Nares the Regius Professor of Modern History at Oxford, where he later failed to give any lectures for many years. Nares recurs in this book in chapter 10.

Landscape gardening provided settings for stately homes while the parks (grounds) served as an important boundary between the house and the wider world, including the poor. The much discussed ethos and practice of landscape gardening represented an Anglicization of classical notions of rural harmony, retreat, and beauty, as well as what was understood as nature tamed by taste and reason. The rigid formality associated with geometric Continental models was swept aside, notably by Lancelot "Capability" Brown (1716–83). He contrived settings that appeared natural but nevertheless were carefully designed for effect. Brown's deliberately asymmetrical landscapes of serpentine lakes, sweeping lawns, gentle hills, copses on the brow of hitherto bare hills, and scattered groups of newly planted trees swiftly established a national fashion. His work for Lord Clifford, whose seat was in Devon, was celebrated in "A Poem on Ugbrooke" by Joseph Reeve, a Clifford chaplain:

> To shade the hill, to scoop and swell the green,
> To break with wild diversities the scene
> To model with the Genius of the place
> Each artless feature, each spontaneous grace.

François de la Rochefoucauld, a visiting French aristocrat, observed in 1784:

> It is usually fine grass and beautiful: above this verdure, which continues the existing slopes of the hills, stand mature trees distributed in masses; they are massed so as to reveal views, a view of a picturesque bell-tower, an attractive village, etc. The woods hide anything that could offend the eye, where the landscape is disagreeable. A bridge, or a pagoda, or a little temple, may be built in order to arrange a view; when the hills don't slope together smoothly enough, a junction is arranged entirely at whim: if necessary, the whole hill can be moved. Above all, one does not forget to bring all the streams to a confluence and turn them into a river, the course of which seems so natural that one could believe it had always been there; and one creates islands, pleasant places; in short, nothing is forgotten. In a well-tended garden there is sometimes not an ugly weed to be seen in the entire vista, which is immense. That is what the English mean by "a park."[61]

The details of individual parks throw considerable light on contemporary interests and tastes. At Osterley Park near London, a house that can still be visited, an unknown designer was responsible for major changes between 1760 and 1790. In place of the formal ponds and canals, three long lakes created the appearance of a river curving around the house. Lawns and pasture with clumps of trees replaced the formal garden, and the planting—about three thousand trees—was extensive. The grounds at Osterley were enhanced with buildings designed to provide interest for those strolling in them, including a "tea room," which was really a summer house; a pine house; a windmill; and temporary structures, including a flower stage and another summer house. Boating on the lake and a menagerie with rare birds, including from the Orient, added to the interest.

The painterly quality of the landscape was referred to in 1798 by the popular travel writer William Gilpin (on whom see chap. 11) when he wrote of "that kind of beauty which would look well in a picture." Austen was observant in her fictional seats. Thus, meeting significant requirements of contemporary taste, the windows of the salon at Pemberley, which opened to the ground, "admitted a most refreshing view of the high woody hill behind the house, and of the beautiful oaks and Spanish chestnuts which were scattered over the intermediate lawn." In contrast, at Sotherton Court, "the situation of the house excluded the possibility of much prospect from any of the rooms."[62] A hill was indeed important. At Henry Crawford's seat, Everingham, there was "a happy fall of ground... the natural advantages of the ground."[63]

Fashions in landscape gardening, as in novels, changed. Sir Uvedale Price (1747–1829) criticized Capability Brown's system for the formalism it still retained. He argued, in his *An Essay on the Picturesque* (1794), in favor of a wilder, less regular and smooth, and more natural and "picturesque" beauty that, he claimed, would accord with "all the principles of landscape painting." Price was supported by Richard Payne Knight in *The Landscape: A*

Didactic Poem (1794). The concept of the "picturesque" stressed the individual character of each landscape, an English form of romanticism, and the need to retain it while making improvements to remove what were judged blemishes and obstructions and to open up vistas.

Their arguments influenced Humphry Repton (1752–1818), who developed Brown's ideas in accordance with a more functional and less extravagant treatment of the "picturesque" and transformed about 220 gardens. Repton was referred to in *Mansfield Park*:

> Mr Rushworth had been visiting a friend in a neighbouring county, and that friend having recently had his grounds laid out by an improver, Mr Rushworth was returned with his head full of the subject....
>
> "I never saw a place [Compton] so altered in my life. . . . The approach *now* is one of the finest things in the country. You see the house in the most surprising manner. I declare when I got back to Sotherton yesterday, it looked like a prison—quite a dismal old prison."

Smith had used Repton, who charged five guineas (thirty-three shillings, or just over five pounds) a day, and Rushworth proposes to do the same. He discusses cutting down the avenue at Sotherton in order to open up the prospect, which leads Fanny to remark to Edmund Bertram: "Cut down an avenue! What a pity. Does not it make you think of Cowper 'Ye fallen avenues, once more I mourn your fate unmerited,'" a quotation from *The Task* (1785). Trees are living proof of continuity and the values of the past. The dinner conversation opens up to consider the merits of improvement by "an improver" or, the alternative, "an inferior degree of beauty, of my own choice, and acquired progressively."[64] Improvement is an important theme in English agricultural history, with a focus on productivity and efficiency. The word has a slightly different meaning for design that implies preserving as much of the natural as can be done without leaving grounds wild.

Henry Crawford also proposes changing Edmund Bertram's future house at Thornton Lacey, including turning the house to front the east instead of the north, making a new garden, and doing something with the stream; only for Edmund to say that he "must be satisfied with rather less ornament and beauty. I think the house and premises may be made comfortable, and given the air of a gentleman's residence without any very heavy expense."[65]

In practice, improvement was seen at Attingham Park, where Repton also added a weir to maintain the water level in the upper reaches of the River Tern so that a cascade could then enhance the landscape. Repton landscaped Stoneleigh Abbey, the seat of wealthy relatives of Austen whom she visited in 1806, and this might have been the original of Sotherton Court in *Mansfield Park*. She also knew of his work at Adlestrop, where the rector (vicar) was her mother's cousin, Thomas Leigh. She visited it in 1806. Repton improved the garden. Austen had access to Repton's *Observations on the Theory and Practice of Landscape Gardening* (1803), which included his design plans for Adlestrop.[66] The density of the English literary language, and thus of cultural references, is indicated by Edward Thomas's poem *Adlestrop*, based on a rural railway journey he made in 1914 when the train stopped there.

Other designers went in the same direction as Repton. Thus, at Bowood in Wiltshire, the home of the Marquess of Lansdowne and one of the great seats close to Austen's rural England, Brown's work was enhanced in the mid-1780s by a "picturesque" landscape designed by Charles Hamilton, including a cascade, grottoes, and a hermit's cave. As Earl of Shelburne, William, first Marquess, had been prime minister from 1782 to 1783.

Status was both reflected and reinforced by the parks that surrounded stately homes. Although park landscape had some economic value, as sheep served as more than natural lawnmowers, considerable labor was required to excavate basins for artificial hills, to create hills, and to move huge, living trees. Thus,

major expense was incurred in landscaping. Moreover, there
was opportunity foregone in the case of timber that was not cut
down. In contrast, in Mr. Knightley's Donwell Abbey, which
Austen locates in Surrey, the emphasis was on usefulness and
not on modernity. More generally, there is (Tory) continuity at
Donwell:

> Its ample gardens stretching down to meadows washed by a stream,
> of which the Abbey, with all the old neglect of prospect, had scarcely
> a sight—and its abundance of timber in rows and avenues, which
> neither fashion nor extravagance had rooted up.—The house was
> larger than Hartfield, and totally unlike it, covering a good deal of
> ground, rambling and irregular, with many comfortable and one
> or two handsome rooms.—It was just what it ought to be, and it
> looked what it was—and Emma felt an increasing respect for it, as
> the residence of a family of such true gentility, untainted in blood
> and understanding.[67]

New and fashionable developments in horticulture, especially
imports, mainly from North America, greatly extended the range
of possible trees, shrubs, and flowers that could be planted. These
flowers included the fuchsia in 1788, the strelitzia in the 1780s, and
the dahlia in 1798. The cultivation of imported plants reflected
affluent taste and attracted interest. Landscape gardening also
responded to, and helped create, a new aesthetic that was interested in nature. However, this was an altered nature that reflected
and enhanced aesthetic judgments, enabling those who viewed
and perambulated the landscape to display their own worth and,
with it, that of nature. In 1807, Austen observed of the garden
at Castle Square: "Our Garden is putting in order . . . he pro-
cures us some syringas. . . . We talk also of a laburnum . . . cur-
rants and gooseberry bushes, and a spot is found very proper for
raspberries."[68] In *Lady Susan*, "we pace the shrubbery for hours
together,"[69] an activity frequent in Austen's novels—extolled, for
example, by Lady Bertram in *Mansfield Park*—that drew together
exercise, privacy, and the outdoors.

Austen's approach was that of her age. In her poetic account of an English country house, *Crumble Hall*, Mary Leapor, a kitchen maid, wrote of climbing up to the roof to view the "beauteous order" of a landscaped park. Visiting Torbay in 1793, John Swete claimed that the influences of Brown and others enabled society to "trace the path of nature without the aid of geometric art,"[70] the latter a dig at traditional French-based systems of design. In contrast, the Brontë sisters favored rugged Yorkshire moors.

The park ceased primarily to be a place to hunt, becoming, instead, a landscape—a source for, and site of, contemplation. Like gardens, these were conspicuously luxurious spaces since they were not economically productive. In the grounds of stately homes, parks were also embellished with grottoes, follies, shell houses, columns, and classical statues. The new fashion in landscaping was less rigid and less formal than its predecessor, and this change permitted a more personal response by visitors to the tamed natural environment presented. This response led to the more individual reaction to nature, or at least a very much reworked nature, that was to be such a major theme in romanticism and that characterizes Elizabeth Bennet's experience of Pemberley. In accordance with the fashion of the period, she is more taken by the grounds than the inside of the house. Less positively, the gushing Augusta Elton compares Hartfield's grounds to her brother-in-law's seat of Maple Grove near Bristol, "The laurels at Maple Grove are in the same profusion as here, and stand very much in the same way—just across the lawn; and I had a glimpse of a fine large tree, with a bench round it, which puts me so exactly in mind! My brother and sister will be enchanted with this place. People who have extensive grounds themselves are always pleased with any thing in the same style," a view Emma doubts.[71]

Display included welcoming respectable-looking visitors to stately homes. This was true of Blenheim, Castle Howard, Chatsworth, Houghton, and Stourhead, all of which were private homes, as well as of many other stately houses. There was no equivalent then to the National Trust to enable all to visit, but many houses were open. Holkham Hall was open every day, bar Sunday, to "the quality." Over 2,300 people visited the Earl of Pembroke's house Wilton in 1776. Guidebooks for the most notable houses were published from mid-century. Kedleston was always open to the public and was perhaps the most admired. Revisiting it in 1777, Samuel Johnson was shown around by a housekeeper who had a printed list of the many pictures.[72]

Pemberley, also in the Peak District, is similarly shown to the visitors in *Pride and Prejudice* while, with Lady Denham absent, Mrs. Parker and Charlotte Heywood are shown around Sanditon House. In *Sense and Sensibility*, there is a proposed visit to Whitwell, "belonging to a brother-in-law of Colonel Brandon, without whose interest it could not be seen, as the proprietor, who was then abroad, had left strict orders on that head." A note by Brandon to the housekeeper does not suffice for entry.[73] In *Mansfield Park*, Mrs. Rushworth shows Sotherton Court. She "had been at great pains to learn all that the housekeeper could teach, and was now almost equally well qualified to shew the house."[74]

The less affluent gentry provided an important way in which new styles, whether in clothes or portraits, buildings or gardens, were disseminated. The Palmers' Cleveland

> was a spacious, modern-built house, situated on a sloping lawn. It had no park, but the pleasure-grounds were tolerably extensive; and like every other place of the same degree of importance, it had its open shrubbery, and closer wood walk, a road of smooth gravel winding round a plantation, led to the front, the lawn was dotted over with timber, the house itself was under the guardianship of the fir, the mountain-ash, and the acacia, and a thick screen of them altogether, interspersed with tall Lombardy poplars, shut out the offices. . . . A distant eminence . . . its Grecian temple.[75]

Edward and Elinor Ferrars were able to improve his parsonage at Delaford, including projecting shrubberies and devising a "sweep," or curved drive,[76] which was necessary for those arriving or leaving by carriage to do so in style.

If less affluent gentry could not emulate the patronage of the elite, they were still of considerable importance in rural regions and in aggregate terms sometimes more significant. Houses built or rebuilt for the less affluent gentry looked toward not only more impressive seats but also the less grand farmhouses of a wider segment of the rural population; similarly, parks looked toward paddocks. La Rochefoucauld noted: "Gentlemen who are not wealthy enough to have parks have what they call lawns, a small area of land round their houses, with bordered walks, beautiful turf, and a small clump of trees, all kept in extremely neat order. They themselves design these garden walks. It's everything they need for the surroundings of the house, to give them an air of ownership and to walk in for half an hour after dinner."[77] In *Northanger Abbey*, Henry Tilney is improving the grounds at Woodston, at the scale he can afford, to the pleasure of Catherine Morland: "The ornamental part of the premises, consisting of a walk round two sides of a meadow, on which Henry's genius had begun to act about half a year ago. . . . Prettier than any pleasure-ground she had ever been in before, though there was not a shrub in it higher than the green bench in the former."[78] In contrast, those manor houses that were not improved risked becoming, or at least being regarded as, farmhouses, a serious fall in status.

Alongside offering access to visitors, the landed elite lived behind the protective infrastructure of gates, walls, and lodges. The reorganization of much of the countryside through enclosure reflected elite power, not least by disrupting traditional rights and expectations. So even more with the demolition of villages to create parkland.

To improve the park at Attingham, Tern Mill was demolished from 1787 to 1789, the village of Berwick Naviston was pulled down in 1802, and part of the town of Atcham was disassembled in 1806. Villages were also swept aside for Bowood, Kedleston,

Nuneham Courtenay, Shugborough, Stowe, and Wimpole. Oliver Goldsmith complained in *The Deserted Village* (1770) about the tyrant that had destroyed "sweet Auburn" village:

> The man of wealth and pride
> Takes up a space that many poor supplied;
> Space for his lake, his park's extended bounds
> Space for his horses, equipage and hounds.

Although a benign account of the countryside drew on the conventional contrast of rural virtue with urban vice, there was also an awareness of rural bleakness and the harshness of nature, as in George Crabbe's poem *The Village* (1783). Based on the poet's experience of Suffolk poverty, it was a stark rejoinder to the pastoral and the sentimental:

> Fled are those times, when, in harmonious strains,
> The rustic Poet prais'd his native Plains . . .
>   . . .
> Theirs is yon House that holds the Parish Poor,
> Whose walls of mud scare bear the broken door.

The pictorial quality of Crabbe's account offered a criticism of painters who offered bucolic accounts of rural life. The well-read Austen herself knew and liked the work of Goldsmith, Crabbe, and William Cowper.

The differences of rural life can be glimpsed today on the Gunby Hall Estate in Lincolnshire. Alongside the red-brick-paneled Gunby Hall is Whitegates Cottage. A small thatched home built in about 1770 to provide accommodation, it would have been colder, darker, and wetter as a dwelling. In William Redmore Bigg's painting *A Cottage Interior* (1793), walls are of brick, not mud, but the face of the woman shows toil and anxiety, and her figure is scarcely buxomly. Maria Bertram thinks the cottages near Sotherton Court "really a disgrace" but, of course, does not criticize the system that left them thus.[79] Rustic scenes, including cottages, dominated the paintings of George Morland

(1763–1804), whose talents could not protect him from debtors' prison.[80]

People at this rank were not Austen's subjects. She deals with what John Willoughby terms "comparative poverty," which comes from lacking the strength of character and purpose not to be disorientated by "the habit of associating with people of better income," and not with true poverty.[81] The life of the poor was a background that would have been readily apparent in Austen's world, but that did not mean people met socially across the divide of poverty unless through employment. Instead, in common with earlier and contemporary novelists, much of Austen's fiction relates to the nuances and consequences of social distinctions among those who were not poor. So also with her correspondence. Thus, in a letter of 1814 to Cassandra, Austen comments on the Lent Assizes for Hampshire as likely to "hasten an intimacy" between her brother Edward's family and that of William Wickham, a prominent public figure.[82]

Austen herself had an extensive, albeit indirect, knowledge of the peerage.[83] This was strengthened by developing connections. Thus, in 1813, John Austen, a second cousin, became rector of Chevening, the seat of Charles, third Earl Stanhope, a socially prominent man of science and an eccentric, as well as the cousin of William Pitt the Younger. Although referred to as "Citizen Stanhope" for his radical beliefs, Stanhope was annoyed when his daughter Lucy married a surgeon from Sevenoaks.[84] Also in Kent, Austen's favorite niece, Fanny, in 1820 married Sir Edward Knatchbull, a member of a prominent and long-established country family.

To a degree, the social distinctions of the past (and present) have been sidelined due to pushing gender concerns to the fore and because modern society is less comfortable with overt social distinctions. Nevertheless, Austen was well aware of them. Thus, in August 1814, she wrote to her niece Anna, who was working on a novel, that the meeting of a lord and his brother with a doctor had to be "scratched out" as a "country surgeon . . . would not be introduced to men of their rank." They were very much socially inferior to physicians.

While dealing in part with men, Austen focused on social distinctions and personal relations from the female perspective. However, male approaches to women repeatedly complicated the situation and helped set the narrative. These approaches and the responses could be deliberately used for social advancement, but much else was also at play, and Austen focused on the latter, as with Fanny Price's rejection of Henry Crawford. More generally, matrimony, like friendship, could both affirm and dissolve social distinctions, if not barriers.

Social distinctions were very much present throughout the novels and offered an opportunity for the play of personality. Thus, the Westons' visit to Hartfield provides Emma with the opportunity to discuss the burning question posed by the presumption, as she saw it, of the Coles choosing to invite "the superior families" to visit. Visiting, more generally, is a minefield for, in offering a way to demonstrate, indeed, assert status, it also risks compromising it. That factor interacts with those of self-interest in visiting or, indeed, convenience or preference. All these issues are addressed in the discussion in the first chapter of *Pride and Prejudice* of whether to visit Mr. Bingley. This is not only a matter of form for the Bennets. As Mrs. Bennet notes when pressing her husband to visit: "Consider your daughters. Only think what an establishment it would be for one of them. Sir William and Lady Lucas are determined to go, merely on that account; for in general you know they visit no newcomers."

In *Emma*, the Coles themselves apparently represented the corrosive quality of money, which posed the prime threat to traditional rural values. In this case, the money was that of a mercantile or financial company or "house," such as a bank:

> The Coles had been settled some years in Highbury, and were very good sort of people—friendly, liberal, and unpretending; but, on the other hand, they were of low origin, in trade, and only moderately

genteel. . . . The last year or two had brought them a considerable increase of means—the house in town had yielded greater profits and fortune in general had smiled on them. With their wealth, their views increased; their want of a larger house, their inclination for more company. They added to their house, to their number of servants, to their expenses of every sort; and by this time were in fortune and style of living, second only to the family at Hartfield.[85]

The extent to which the Coles represented the corrosive quality of money in Austen's view, as opposed to Emma's, is unclear. It is indicative that Mr. Knightley appears to get on well with Mr. Cole, who is included in discussions of parish business. Nobody but Emma seems to think the Coles ought not to send her an invitation, and in the end she accepts anyway and is rather pleased by their deference toward her. They seem to be an example of new money managing to incorporate social change into rural society without threatening its traditional values.

Emma offers concern about such relationships throughout, as when the Churchills opposed the marriage of his sister to the less exalted Captain Weston, this dissatisfaction extending to the sister: "She wanted at once to be the wife of Captain Weston, and Miss Churchill of Enscombe,"[86] from whence she came. In *Pride and Prejudice*, the unacceptability of introducing oneself to a social superior, an issue that does not really arise today, or at least not to the same extent, is a theme at the Netherfield ball. As that fault is committed by Mr. Collins, who is being oleaginous, the convention is thereby affirmed. Darcy responded with but "distant civility." Augusta Elton is overly familiar in her failure to use titles, as in "Knightley" and "Jane Fairfax": "Let us now suppose that she dares go about, Emma Woodhouse-ing me!"[87]

In a quieter way, Austen shares Tobias Smollett's assumption that positive social values are embodied in the country gentry and like him is uneasy about both social mobility and aristocratic privilege.[88] Her ironic critique is most strongly captured with the portrayal of arrogant and designing women of rank, compared to whom the men can appear arrogant and manipulated. Thus, Mr. Parker's partner in the development of Sanditon is described as a woman who

> knew the value of money . . . Lady Denham had been a rich Miss Brereton, born to wealth but not to education. Her first husband had been a Mr Hollis, a man of considerable property in the country, of which a large share of the parish of Sanditon, with manor and mansion house made a part. He had been an elderly man when she married him;—her own age about thirty.—Her motives for such a match could be little understood at the distance of forty years, but she had so well nursed and pleased Mr Hollis, that at his death he left her everything—all his estates, and all at her disposal. After a widowhood of some years, she had been induced to marry again. The late Sir Harry Denham . . . had succeeded in removing her and her large income to his own domains, but he could not succeed in the views of permanently enriching his family, which were attributed to him. She had been too wary to put anything out of her own power—and when on Sir Harry's decease she returned again to her own house at Sanditon, she was said to have this boast to a friend "that though she had *got* nothing but her title from the family, still she had *given* nothing for it."[89]

Yet there is meanness at other ranks and ages, an almost instinctive desire or instinct on the part of some to look down on those less fortunate, as when Mrs. Norris opposes the provision of a horse for her niece Fanny Price while her affluent cousins, the Miss Bertrams, would not let her ride theirs: "The Miss Bertrams regularly wanted their horses every fine day, and had no idea of carrying their obliging manners to the sacrifice of any real pleasure."[90] This is Austen being very observant on the difference between true and false politeness.

Ironically, George III was widely considered as middle class. His lifestyle, notably as "Farmer George," was more cautious and less social than that of many of the great Whig aristocrats. At the same time, George, like Austen, was socially and morally

conservative, which he would have associated with an emphasis on the importance of duty and merit. His correspondence
on military promotions was indicative of his attitudes. After the
capture of a French frigate in 1795, George wrote to George, second Earl Spencer, the first lord of the admiralty, applauding the
promotion of the captain and the first lieutenant, adding: "As the
Second Lieutenant Mr Maitland conducted himself very well, I
trust he will soon meet with the same favour, being a man of good
family will I hope also be of advantage in the consideration, as
it is certainly wise as much as possible to give encouragement if
they personally deserve it to gentlemen."[91] Frederick Maitland
was indeed a brave officer and was to have a distinguished naval
career, rising to the rank of rear admiral. His father, Frederick,
the godson of George's father, was a son of Charles, sixth Earl of
Lauderdale, and had been commander of the royal yacht. Austen's attitude was similar: merit and birth ideally aligned.

In *Pride and Prejudice*, Darcy comes to reflect that he was
almost taught "to care for none beyond my own family circle; to
think meanly of all the rest of the world; to wish at least to think
meanly of their sense and worth," only for Elizabeth Bennet to
teach him the error of his ways.[92] Darcy's social condescension
matches the sanctimonious moral condescension of Mr. Collins
after Lydia's elopement. Darcy, however, can learn to do better, whereas Collins has to be contained by his wife. Thanks to
Darcy's transformation, the novel shows the defeat of social and
moral condescension, more particularly in the nexus of Lady
Catherine de Bourgh, who thus provides further coherence in
the novel. Such placing of individuals happens more generally
in Austen's work, both leading to and reflecting the interdependence within each novel.

Collins himself is encouraged by Mr. Bennet to reflect that
he needs to turn to Darcy, rather than Lady Catherine, in order
to achieve further preferment. This provides an explanation of
the superiority of money in the shape of the greater value of

additional livings, but, looked at differently, it is the traditional issue of patronage that comes to the fore. Certainly, Mr. Bennet reads Mr. Collins aright, as he has done throughout the story. To that extent, Mr. Bennet is a wiser custodian of his family than his wife, who would prefer Collins to be won over via marriage to a Bennet daughter.

Status and honor are key issues. Indeed, the lack of dependence "on the appearance of either merit or sense" to which Elizabeth Bennet refers might have been even more the case in Austen's novels had they engaged with honor culture in the shape of dueling, other than in the somewhat absurd idea that Mr. Bennet would fight a duel with Wickham over his seduction of Lydia.[93] The duel between Colonel Brandon and John Willoughby is mentioned but is neither described nor made a topic of conversation.[94] Austen's treatment, almost nontreatment, of dueling was probably an indication that for her it was an outmoded custom that belonged in silly romantic fiction. Her novels assume a world in which dueling is an absurd idea, as indeed it was.

Dueling in practice was a product of concerns with rank, reputation, and masculinity and, arguably, an aspect of the British imperial state, with its aspirations fronting a society in which status had to be affirmed while masculinity was linked to display and aggression.[95] A duel removes Delamere in Charlotte Smith's novel *Emmeline*. The arbitrary nature of the result of duels, and the peculiar concepts of bravery, honor, and masculinity that were involved, served to underline some of the major problems with male culture. There was an arbitrariness that was scarcely contained by reason, and this helped encourage moves to outlaw dueling. The report in the *Carlton House Magazine* of August 1792 of a duel in Hyde Park with pistols and then swords between Lady Almeria Braddock and Mrs. Elphinstone, over the latter questioning the age of the former, was a fiction, although one woman was nearly beaten to death in a duel-like fight the following year near Chelmsford.[96]

Status and honor are matters of character and language as well as action. Indeed, the interplay of themes in Austen's writings was seen not only in the plots but also in the related characterization. Moreover, the differentiation of the latter was deeply "embedded in the plain stuff of the language."[97] More generally, the moral vibrancy of the novels is linked to the response elicited by the characters and their interaction. Today, film captures the context of this interaction, but it requires fine acting to accompany Austen's dialogue in order to do the rest.

NOTES

1. D. Le Faye, *Jane Austen's Country Life* (London, 2014).
2. *Sanditon* 2.
3. *Sanditon* 11.
4. *Sense* II, 11.
5. *Persuasion* I, 1.
6. D. Greene, "Jane Austen and the Peerage," *PMLA* 68 (1953): 1017–31.
7. *PP* II, 10.
8. *Persuasion* I, 2.
9. *Sense* II, 12.
10. I. R. Christie, *Stress and Stability in Late Eighteenth Century Britain* (Oxford, 1984).
11. *PP* III, 14.
12. J. Cannon, *Aristocratic Century: The Peerage of Eighteenth-Century England* (Cambridge, 1984).
13. W. T. Gibson, "'Withered Branches and Weighty Symbols': Surname Substitution in England, 1660–1880," *British Journal for Eighteenth-Century Studies* 15 (1992): 17–33.
14. *PP* I, 1.
15. *PP* III, 14.
16. *PP* I, 9.
17. *PP* I, 13.
18. *Sense* II, 11.
19. *PP* I, 14.
20. *PP* I, 18.
21. *Emma* I, 16.
22. *Emma* I, 16.

23. *PP* III, 1.

24. Trevor to William, Lord Grenville, Foreign Secretary, October 8, 1792, NA. FO. 67/10.

25. *Emma* II, 8; III, 3, 13.

26. A. M. Duckworth, *The Improvement of the Estate: A Study of Jane Austen's Novels* (Baltimore, MD, 1994).

27. *PP* I, 4.

28. *PP* I, 4.

29. *PP* I, 6.

30. *Emma* I, 2.

31. *Persuasion* I, 9.

32. *Sense* III, 1.

33. *MP* I, 3.

34. *MP* I, 3.

35. *MP* II; 4, III, 9.

36. *Persuasion* I, 1, II, 5.

37. D. Rapp, *Samuel Whitbread (1764–1815). A Social and Political Study* (New York, 1987); *Sense* II, 11.

38. *Emma* II, 4.

39. *Collected Novels and Memoirs of William Godwin V* (London, 1805, 2nd ed. 1832), 173. For a different view, J. A. Jones,"Tax and Taxability: 'Trade, Profession or Vocation' Seen Through the Eyes of Jane Austen," in P. Hart and D. de Cogan, eds. *Studies in the History of Tax Law*, vol. 9 (Oxford, 2019), 123–58.

40. T. Carlyle, *Chartism* (London, 1839), chapter 6.

41. A. L. Cohen, "The 'Aristocratic Imperialists' of Late Georgian and Regency Britain," *Eighteenth-Century Studies* 50 (2016): 5–26.

42. *PP* III, 2.

43. Earlier, there had been a baron-bishop, Crewe of Durham.

44. *PP* II, 5.

45. *MP* I, 6.

46. *MP* I, 9.

47. *Sanditon* 4.

48. *PP* III, 1.

49. P. Lindfield, *Georgian Gothic: Medievalist Architecture, Furniture and Interiors 1730–1840* (Woodbridge, UK, 2016).

50. *Sense* II, 14.

51. *Letters*, 117.

52. D. Stillman, *English Neoclassical Architecture* (London, 1989).

53. *MP* I, 5.

54. *Northanger* II, 5.

55. *Persuasion* I, 1.

56. *Sanditon* 12.

57. *MP* I, 9.

58. *PP* III, 1.

59. *Sanditon* 12.

60. *Persuasion* I, 1.

61. N. Scarfe, ed., *A Frenchman's Year in Suffolk* (Woodbridge, UK, 1988), 34.

62. *PP* III, 3; *MP* I, 9.

63. *MP* I, 6.

64. *MP* I, 6.

65. *MP* II, 7.

66. M. Batey, *Jane Austen and the English Landscape* (Barn Elms, UK, 1996).

67. *Emma* III, 6.

68. *Letters*, 119.

69. *Lady Susan*, letter 16.

70. T. Gray, ed., *Travels in Georgian Devon: The Illustrated Journals of the Reverend John Swete, 1789–1800* (Exeter, UK, 1997), xv.

71. *Emma* II, 14.

72. J. Harris, "English Country House Guides, 1740–1840," in *Concerning Architecture: Essays on Architectural Writers and Writing Presented to Nikolaus Pevsner*, ed. J. Summerson (London, 1968), 58–74.

73. *Sense* I, 12–13.

74. *MP* I, 9.

75. *Sense* III, 6.

76. *Sense* III, 14.

77. Scarfe, *Frenchman's Year*, 36.

78. *Northanger* II, 11.

79. *MP* I, 8.

80. D. Winter, *George Morland: 1763–1804* (Stanford, CA, 1977).

81. *Sense* III, 8.

82. *Letters*, 259.

83. R. Vick, "Jane Austen and Lord Howard," *Notes and Queries* 239, no. 3 (September 1994): 324–25.

84. A. Newman, *The Stanhopes of Chevening* (London, 1969), 188–89. There are very few such works by academics.

85. *Emma* II, 7.

86. *Emma* I, 2.

87. *PP* I, 18; *Emma* II, 15.

88. I. C. Ross, "Tobias Smollett: Gentleman by Birth, Education, and Profession," *British Journal for Eighteenth-Century Studies* 5 (1982): 188.

89. *Sanditon* 3.

90. *MP* I, 4.

91. George III to Spencer, March 17, 1795, BL. Add. 75779.

92. *PP* III, 16.

93. *PP* II, 1.

94. *PP* III, 5.

95. S. Banks, *A Polite Exchange of Bullets: The Duel and the English Gentleman 1750–1850* (Woodbridge, UK, 2010).

96. J. L. Wood, "The Petticoat Duellists," *Factotum* 29 (August 1989): 11–13.

97. J. F. Burrows, "'Nothing Out of the Ordinary Way': Differentiation of Character in the Twelve Most Common Words of *Northanger Abbey, Mansfield Park*, and *Emma*," *British Journal for Eighteenth-Century Studies* 6 (1983): 17–41, esp. 40.

AGRICULTURE AND AGRICULTURAL CHANGE

Many of the farmers of that part of the country [Pewsey]
have very humanely supplied their labourers with wheat
at 6 shillings per bushel, and that with equal humanity
and good policy, they have now agreed to a temporary
increase in the wages of those who have large families.
May these laudable examples be everywhere followed.[1]

—*Salisbury and Winchester Journal*, May 3, 1790

THE DOMINANCE OF BOTH CENTER and localities by the
landed elite was expressed, clearly and repeatedly, in the life of
the population and the molding of the landscape. In the latter
case, the key instance arose not so much from the landscaping
of the grounds of stately homes and other houses that interested
those presented by Austen but rather from Acts of Parliament
providing for the enclosure of open land, classically with hedges
that divided individually owned properties. Passed in a Parliament dominated by the elite, this legislation facilitated a total
reorganization of the rural landscape covered by each act in
order to enhance the control and profits of landlords. As freehold tenure thus became more important, the sense of place and
identity of others, indeed of the overwhelming majority of the

rural population, who worked on the land was challenged. This challenge was taken furthest where, as happened occasionally, settlements were moved or, less infrequently, when individual homes were replaced.

Enclosure acts were part of a more general process by which, in many parts of the country, landholding and control over land, already concentrated, were now further concentrated in fewer hands. Thanks to demand from a rapidly increasing population, land had become more productive and thus a better investment. If most of the elite, in this and other respects, preferred to gain their ends in a consensual fashion and managed their localities in a reciprocal manner, they did both in their own interest. Consensualism and reciprocity were only taken so far, and most were excluded from its scope or only admitted on a deferential basis.

Enclosure, and agrarian change more generally, were driven by rising demand for food as a result of the growing population and in a context where most food was produced in England, or at least the British Isles, and not imported from further afield. This rising demand benefited landlords and tenant farmers but not the landless poor. Indeed, agricultural wages remained low in part because there was no shortage of labor and in part because agricultural workers were not able to secure better conditions. The rural population was dominated by an economy of proprietary wealth: a system built around rent and poor remuneration for labor, and, in the context of a markedly unequal distribution of land, a situation that did not change. As a woman, Lady Catherine de Bourgh could not be a justice of the peace, but, assisted by information from Mr. Collins, she controlled her tenants and the local people: "Whenever any of the cottagers were disposed to be quarrelsome, discontented or too poor, she sallied forth into the village to settle their differences, silence their complaints, and scold them into harmony and plenty."[2] The last was a classic instance of Austen's irony.

The situation could be even less attractive. In *Henry and Eliza*, Austen began: "As Sir George and Lady Harcourt were superintending the labours of their haymakers, rewarding the industry of some by smiles of approbation, and punishing the idleness of others, by a cudgel."[3] The prospect of Lady Harcourt doing so was improbable, but physical violence, in reality, prospect, or threat, could underlay social relations. It was mentioned on several occasions in Austen's juvenilia.

It was not possible for the poor to change the situation. Riots against enclosure had scant consequence. The French husband of Austen's cousin Eliza Hancock met more opposition in the 1780s when trying to enclose land in the Landes in southwest France. He was later guillotined in February 1794 during the "Terror," when the French Revolution was at its height.

Agrarian prosperity was of crucial significance to Austen's family because tithes, a tenth of annual produce taken by law to support the Church, were the foundation of clerical income. This was true both for those with wealthy livings and for those, such as Austen's father, with poor ones. For the latter, the tithes were even more significant. This was especially so because George Austen was very much part of the universal world of credit and debt, a world that reached from the pauper to the peer. Indeed, he borrowed heavily within his family network, including from his brother-in-law, James Leigh-Perrot, and his sister Philadelphia. Cobbling together his income from a number of sources, as most did, George had to rely on the sale of his own farm produce, principally grain, which linked him even more intimately to the rural economy and would have made his children knowledgeable about the latter.

Like the others who lived on the land, Austen's parents fed themselves from their land and that of their neighbors. They did not buy everyday food (as opposed to items such as sugar, spices, and chocolate) in shops. Thus, there was not the specialization of modern agriculture. The limited nature of communication links ensured there was a greater need for all-around agricultural production than would be the case by the late nineteenth century and, still more, today. Indeed, the detailed pattern of land use was far more complex than might be suggested by upland pasture and lowland arable, which was the most common distinction. In upland areas, grain was grown in small quantities as a subsistence crop, as it is not today. Livestock were kept in lowland areas to provide meat, milk, manure, wool, leather, and motive power. At the level of the individual farmstead, and again of the village, there was a degree of self-reliance totally alien to modern farmers. This reflected the relative difficulty of preservation and transport in an age before refrigeration and motor vehicles but also the degree and intensity of local systems of exchange, as well as the extent to which reliance on self and the local made more economic sense than in the modern age of specialization through comparative profit margins.

The Austens produced their own bread, milk, vegetables, and eggs. Indeed, their household, like many others, functioned as an enterprise in the making of beer and bread. Dilute beer was a way to avoid the health risks from bad—contaminated—water. The harvest was a key annual event for the Austens and others, but farming also brought other annual events, as well as daily chores such as collecting eggs and milking cattle. This situation created a frame of reference and a pattern of activity. The impact can be seen in the life of her characters. Elizabeth Bennet mistakenly thinks a whole house in confusion means "at least that the pigs were got into the garden"[4] and therefore able to eat the vegetables, whereas it is in practice due to a visit by Miss de Bourgh. Charlotte Collins, the daughter of a knight, devotes herself to "her poultry,"[5] which reflects the groundedness she displays throughout the novel. Poultry were a valued source of meat and eggs and thus were crucial for protein.

The majority of the population lived in, and on, the countryside. Although the rise of industry and the development of the service sector altered percentages and perceptions, agriculture was the principal source of employment and wealth, the most significant sector of the economy, and an important support of the taxation—whether governmental, ecclesiastical (tithes), or proprietorial (rents)—that funded many other activities. Land, and its products, provided the structure of the social system and the bulk of the wealth that kept it going.

The opportunities provided by agriculture were enhanced, and exploited, by interrelated changes in inputs, land use, and agricultural organization. There was a spread of fodder crops, both "artificial grasses" and root crops—for example, sainfoin, clover, coleseed, and turnips. These crops helped eliminate fallow and increase the capacity of the rural economy to rear more animals, which, in turn, produced more manure and further raised crop yields and thus productivity and profitability. Separately, important advances in animal breeding, notably of cattle, sheep, and pigs, led to an improvement in meat yields, as celebrated by paintings of owners with their large animals.

Changes were aided by the practice of enclosing land, although that was expensive. Indeed, most small farms lacked the capital and willingness to accept risk that were necessary for a program of improvement, to return to a term used by contemporaries in a different fashion in the previous chapter. Consolidated, compact, and enclosed holdings were far from new, especially in the West Country and the Southeast, but became far more common from the 1760s. Steventon itself was enclosed in about 1741.[6] Enclosure was frequently linked to changes in naming, not least of field names, local terrain features, and roads. This naming reflected major and often fundamental alterations in layout, land use, and agricultural practices. There was a linear aesthetic of form and function that corresponded with the usefulness of enclosure. Enclosure has been presented as leading to the proletarianization of the rural labor force. In practice, though, the situation varied by region, locality, and estate. *Persuasion* includes a walk, in part, "through large enclosures,"[7] although it is unclear if these were the product of recent enclosure acts.

There were also relevant national trends. In particular, the continued growth and integration of the market economy was a product of improved transport links and the rise in population and, therefore, demand—a demand these links could address. As the national market developed, the relative importance of local consumption declined, and regional variations in price became gradually less pronounced.

Elite power and wealth remained key facets of the agrarian economy. John Parker, first Earl of Morley (1772–1840), was able to mortgage his Saltram estate near Plymouth in order to raise over fifteen thousand pounds to drain the wetlands to the southwest of his house in 1806–7. As a reminder of multiple links, George III, who made Parker an earl, had stayed at Saltram in 1789 during his visit to Plymouth, and Joshua Reynolds was a friend of Parker's father and painted the young John, and the 1995 film of *Sense and Sensibility* was partly filmed at the house. Elite power was reflected in the concentration of landownership, in electoral politics, and in the crucial role of prominent local figures in the administration and operation of the Land Tax.

However, at the same time, as a reminder of the nuances of Austen's England, much of the work on electoral interests over the last quarter century has emphasized the extent to which the sway of the elite was conditional and often, although not always, contested. Tenants and other dependents did not necessarily conform to the views of the landowners. The sway of the elite within parliamentary boroughs, although important, was also conditional. Negotiation was the means of maintaining social mores and structures and handling disputes. Linked to this, continuity among the farming population through regularly renewed leases was crucial in assisting the development of the land's potential.

The counties that had the most enclosure acts were, in order, the West Riding of Yorkshire, Lincolnshire, and Norfolk.

Northamptonshire, the setting for *Mansfield Park*, was another county with enclosures, but less prominently. Austen asked Cassandra in January 1813 to find out "whether Northamptonshire is a country [*sic*] of hedgerows."[8] An alliance there of small occupiers and landless commoners resisted parliamentary enclosure with petitions; threats; attacks on gates, posts, and rails; and other crimes. This was not a rural society of deference and order but one in which elite hegemony was seen by some as selfish and disruptive. At the same time, the social elite was also the source of employment, patronage, and philanthropy, as well as a symbol of stability and a defender of custom and the Church.

Austen not knowing about Northamptonshire was an aspect of the limited span of her traveling, unlike the unmarried Celia Fiennes (1662–1741),[9] but such a limited span was far from atypical. George III (1738–1820, r. 1760–1820) never visited Northamptonshire. Indeed, although he got to Portsmouth, Exeter, Plymouth, and Oxford, he never went further north than Worcester. No eighteenth-century monarch toured Scotland, Wales, Ireland, or the north of England. Austen also never visited any of these four, although she visited Stoneleigh Abbey, Warwick Castle, Kenilworth, and Hamstall Ridware in 1806 and may have pressed on to Chatsworth, the possible basis of Pemberley,[10] although that identification is not accepted by all commentators.

Moreover, knowledge of geography, while spread by the world of print, could also be limited, although not necessarily less than today.[11] Austen had sufficient knowledge to make a joke in her juvenilia about a character ending up in a totally wrong county because of not knowing the way. However, there is little sign that geography, notably of abroad, but also of England, played much of a role in her extensive reading, other than in Gilpin's travels. So also with other novelists. The group who tended to show such knowledge set their action abroad or wrote specifically on the subject of travel, as did Smollett. It was not necessary to have traveled in order to pursue such a setting, but Austen was not interested in letting her imagination roam in this fashion.

The process of obtaining enclosure acts reflected the social politics of the period. Once the major landowners were convinced of the value of enclosure, they would petition Parliament for an act, and 1,532 enclosure acts were passed between 1760 and 1797. Although about a third of these acts brought waste land into cultivation for the first time, the extent to which there was a peasantry with a proprietary interest in the soil was also reduced. Freehold tenure became more important, and other "rights" over land were downgraded. This loss of security of tenure increased uncertainty, not least by dislocating the senses of place and identity for many who worked on the land. The radical Newcastle bookseller Thomas Spence wrote in 1800: "Are not our legislators all landlords? . . . It is childish to expect ever to see small farms again, or ever to see anything else than the utmost screwing and grinding of the poor, till you quite overturn the present system of landed property." However, this was very much a partisan comment and exaggerated.[12] The view that enclosure drove the small farmer out of existence is a myth.

This was not the subject of Austen's novels. She was well aware of control by those of birth, connection, and wealth but looked at other aspects of it. Yet her settings rest on the wealth of a rural economy—for example, the attractive Abbey Mill Farm in *Emma* during the last stages of the Napoleonic wars when grain prices were high, a process further aided because the War of 1812 blocked grain imports from the United States from 1812 until early 1815. So also in *Emma*, with Knightley's knowledge of the home farm at Donwell Abbey, which he keeps under his own care. Visited by his brother, "he had to tell what every field was to bear next year, and to give all such local information as could not fail of being interesting to a brother whose home it had equally been the longest part of his life, and whose attachments were strong. The plan of a drain [drainage ditch], the change of a fence, the felling of a tree, and the destination of every acre for wheat, turnips, or spring corn, was entered into with as much equality of interest by John."[13] Thus, Knightley was a modern farmer. Turnips were an important fodder crop and had been incorporated in the crop rotations popularized in the 1730s by Charles, second Viscount Townshend, "Turnip Townshend," a major Norfolk landowner and former prominent minister. Subsequently, Knightley gives Harriet "information as to modes of agriculture," which are his concern, and talks to Robert Martin of "business, shows of cattle, or new drills,"[14] the last a reference to seed drills. In *Sanditon*, Mr. Heywood is found at the outset "among his haymakers." Returning to Mansfield Park, Sir Thomas Bertram rapidly had "to reinstate himself in all the wonted concerns of his Mansfield life, to see his steward and his bailiff—to examine and compute—and in the intervals of business, to walk into his stables and his gardens, and nearest plantations,"[15] the last a reference to new timber. John Dashwood encloses Norland Common, and "the variety of politics, enclosing land, and breaking horses" is the after-dinner conversation when he entertains Sir John Middleton and Colonel Brandon, two other landowners. Once at Delaford, Edward and Elinor Ferrars regret that they do not have "better pasturage for their cows."[16]

In contrast, Mr. Rushworth is "ignorant in business," making him an unattractive prospect as a son-in-law to Sir Thomas Bertram, and Mr. Palmer "idled away the mornings at billiards, which ought to have been devoted to business,"[17] while Kellynch Hall in *Persuasion* is managed poorly, which obliges the unimpressive Sir Walter Elliot to leave his estate. This departure leads to a discussion of social mobility. Sir Walter is reluctant to let his house. When the possibility of doing so to naval officers who have made money from the war, notably by winning prize money from captured ships, both the term and the concept a measure of merit, is mentioned, he also attacks upward social mobility. Sir Walter disdains "bringing persons of obscure birth into undue distinction, and raising men to honours which their fathers and grandfathers never dreamt of.... A man is in greater danger in the navy of being insulted by the rise of one whose father, his father might have disdained to speak to, and of becoming prematurely an object of disgust himself, than in any other line."[18]

This is Sir Walter as impolite, as well as a poor custodian of his property and inheritance. He presses on to personalize this harshness, adopting an approach, clearly criticized by Austen, prefiguring that of Antony Trollope in his account of aristocratic snobbery, notably with the impecunious Longestaffes in *The Way We Live Now* (1874–75): "One day last spring, in town, I was in company with two men, striking instances of what I am talking of, Lord St Ives, whose father we all know to have been a country curate, without bread to eat; I was to give place to Lord St Ives, and a certain Admiral Baldwin, the most deplorable looking personage you can imagine."[19] This is because, as Sir Walter knows, the admiral had seen extensive sea service on behalf of his country that had roughened and reddened his skin as a result of exposure to wind, rain, and sun. This was particularly the case with naval officers, who, in a face-to-face society and also facing the enemy, very much commanded from the open deck. Here and elsewhere, Austen, in this case in her presentation of Sir Walter, captures the distinction noted in *Pride and Prejudice* between being gentlemanlike and "merely" looking "the gentleman."[20] The former was not a matter of presentation to the eye, and thus of bearing, but rather of conversation and conduct, of content and tone. Austen's point and commitment were clear, not least because of her brothers in the navy.

Agrarian care is part of the question of appropriate behavior. When Admiral Croft takes over Kellynch, he at once improves on Sir Walter in every respect. He and his wife "were generally out of doors together, interesting themselves in their new possessions, their grass, and their sheep."[21] Similarly, in valuing prospects, it was, more generally, assumed that it would be known which farms were "some of the best land in the country,"[22] meaning county. However, utilitarianism can be taken too far. When John Dashwood sees Delaford Hanger, a fine wood, he can only think of the timber it represents.[23] This is unattractive and depredatory and not part of the trust between the generations that Austen supports. This trust was crucial to Tory ideas of stewardship, service and trusteeship, ideas that were both religious and secular.

Austen's mature novels do not deal with a key aspect of the rural economy, poaching, although an unattractive aspect of both hunting and the social hierarchy is captured in *Jack and Alice*, an early work. Alice and Lady Williams meet Lucy, a young woman whose leg is entirely broken by "one of the steel traps so common in gentlemen's grounds"—a steel mantrap deployed against poachers.[24] Poaching is alluded to in Austen's correspondence in an account of a visit to Kent in 1805 when she refers to the danger of troops poaching.[25] The game (meat from hunted animals) trade, although illegal under the game laws, flourished in the second half of the century as game that had been poached reached urban markets, especially London, in increasing quantities, in part through the developing network of coach services. Alongside poaching "for the pot"—in other words, for one's own food—there was national business for the poacher. The government responded with an Act of 1755 that made the sale of game illegal by those allowed to hunt and by others. This act also failed, but it made those who wanted to buy game dependent on poachers.

Hunting was very important to the rural society in which Austen grew up. In her letter of September 15, 1796, Austen refers to her brother Edward going shooting. So also in the novels. When, in *Lady Susan*, Reginald from Kent, visiting his sister in Sussex, decides to stay for a while, he summons his "hunters"—in other words, his horses for hunting. Having such horses is very much an indication of wealth. The prelude to his intended departure is him telling his sister, "I am going to send James forward with my

hunters immediately."[26] Masculinity was linked to horsemanship, although the proper nature of the latter was debated.[27]

And not only horses. In *Pride and Prejudice*, a young Lucas
declares that he would keep a pack of foxhounds if he was as rich
as Darcy.[28] This is a ready measure of wealth and its consequences,
notably the opportunity to acquire social status by means of the
patronage of elite male sociability. Owning a pack of foxhounds
would be expensive and would require staff, buildings, and land.

In *Mansfield Park*, Henry Crawford shoots and sleeps when
he returns to his seat at Everingham while Mr. Rushworth at
Sotherton Court provides "the repeated details of his day's sport,
good or bad, his boast of his dogs, his jealousy of his neighbours,
his doubts of their qualification [reference to the game laws],
and his zeal after poachers."[29] Austen's comment about "repeated
details" presumably captures the boredom of those, principally
women but also men, who had to listen to such accounts. Later,
trying to distract his returned father, Tom Bertram complains
about the shooting:

> We have had such incessant rains almost since October began, that
> we have been nearly confined to the house for days together. I have
> hardly taken out a gun since the 3d. Tolerable sport the first three
> days, but there has been no attempting any thing since. The first day
> I went over Mansfield Wood, and Edmund took the copses beyond
> Easton, and we brought home six brace between us, and might each
> have killed six times as many; but we respect your pheasants, Sir, I
> assure you, as much as you could desire. I do not think you will find
> your woods by any means worse stocked than they were. I never saw
> Mansfield Wood so full of pheasants in my life as this year. I hope
> you will take a day's sport there yourself, Sir, soon.[30]

The following morning, Tom and his friend John Yates take
their guns to shoot in Mansfield Wood. Subsequently, when
Henry Crawford and Edmund Bertram meet at dinner, they
discuss hunting, and the next day Henry sends for his hunters
from Norfolk.[31] With limited talent and taste, Sir John Middleton

"hunted and shot." When Marianne Dashwood falls, John Willoughby is nearby out shooting,[32] but the cost of his "hunters"—horses for hunting—is one of the reasons Willoughby seeks the wealthy Miss Grey as a wife and not Marianne. This is yet another poor choice of priorities. As the boldest rider in England, Willoughby had gained the respect of Sir John Middleton, earning a promise of a pointer (a gundog) puppy to help in his hunting. At the end, Willoughby reconciles himself to marriage: "In his breed of horses and dogs, and in sporting of every kind, he found no inconsiderable degree of domestic felicity."[33]

In *Northanger Abbey*, a lack of shooting means a "dead time in the year" such that General Tilney could not hold a ball: "The Lady Frasers were not in the country."[34] Henry Tilney receives his guests with the "friends of his solitude," who are hunting dogs.[35] In *Persuasion*, when Anne Elliot arrives at Uppercross, Charles Musgrove is out shooting. Indeed, "the Mr Musgroves had their own game to guard, and to destroy," and were engaged with horses and dogs as well as newspapers. Charles Musgrove's "zeal" focuses on sport—in other words, hunting and shooting. He subsequently goes shooting with Captain Wentworth, and shooting is crucial to his male socializing. This again is a silent critique of much rural male sociability as repetitive and boring, if not boorish. Women are excluded. As such, male authority looks less positive. Moreover, in contrast, female socializing appears more positive.[36]

The rural economy was far from static. The wars with France from 1793–1802 and 1803–14 and in 1815 had a serious impact on the national economy, affecting export markets as a whole and hitting the woolen industry. Charlotte Brontë's novel *Shirley* (1849) was set in Yorkshire during the industrial depression in 1811–12, more particularly the Luddite uprisings in the textile industry. However, wartime agriculture benefited from buoyant domestic demand. In Austen's last years, a serious postwar depression saw an accentuation of the general difficulties of society. In particular, a rising population faced low wages. Dominated by the landed interest, Parliament in 1815 passed the Corn Law legislation, which, in response to the marked fall of grain prices after the end of the wars with France and the United States as foreign sources became accessible, prohibited the import of grain unless the price of British grain reached eighty shillings (four pounds) a quarter. This protectionism on behalf of the elite rural interest—or, rather, the well-off who benefitted—kept the price of food artificially high, leading to urban radicalism and food riots among hungry agricultural laborers, with attacks on farmers and corn mills and demands for higher wages. "Bread or blood" was their call. Robert Sharp, a Yorkshire village schoolmaster, complained in his diary: "I have seen long and said often that the rage for enclosing open fields and commons was one great cause of the ruin or poverty of the rural population . . . crowds of labourers, who now as a boon ask for employment and cannot have it, but at such a rate that hunger is always in their train."[37] The spread of machines that replaced handwork, such as threshing machines, further increased tension and led to destructive attacks on the machines.

Throughout, agrarian society rested on a network of towns, and Austen's fiction captures the interplay between life in the country and these settlements. The latter were the prime means for the diffusion of the goods and practices of larger cities. They were particularly significant, like the fictional Meryton, for their shops.[38] Most of England was within a day's journey of a market, and these markets acted as crucial foci for the local economy and society. Goods were traded, animals sold, servants hired, and opinions exchanged. The markets acted as a link between localities and the wider world, a link where the influence of landlord and parson was less direct than in the parish.

Nevertheless, although often regarded today as an urban culture, and considered in terms of urban sites, notably Bath and the West End of London, Hanoverian England also had a pronouncedly rusticity and pastoralism. These were seen in such aspects as the parks of stately homes, songs, and poetry, such as that of James Thomson, Thomas Gray, and John Dyer. Austen makes fun of pastoralism, or at least faddism, in the shape of Mrs. Dashwood's response to Barton Cottage: "As a house, Barton Cottage, though small, was comfortable and compact; but as a cottage it was defective, for the building was regular, the roof was tiled, the window shutters were not painted green, nor were the walls covered with honeysuckles."[39]

The engagement of novels with more picturesque, and thus rugged, landscape by the late eighteenth century led to a downplaying of agrarianism and the rural. However, a rural context continued to be important to many novels, including very much those of Austen. Indeed, she drew on James Thomson's poems *The Seasons* (1730) in *Persuasion*, when Anne Elliot's response to a walk is described. This is a response in which the reader is invited in, to join, as it were, Anne and Jane, through the resonances of description and quotation: "Her *pleasure* in the walk must arise from the exercise and the day, from the view of the last smiles of the year upon the tawny leaves and withered hedges, and from repeating to herself some few of the thousand poetical descriptions extant of autumn, that season of peculiar and inexhaustible influence on the mind of taste and tenderness, that season which has drawn from every poet, worthy of being read, some attempt at description, or some lines of feeling. She occupied her mind as much as possible in such like musings and quotations."[40]

NOTES

1. Pewsey in Berkshire was not far from Steventon.
2. *PP* II, 7.
3. *Juvenilia*, 38.
4. *PP* II, 5.
5. *PP* II, 15.

6. R. Clark and G. Dutton, "Agriculture," in *Jane Austen in Context,* ed. J. Todd (Cambridge, 2005), 187; T. Williamson, *The Transformation of Rural England—Farming and the Landscape 1700–1870* (Exeter, UK, 2002).

7. *Persuasion* I, 10.

8. *Letters,* 202.

9. C. Morris, ed., *The Illustrated Journeys of Celia Fiennes, 1685–c. 1712* (London, 1947).

10. D. Greene, "The Original of Pemberley," *Eighteenth-Century Fiction* 1 (1988): 1–23.

11. J. Black, *Geographies of an Imperial Power: The British World, 1688–1815* (Bloomington, IN, 2018).

12. R. A. Butlin, *The Transformation of Rural England c. 1580–1800: A Study in Historical Geography* (Oxford, 1982); A. Sevilla-Buitrago, "Territory and the Governmentalisation of Social Reproduction: Parliamentary Enclosure and Spatial Rationalities in the Transition from Feudalism to Capitalism," *Journal of Historical Geography* 38 (2012): 219.

13. *Emma* I, 12.

14. *Emma* III, 6, 18.

15. *MP* II, 2.

16. *Sense* II, 11–12, 14.

17. *Sense* III, 6.

18. *Persuasion* I, 3.

19. *Persuasion* I, 3.

20. *PP* I, 3.

21. *Persuasion* I, 9.

22. *Persuasion* I, 9.

23. *Sense* III, 14.

24. *Juvenilia,* 24.

25. Letter 47.

26. Letter 23.

27. M. Mattfeld, *Becoming Centaur: Eighteenth-Century Masculinity and English Horsemanship* (University Park, PA, 2017).

28. *PP* I, 5.

29. *MP* I, 12.

30. *MP* II, 1.

31. *MP* II, 2, 5.

32. *Sense* I, 7, 9.

33. *Sense* II, 8, 10; III, 8, 14.

34. *Northanger* II, 11.

35. *Northanger* II, 11.

36. *Persuasion* I, 5–6, 10.

37. J. E. Crowther and P. A. Crowther, eds., *The Diary of Robert Sharp of South Cave: Life in a Yorkshire Village, 1812–1837* (Oxford, 1997).

38. P. J. Corfield, "Small Towns, Large Implications: Social and Cultural Roles of Small Towns in Eighteenth-Century England and Wales," *British Journal for Eighteenth-Century Studies* 10 (1987): 125–38.

39. *Sense* I, 6.

40. *Persuasion* I, 10.

FOUR

—⚊—

FAMILIES, WOMEN, AND MEN

About thirty years ago, Miss Maria Ward of Huntingdon, with only seven thousand pounds, had the good luck to captivate Sir Thomas Bertram, of Mansfield Park, in the county of Northampton, and to be thereby raised to the rank of a baronet's lady, with all the comforts and consequences of an handsome house and large income.

—Start of *Mansfield Park*

I would rather work for my bread than marry him.

—Frederica Vernon in *Lady Susan*, letter 21

AS THE CASE OF CAROLINE of Brunswick (1768–1821) showed, Austen was happy to identify with women but was also aware of the need to compromise. Married in 1795, Caroline had poor relations with her unattractive and unfaithful husband (and first cousin), George, the prince regent, later George IV. The faults were on both sides but principally his, and Jane supported Caroline, writing in February 1813: "Poor woman, I shall support her as long as I can, because she *is* a woman, and because I hate her husband." Initially, indeed, in November 1815, Austen was reluctant to accept the invitation to dedicate *Emma* to the prince regent, a fan of her work. However, her reluctance was sidelined, and the dedication was duly carried in the book. This dedication would have been commercially valuable, as well as socially important and probably, in the event, a psychological help. Recognition was doubtless more important to her than is now appreciated.

The position of women in English society was defined in large part by social presence and pressure, but much else was at stake. Gender and social issues could easily, almost automatically, combine to a damaging extent. The lives of individual novelists made this readily apparent. Charlotte Lennox (c. 1730–1804), whom Austen admired, suffered both from the social system, in particular her need for patrons, alongside the difficulties this posed for someone of an independent mind, as well as from the more general problems of the female economy. Although she was married, Charlotte was the earner; her husband, Alexander, was feckless (an issue Austen underplays in her own novels), and she was short of money, relying, in her last years, on money from the Literary Fund for writers set up in 1790.[1]

The relationship between population and household structure was very different from that of modern England. Barring occasional bigamies, annulments, wife sales, and aristocratic bills of divorce, marriage was irreversible. As a consequence, marriage generally ended only with the death of one of the partners or with a desertion that involved flight from the community. Both were common, especially the first.[2] For most people, and certainly in terms of the norms of society, marriage was fundamental to sex, procreation, and the upbringing of children, and most childbearing was within marriage. Despite the absence of readily available effective contraceptives and safe, let alone legal, abortion, recorded illegitimacy rates were low, especially by modern standards, although it is impossible to say how much illegitimacy was concealed by infanticide. Moreover, alongside the size of the population and the rate of population growth, the rate of illegitimacy rose during the eighteenth century.

Celibacy was common. Indeed, many people never lived in a sexual relationship, and suggestions to the contrary about Austen, the devout daughter of a clergyman, are totally unconvincing, however conflicted some of her characters might have been. Reputation and respectability were key elements in society. The position of most women recalled Dr. Johnson's celebrated judgment as to matrimony and celibacy, which very much favors the former: "Marriage has many pains, but celibacy has no pleasures."[3] No other alternative is offered. As a celibate, Austen could have no children, which helped explain her fondness for younger relatives and her habit of referring to her novels as children. Thus, *Sense and Sensibility* was termed "her sucking child" and *Pride and Prejudice* as "my own darling child" in letters of 1811 and 1813 respectively. Suggestions that Austen did not have sex because of the shortage of men due to the war with France, as a result of both military service and casualties, are ludicrous.

Marriage became more common during the eighteenth century, and, by the end, fewer than 9 percent of people remained unmarried, compared to nearly a quarter of the population earlier in the century. In addition, less of adulthood was now spent in the unmarried state. The average age at marriage fell to 25.5 and 23.7, for men and women respectively, which greatly increased the possibility of having more children. Economic growth, and the rise of urban employment and living, contributed greatly. Thanks to this, the link between marriage and the availability of land declined, although this decline was far less apparent in rural areas that lacked household industries such as spinning.

Despite a falling death rate in Austen's lifetime, death and disease remained a constant presence and were particularly serious in infancy, especially in the first months of life. This meant that life expectancy at birth provides only a limited guide to the better long-term survival rates for those who reached age five. In addition, giving birth was hazardous. In September 1814, Fanny Austen, the wife of Jane's brother Charles, died soon after giving birth to her daughter Elizabeth, and Elizabeth herself died at three weeks old. Nevertheless, unlike Mary Price in *Mansfield Park*, who died before the age of ten,[4] none of Austen's siblings died young. Furthermore, this impressive outcome was the case despite the family practice of paying local village women to look after the children from soon after birth until they were about one.

This practice ensured that formative experiences at that stage did not occur at home. In addition, sending children out, although normal, may well have had serious psychological consequences, especially in terms of relationships with mothers, fathers, and siblings and a sense of self. An individual's personal narrative would have included the consequences of separation. In Austen's case, the separation was not far, either physically or psychologically, as she visited her parents and was visited by them, but the consequences are unclear. The Austen children were impressive as adults, particularly self-reliant and keen to succeed. More prosaically, thanks to this care, Austen would have become even more used to the Hampshire dialect of the village people. However, due to the strength of local culture, accent was less likely to denote class than in the early twenty-first century.

The average age of life experiences for people of the period was younger than for their descendants today, and these experiences were shaped within a context of the ever-present threat of death, disease, injury, and pain. Death was often sudden, as in 1801 for Marianne Mapleton, a daughter of Austen family friends, and for Austen's father in 1805. So also across the social spectrum. Of the Parkers of Saltram, members of the landed elite in Devon whose house was visited by George III in 1789, four of the five who headed the family between 1649 and 1840 had more than one marriage. Several of these wives died young: after Frances, first wife of John, first Lord Boringdon (1735–88), died in 1764, he married Theresa (1744–75), but she died soon after the birth of her second child, another Theresa. Other, fifth Earl of Plymouth (1751–99), was very ill by the early 1790s, and his son and heir,

Other, sixth Earl, had an even shorter life: 1789–1833. Other was a family name. After the sudden death of his wife Anne in May 1795, Austen's brother James married again in January 1797. As a result of such deaths, many children had stepmothers, which could be a difficult relationship. James's second wife, Mary Lloyd, got on badly with Anna, the daughter of his first marriage.

Alongside a falling death rate, marital fertility among women aged thirty-five and over rose, probably due to better maternal nutrition. The lack of easy birth control, moreover, ensured that a large number of children were born to healthy women. Austen's mother had eight children, which imposed heavy costs on the family economy. George III's wife, Queen Charlotte, had fifteen. The shock of the fatal illness of the youngest daughter—the king's favorite, Amelia (1783–1810)—proved crucial to the permanent collapse of George's mental health.

Austen treats a large number of children as a normal sign of affection between parents. Indeed, although the Crofts in *Persuasion* have no children and appear to be one of the happiest married couples in her work, children are usually emphasized for couples who are presented as happy. The converse could be the case. Of the three Miss Wards, Frances, who becomes Mrs. Price, has a large family, nine children in twelve years, and her sister Maria, now Lady Bertram, has several, but the Miss Ward who marries the Reverend Norris has none. The last is presented as repeatedly selfish and not aware of "how to be pleasant to children." Indeed, there is the suggestion that she would treat the loss of three or four of the Price children as "a great blessing."[5] Mrs. Jennings predicted of a happy clerical marriage that "they will have a child every year! . . . and . . . how poor they will be!"[6] In practice, the marriage of Samuel and Susanna Wesley, a famously unhappy one, saw nineteen pregnancies.

Despite improving average conditions, those who survived infancy were fully aware of their vulnerability. Defenses against disease remained flimsy, not least because of the limited nature of medical knowledge. Accounts of the extraction of teeth using pliers underline the frequency of pain and discomfort. The poses adopted in portraits, whether heroic or familiar, provide no hint of the suffering, indeed tragedy, of individual lives: of Dr. Johnson lancing his own swollen testicles[7] or Queen Anne unsuccessfully suffering through numerous pregnancies in her search for a child who would survive sufficiently long to be her heir. For many, prayer or folk cures were the only remedy for disease and pain. At the same time, a large number of people turned to patent medicines, which were extensively advertised in the press, and this use suggests that confidence in folk remedies and prayer only went so far, especially in towns.

Progress, however, was made in the prevention of smallpox. Inoculation (ingrafting) became safer and popular from the late 1760s. Vaccination, a safer method, was not performed until 1796, but, despite debates over its effectiveness, inoculation lessened the potential breeding for smallpox. No comparable progress was made in fighting other serious problems. Those who survived still often had smallpox scars—for example, Austen's sister-in-law, Mary Lloyd.

Other serious problems included diseases, such as intestinal ones, that would no longer be fatal to the healthy with access to good medical care. In Austen's age, typhus, typhoid, influenza, dysentery, chickenpox, measles, scarlet fever, and venereal diseases were all serious. There was a typhus epidemic from 1782–85. From the 1730s, epidemics of "putrid sore throat"—scarlet fever or diphtheria—occurred for the rest of the century. In January 1807, Austen observed "the Welbys have lost their eldest son by a putrid fever at Eton."[8] Every year, indeed, could be readily divided by the prevalence of different diseases and by how they were experienced.

Other nonfatal diseases, including rheumatism, scurvy, and jaundice, were debilitating and had few or no cures. Alcohol and opium were the only painkillers, and cheap, opium-based laudanum was a universal panacea and the basis of standard medicines. While bishop of Bristol from 1735–37, Thomas Secker spent a quarter of his income on laudanum for his wife's addiction.

There was no system of health provision. Skilled practitioners were few, generally concentrated in the towns, and expensive, although most parishes were within reach of a doctor. Medical training could be very good. Nevertheless, medical treatments, such as blistering or mercury, could be inappropriate and were often painful, dangerous, or enervating. They were also no respecter of class. Aware of the likely pain, some patients refused treatment. Surgery, such as the mastectomy performed without anesthetic on Fanny Burney by Napoleon's surgeon in 1811, was primitive by modern standards. There were anyway no effective anesthetics. Everyone was at the very least threatened by great pain. Austen's last days certainly were very painful, which was one reason she welcomed death. Religious conviction was also an important factor in her attitude.

Widespread trust in quack medicines and herbal remedies reflected the sense that something could, and should, be done at the individual level, and there was no simple acceptance of the grim will of God. However, at the collective level, there was no real pressure for any sweeping improvements in public health.

The virulence of diseases, the impact of accidents, and the potency of crippling medical conditions were due to more than a lack of knowledge and relevant treatments, particularly in terms of antibiotics and anti-inflammatory drugs. Living conditions were also a major problem. Crowded housing, especially the sharing of beds, helped spread diseases, notably respiratory infections. Sharing a bed was common at boarding schools. Austen was sent to one at age seven. However, her near-fatal ill-health there in Southampton in 1783 was due to troops returning from the American Revolutionary War. The movement of troops was a common cause of the spread of infections, a theme that is understandably not present in *Pride and Prejudice*.

Most dwellings, notably those of the poor, were neither warm nor dry, and it was very difficult to get clothes aired. This discouraged washing them and led to the wearing of layers of clothes, many of them thick, so exposure to the damp would not lead to wet skin. The prevalence of outdoor work and transport on foot or horseback greatly exposed people to adverse weather. Furthermore, by modern standards, breath, teeth, and skin must have been repellent; this explains Robert Ferrars' insistence on buying toothpicks in Sense and Sensibility, although it also would have been for show. Houses would have been smelly. Moreover, poor nutrition lowered resistance to disease and the psychological impact of adversity. Fruits and vegetables were both seasonal and expensive. The poor ate less meat.

Austen, however, was more interested in very different sociomedical issues, notably psychological perceptions and drives[9] and how they played through in terms of the events of plots and the development of character. In these, the demographics of the period were less important than the interplay of social and cultural structures and practices with the events of personality and plot.

Social relationships and attitudes reflected a clear cultural inheritance as well as the prevalent economic and technological environment. The Judeo-Christian inheritance, clearly enunciated in the laws and teachings of the churches, decreed monogamy; prohibited marriage between close kin; stipulated procreation as a purpose of matrimony while condemning it outside; forbade abortion, infanticide, homosexuality, and bestiality; made divorce very difficult; enforced care of children; venerated age; and ordered respect for authority in all forms, religious and secular, legal and law enforcing, familial and community. Other issues that would be more regulated today, such as spousal abuse and rape within marriage, were ignored or viewed within a patriarchal sense of the right ordering of authority by God and king. The dominant ethos was patriarchal, hierarchical, conservative, religious, and male dominated, although each involved both tensions and compromises and, related to the latter, a variety of means of expression. For example, some women became more politically active, with abolitionism the first major political campaign in England in which women played a prominent role.[10] Sugar was boycotted, and alternative cooking recipes were published. Thanks to the press, controversy over the slave trade reached the distant corners of the country. In 1793, women also played a key role in prompting and responding to a newspaper appeal for flannel waistcoats and other clothes for British troops in the Low Countries.

The majority of the population was female. The ratio of women to men in England and Wales, as revealed by the census figures, was 109:100 in 1801 and 1811 and 105:100 in 1821.[11] Many women faced grueling labor and debilitating diseases, as did men, but the women were in a society that awarded control and respect to men and left little acknowledged independent role for female merit or achievement.

The arduous nature of most work, and the confining implications of family and social life and its gender and age dimensions, together defined the existence of the majority of women. Social and economic pressures helped drive women toward matrimony and, regardless of marital status, employment.

For unmarried men and women, domestic service was a common form of work. This was understandably so in a society where household tasks were arduous and manual and the contribution from machines minimal. Hard physical labor was involved in many domestic tasks, such as carrying water and washing clothes. Wet clothes and bedding were very heavy and difficult to handle. In *The Watsons*, a "great wash" takes place.

It was possible to gain promotion in the hierarchy of service, but most domestic service was unskilled rather than a career, and married servants were relatively uncommon. Wages were poor; pay was largely in kind—in other words, in food and accommodation—and there was no chance of retirement. In addition, social norms greatly affected the type of work that could be done.

Agricultural servants were also vital. They frequently lived with their employers, although less so than in the past, and gave many nuclear families the character of an extended family. This was a variant to the more widespread pattern of families, with very marked differences in status, wealth, and prospects. That was certainly true of Austen's family and of the casts of characters she successively created.

The most striking aspect of the contribution of the female labor force was its variety. Women had only a relatively small role in the churches—save with the Quakers, as Methodist preachers, and in charitable works—and no role in the armed forces, with the exception of the important place of wives and the informal one of camp followers. Nevertheless, women were found in most spheres of employment. This was particularly so in domestic manufacturing, notably spinning. Women also did hard physical labor—for example, as coal heavers, taking coal to the surface, and as fish and salt carriers. Thus, increased demand for coal led to the growing employment of women and children in mining jobs formerly done by men, such as working underground to tend the roads and the horses. In 1802, 124 women aged nine to eight-one, over a quarter of the workforce, were on the payroll of Howgill Colliery in Cumbria.

Women were generally given the lower-paying jobs. In many industries, such as glove making, women had the less skilled jobs; at times (very differently) their employment was defined as less skilled and therefore was paid less. Reflecting the impact of differential job opportunities, as well as the consequences of widowhood, spinsterhood, and unwanted pregnancy, the majority of the poor were women.[12]

Not all women, however, were confined to poor jobs. A minority had interesting careers, and some benefitted from the expansion of the commercial economy. Women were unabashedly listed as proprietors of a host of businesses in directories, from printers to grocers. Elizabeth Raffald (1733–81), a former housekeeper, the author of the cookbook *The Experienced English Housekeeper* (1769), and proprietor of a coffeehouse, produced *The Manchester Directory* (1772). In the theater, from the late seventeenth century, actresses took over female roles, leading to a more realistic presentation of women and gender relationships. Both became more relevant to women playgoers. In the late eighteenth century, the radical writer Catharine Macaulay and the painter Angelica Kauffmann, a founding member of the Royal Academy, were among those who "made the weather" in the sense of playing a major role in developments. Women wrote across the genres, largely for money, but most female writers suffered from a lack of funds and self-confidence.[13]

Yet there were also long-standing issues in the experience of women and the treatment they received. These issues reflected traditional constraints and controls as well as the anxiety directed at women who were apparently outside their proper role. Thus, Eliza Haywood (1693–1756), who offered frank discussions of female desire in her plays *The City Jilt* (1726) and *The Mercenary Lover* (1726), could be seen by men as a threat or, at least, a challenge. Haywood's *Anti-Pamela* (1742) was less successful than Samuel Richardson's *Pamela* because it was more disturbing and less didactic. Haywood's works were not reprinted in the late eighteenth century but have received greater attention since the 1980s. A different form of subversive womanhood was offered by the warrior women presented in popular ballads.[14]

Households tended to be dominated by men, who were regarded as heads when they were present and in the legacy of accounts of the past. The legal rights of women were limited, not least their rights to own and dispose of property. Marriage was central to property, and legal devices encouraged patrilineal inheritance and primogeniture in the sense of inheritance by the eldest man. In contrast, Lady Catherine de Bourgh is powerful because she is a widow and also only has a daughter, Anne.

The Strict Settlement was particularly important and circumvented common-law rules of inheritance that would otherwise have left more land inherited or held by women. The Strict Settlement preserved estates by limiting charges for subordinate members of the family. Indeed, John Galt's novel *The Entail: or the Lairds of Grippy* (1823) focused on the protagonist's attempt to ensure the estate remained with his family forever.

The Strict Settlement did not necessarily imply that landowners lacked concern for the members of their nuclear families or that children and wives were casually or indifferently treated.[15] However, as Austen makes clear in her novels, the consequences could be a lot less attractive than that situation. This was especially true for widows, and there was a clear family link for Austen. Her paternal great-grandmother, Elizabeth Austen, had been left a young widow with seven children in 1704, but her husband's sisters' husbands had been the executors while her father-in-law had promised to help. In the end, she was badly let down by all three, not least because the father-in-law left money for her eldest son but not for the other children, who ended up neglected by the fortunate one. Elizabeth had to sell and borrow just to cope and manage her husband's debts. In the end, she survived by becoming, in effect, the housekeeper of a school in order to get her other sons educated. She did so and set an exemplary standard for her descendants.

Hardship, however, continued. Elizabeth Austen's fourth son, William, the father of Austen's father, George, had a wife die in childbirth and himself died young. His second wife did not care for her orphan stepchildren, and they were sent away from their father's home. One, Leonora, never married, probably became a companion, was left poor, and disappeared from sight. In contrast, Philadelphia went to India and married an older man for money. George's talent took him, with scholarships, to Tonbridge School and then Oxford. He was Austen's father.

Such individual and family narratives exemplified and complicated relations between men and women. Particular strains were created by the matrimonial demands of empire or being a military or naval spouse or partner—circumstances faced by a large number of women during Austen's lifetime and several of the fictional characters she created.[16]

At the same time, the discussion of individual and family relations certainly changed during the eighteenth century. Male attitudes to women softened and became more sympathetic to female feelings, at least in theory. This was as a crucial part of the process by which more "polite" and genteel social norms were encouraged. The good manners implied by the term *gentleman* were thus redefined. At the same time, as Austen shows, there is precious little "politeness" in the degree of control to which women are exposed by their dependence. This control is patriarchal and social and is expressed through family and money. Thus, the very different fates of the three Ward sisters at the outset of *Mansfield Park* capture the significance of matrimonial choices that, in practice, were highly constricted and constrained. These different fates, in turn, affect the children of the two sisters who have them.

An aspiration toward politeness was definitely a keystone of various *public* discourses but not necessarily private ones. Politeness fostered particular ends of moral improvement, Christian purpose, and social order. Propriety and the developing cult of politeness were used to help manage, and make more agreeable, the symbolic authority of fathers and husbands and to try to define gentlemanly behavior.[17] Moreover, heterosexual sociability was fostered. This raised the prestige of those activities and places that offered women a place beside their men and the profile of the gentleman who could do a woman honor.

However, politeness partly meant female passivity, which was an aspect of the wider social passivity, or order, implied by politeness. Although much late seventeenth-century literature presented women as gleefully manipulating sexual relationships, a century later women were seen as passive foils and victims of a pattern of seduction that had to be contained by changing male behavior and not by increasing female assertiveness. *Lady Susan* was a reversion to the late seventeenth-century model as the protagonist is far from a passive player.

In her *Thoughts on the Education of Daughters* (1787), Mary Wollstonecraft emphasized the problems faced by unmarried genteel women who have been raised beyond the status they will subsequently enjoy. Women had to gauge how to behave and did so in a problematic environment in which they risked compromising their reputation, but they were helped by the friendship born of affection, shared experience, and innate sympathy.[18] Charlotte Lucas, eager to marry, pressed on Elizabeth Bennet the need not to be overly cautious in showing affection: "If a woman conceals her affection . . . from the object of it, she may lose the opportunity of fixing him; and it will then be but poor consolation to believe the world equally in the dark. There is so much of gratitude or vanity in almost every attachment, that it is not safe to leave any to itself . . . there are very few of us who have heart enough to be really in love without encouragement. In nine cases out of ten, a woman had better show *more* affection than she feels."

This was a grim view, from one woman getting older in the matrimonial stakes to another, of the economy of effort involved in romance. So even more is the addition: "When she is secure of him, there will be leisure for falling in love as much as she chuses." Elizabeth Bennet, characteristically, is quizzical: "Yes, these four evenings have enabled them to ascertain that they both like Vingt-un better than Commerce [card games]; but with respect to any other leading characteristic, I do not imagine that much has been unfolded."[19] In *The Watsons*, Penelope is described in these terms: "There is nothing she would not do to get married—she would as good as tell you so herself . . . she has no faith, no honour, no scruples . . . we must marry."[20]

Alongside this determination, there were the constraints of expectations of behavior. Thus, an emphasis on female restraint can be seen in much of the theater reporting published in magazines and periodicals. The column "The Theatre" in the *Town and Country Magazine* of December 1782 referred to one actress: "She seems to have imbibed too strongly the rantings of a strolling company, to figure in a capital part upon a regular stage . . . she does not seem calculated for the soft feelings of tender passion." Another actress that month had "a powerful voice; but is destitute of the pathos. Her action is not graceful, but rather violent."

Yet, whether on or off the stage, descriptions of Austen's age in terms of a "polite society" are insufficient, not least because evangelicals attacked politeness as encouraging hypocrisy. In fact, the culture was highly ambiguous, although this ambiguity was not fully probed in fiction. Politeness was part of the period's self-image, but a coarseness of utterance, and indeed of thought and action, were also present, as in joke books.[21] Frequent campaigns against swearing, lewdness, and profanity, and the insistence on Sabbath observance, were necessary aspects of the stress on sobriety and restraint. The Reformation of Manners movement, which in Austen's lifetime was dominated by the Proclamation Society and the Vice Society, was, in part, a response to the anxieties that coarse behavior induced in religious and evangelical circles.

Indeed, as a prime instance of such behavior, there was much matter-of-fact acceptance of prostitution, casual sex, and venereal disease. *Harry's List of Covent Garden Ladies*, an annual directory from 1757 to 1795, with a print run of eight thousand copies, provided information on the first.[22] In 1782, Sir Richard Worsley, the comptroller of the king's household, brought a case for adultery with his wife against Captain George Bissett. His connivance in this adultery led to him only being awarded one shilling (five pence) in damages, but it was reported that thirty-four young men of the first quality had also received her favors. The evidence is patchy, but an explicit sexuality was scarcely remote from a society in which large quantities of sex literature were printed. Prostitution was also widespread. Alongside benign ideas of the household, most rapes occurred in the home or at work and were by people known to the victim.[23] The idea of the gentleman in part drew on images of truly unattractive criminal masculinities, notably those of the rake, the highwayman, and the pirate.[24] The idea was both a reaction against these images and, more disturbingly, a product in part of them.

Ostentatiously virtuous aristocrats are presented in such novels as *Munster Abbey* (1797), by Sir Samuel Egerton Leigh, a distant connection of Austen, who died at twenty-six, leaving his novel to be arranged and probably finished by his widow. In practice, as illustrated by the quotation in chapter 8 from the Earl of Buckinghamshire, many men had not internalized the politeness they apparently valued in public, which presaged the public morality and private vice of the Victorians. In Austen's last years, the prince regent, later George IV, presided over this system, a marked contrast to his father, George III, who was an elderly, mad recluse from 1811.

As a result of male conduct, seduction was a frequent danger in the novels of the age. The misleading attraction and false promises of men are a common theme, and the result is often betrayal and the dangers of abandonment and pregnancy, as in Hannah Foster's *The Coquette* (1797). The moral is underlined clearly, as in Susan Rowson's *Charlotte: A Tale of Truth* (1794). So also in the case of the married Henry Elton, who has a mistress in *Wareham Priory; or, the Will: A Novel. Founded on Facts* (1799), a novel possibly by Mrs. Thomas Adams. Austen's brother Edward and his wife, Elizabeth, subscribed to this warning about sin while Austen looked to the novel for the names of characters.[25]

Austen told a friend, Ann Barrett, who asked her, "Which of your characters do you like best? ... 'Edmund Bertram and Mr Knightley; but they are very far from being what I know English gentlemen often are.'"[26] This comment was an instructive reflection on Austen's experiences, on how Austen saw her world and her art, and on her awareness and characterization of men. Politeness was desirable because self-restraint was necessary, a point underlined by Darcy: "There is in every disposition a tendency to some particular evil, a natural defect, which not even the best education can overcome."[27]

This was true for both men and women, and Austen is very good in presenting similarities between male and female characters—for example, John and Fanny Dashwood, an unattractive couple who automatically accentuate each other's flaws. These similarities are important to the plots and, notably, the romance. They also, if the term is not overused, can be seen as subversive. Thus, in a relationship that thwarts family control, both Darcy and Elizabeth Bennet discover an empathy in *Pride and Prejudice*. Earlier, Elizabeth has ignored her mother (although pleased her father) in rejecting Mr. Collins.[28]

Not only men were "addicted to the Bottle and the Dice," as Austen noted in *Jack and Alice*. Moreover, in her frequently lurid juvenilia, Austen includes murder and theft, and she depicts illegitimacy in *Love and Freindship*; the young Jezalinda Fitzroy running off with the coachman in *Frederic and Elfrida*; and Miss Dickins, the excellent governess, eloping with the butler in *Jack and Alice*. In *Sir William Montague*, the protagonist falls for every attractive woman he meets and is willing to commit murder to get his way. His shooting of a rival matches his decision to disappoint an earlier woman because their wedding day clashed with his shooting of game.

This is a caricature of the problems repeatedly posed to seeking a husband by male character and behavior. These problems emerge frequently in Austen's novels, at times, as in *The Watsons*, more bleakly than in her other works. Other issues are not addressed. In *Love and Freindship*, *The History of England*, and *Mansfield Park*, there are references to homosexuality, but they are brief and indirect.

Despite the reality across society of individual poor conduct, public morality was nevertheless important. Politeness was a public act, a show that was thought necessary. Moreover, there was a class dimension. Politeness and gentility were seen as middle-class virtues and discussion about them as characteristic of middle-class writers. At the same time, there was scant real interest in upward social mobility through virtue alone—and certainly not from the lowborn.[29] Instead, politeness edged around the role and consequences of financial differences within the social world, notably the place of the middle class. Austen, however, fully understood both politeness and financial difficulties and their respective impact on social proprieties. In life and fiction, the financial aspects of courtship and matrimony brought out the ambiguities of politeness.

The idea of equality between men and women met with increasing approval, but the general notion of equality was of respect for separate functions and development—literally so in terms of the layout of a house. The arrangement of rooms in stately houses, a topic in chapter 2, reflected what were held to be the separate needs of men and women as well as the creation of spaces where they could be harmoniously together. Drawing rooms, which were originally withdrawing rooms, served, in particular, to provide appropriate settings for female sociability. The rooms in the Bennet household were clearly differentiated by Mr. Bennet in his characteristic fashion, at once truthful but somewhat unkind about the foibles of others: "In his library he had been always sure of leisure and tranquillity; and though prepared, as he told Elizabeth, to meet with folly and conceit in every other room in the house, he was used to be free from them there."[30]

The definition of the distinctive nature of the ideal female condition did not include equality by modern standards. This was true of sexuality. Women, but not men, were expected to be virgins when they married and chaste thereafter, assumptions held by women as well as men. When, on May 4, 1779, the House of Commons discussed the second reading of a bill for the "more effectual discouragement of adultery" that had been sent down from the House of Lords, it was, of course, like the Lords, an all-male body. Charles James Fox attacked the bill "on the doctrine of non-representation . . . the ladies totally unrepresented." Francis, Viscount Beauchamp, an MP because his title—as son of the Earl, later Marquess, of Hertford—was a courtesy one, also opposed the measure, and he complained about "the inequality in punishing the female transgressor only, without inflicting any punishment on her male co-offender. . . . He attributed the increase of adultery, and of course divorces, to the Marriage Act, which laid young people under the restraints of parents and guardians as to be compelled frequently to marry against their inclinations, which brought on these infidelities."[31] On a "thin House" (with few MPs present), the Commons rejected the bill fifty-one to forty.

By European standards, however, British social conventions were not rigid. French aristocratic visitors, such as the Count of Gisors in 1754, were surprised to find young women of quality paying visits alone without loss of reputation.[32] Jane and Elizabeth Bennet's stay at Netherfield is also indicative. The presence of the Hursts, a married couple, makes it more respectable, but they are part of a house party of young people, to whom they are not related, in a bachelor's home, and nobody in the novel considers this worthy of any form of remark.

Moreover, far from women being largely restricted to private spheres and domestic roles, the public profile of women was important. Women could be employers and consumers and, far from being secluded before, during, or after marriage, were able to take their pleasures in public. Furthermore, within the domestic sphere, women were also able to assert independence and self-control—for example, in music making—and this assertiveness was not contained by that sphere. In 1787, Austen's brother James, in his epilogue for the Austen-family Steventon production of Susannah Centlivre's play *The Wonder! A Woman Keeps a Secret*, declared, "Woman holds a second place no more."

Yet, by modern standards, the situation was far from benign. Single women found it difficult to earn sufficient wages to support themselves, and ideas of gentility greatly constrained options for genteel single women. Although having "good sense and merit," Clara Brereton, "a niece . . . a dependant on poverty—an additional burden on an encumbered circle," prepares "for a situation little better than a nursery maid."[33] Mrs. Elton is condescending about Mrs. Weston as a former governess: "I was rather astonished to find her so very lady-like! But she is really quite the gentlewoman," earning the rejoinder from Emma, her former charge: "Mrs Weston's manners were always particularly good. Their propriety, simplicity, and elegance, would make them the safest model for any young woman"[34]—in other words, Mrs. Elton.

The position of Jane Fairfax, an enigma for much of *Emma* and thus a key figure in the narrative, raises the emotive question of slavery. The poised Miss Fairfax is confident: "When I am quite determined as to the time, I am not at all afraid of being long unemployed. There are places in town, offices, where inquiry would soon produce something—Offices for the sale—not quite of human flesh—but of human intellect!" leading Mrs. Elton to reply: "Oh! My dear, human flesh! You quite shock me; if you mean a fling at the slave-trade, I assure you Mr Suckling was always rather a friend to the abolition." This contrast drew on a misunderstanding, as Jane Fairfax makes clear in the next contribution, that she was thinking of intellectual prostitution and not the slavery that had been a key issue in Bristol, where Suckling was in commerce, although not directly anything to do with the slave trade: "'I did not mean, I was not thinking of the slave trade,' replied Jane; 'governess-trade, I assure you, was all that I had in view; widely different certainly as to the guilt of those who carry it on; but as to the greater misery of the victims, I do not know where it lies.'"[35]

As with John Knightley's approving comment on the post office,[36] the emphasis was on the development of a flexible economy and related institutions. Jane Fairfax refers to "advertising offices ... by applying to them I should have no doubt of very soon meeting with something that would do."[37] Jane Fairfax is not the only woman in *Emma* facing difficulties more acute than the protagonist's well-intentioned but condescending meddling. Mr. Knightley presses for compassion for Miss Bates: "She is poor; she has sunk from the comforts she was born to; and, if she live to old age, must probably sink more."[38] It is not surprising that, although she does not wish to go there, the orphaned poor daughter of a clergyman in *Catherine, or the Bower* goes to Bengal to get (unhappily) married.[39] This account is based on Jane's aunt, Philadelphia Austen.

Jane presented social discrimination not only as a matter of the marriage stakes but also of clothes. The two are linked in *A Collection of Letters*, part of the juvenilia, when the unsympathetic Lady Greville comments on Maria looking "very smart" at a ball:

> *My* poor Girls will appear quite to disadvantage by *you*.... Have you got a new Gown on? ... and a fine one too I think ... I dare say it is all very smart—But I must own ... that I think it was quite a needless piece of expense—Why could not you have worn your old striped one? It is not my way to find fault with people because they are poor, for I always think that they are more to be despised and pitied than blamed for it, especially if they cannot help it, but at the same time I must say that in my opinion your old striped Gown would have been quite fine enough for its wearer—for to tell you the truth ... one half of the people in the room will not know whether you have a Gown on or not—But I supposed you intend to make your fortune tonight.[40]

More generally, the varied pressures caused by the need to respond to the previous generation feature repeatedly. In that collection, Henrietta Hatton will not agree to be Tom Musgrove's until her uncle and aunt die and she is thereby placed "in affluence above what" his fortune can provide.[41] This leads on to a discussion about wealth, with Henrietta telling Lady Scudamore, "We young Ladies who are Heiresses must not throw ourselves away upon Men who have no fortune at all," a view with which

Lady Scudamore concurs, only to focus on Musgrove's prospects, not least his estate being "capable of great improvement."[42] In *Sanditon*, Lady Denham emphasizes that her nephew by marriage, Sir Edward, "*must* marry for money."[43]

Austen herself had many difficulties. Her first surviving letter dealt with money problems. In 1796, she wrote to Cassandra: "You say nothing of the silk stockings; I flatter myself, therefore, that Charles has not purchased any, as I cannot very well afford to pay for them; all my money is spent in buying white gloves and pink persian."[44] This concern remained a theme. In 1805, Austen complained to Cassandra: "I find on looking into my affairs, that instead of being very rich I am likely to be very poor, I cannot afford more than ten shillings for Sackree . . . prepare you for the sight of a sister sunk in poverty."[45] No wonder that in 1808 Austen could look forward to a dinner her brother Edward was giving at Godmersham: "I shall eat ice and drink French wine, and be above vulgar economy." Ice was a luxury that was difficult to produce and preserve.

As Austen was well aware from her family history, personal experience, and observation, inheritance laws and practices treated single women harshly. Unmarried women were also subject to disparaging and satirical comment, although Emma argued that it was poverty only that led to public contempt.[46] The treatment of women by many of Jane's characters, notably, but not only, male ones, focused on money and was frequently condescending and harsh. The lack of prospects was treated as a crime. Thus, in *The Watsons*, Robert Watson criticizes his sister Emma because her aunt's marriage does not leave her a well-cared-for widow or Emma wealthy:

> "By heaven! a woman should never be trusted with money. I always said that she ought to have settled something on you, as soon as her husband died."
> "But that would have been trusting *me* with money," replied Emma, "and I am a woman too."

"It might have been secured to your future use, without your having any power over it now.—What a blow it musts have been upon you!—To find yourself, instead of heiress of eight or nine thousand pounds, sent back a weight upon your family, without a sixpence."[47]

In a bleak tale, Emma ends up reflecting on "the dreadful mortifications of unequal society" and "hard-hearted prosperity" such that she has "become of importance to no one."[48]

After the mid-eighteenth century, expectations about what women should obtain from marriage rose, the notion of romantic marriage and domestic harmony came to prevail among the prosperous, and the practice of separation as a result of incompatibility became more common. Nevertheless, alongside this trend, and the somewhat bland confidence it offered, the clear and cogent reasons Charlotte Lucas accepted Mr. Collins remained all too pertinent:

> Mr Collins, to be sure, was neither sensible nor agreeable; his society was irksome, and his attachment to her must be imaginary. But still he would be her husband.—Without thinking highly either of men or of matrimony, marriage had always been her object; it was the only honourable provision for well-educated young women of small fortune, and, however uncertain of giving happiness, must be their pleasantest preservative from want. This preservative she had now obtained; and at the age of twenty-seven, without having ever been handsome, she felt all the good luck of it.[49]

Economics continued to exercise a harsh discipline. Earlier, in pressing his suit on Elizabeth Bennet, Mr. Collins noted: "Your portion is unhappily so small that it will in all likelihood undo the effects of your loveliness and amiable qualifications."[50] The self-sacrificing life seen with Anne Elliot in *Persuasion*[51] appears the sole alternative to a marriage market loaded against those without means. This was true of men as well as women, but the latter had fewer options and fared worse. This was the case not only in these considerations but also in not being allowed to take the initiative and in the commonplace condescension of control.

A clear instance of male dominance, although not about marriage, is when Mr. Parker decides to accept Mr. Heywood's offer of hospitality, an offer made by Heywood without consulting his wife and daughters. In turn, Parker is described as "consulting his wife in the few words of 'Well my dear, I believe it will be better for us.'"[52]

Austen's account of female childhood and education builds on that of Fanny Burney. Alongside the decorous social surface *and* underpinning and the emphasis on the traditional expectation of marriage is a sense of the need for protection in the face of the hazards of society.[53] That some challenges to happiness are from within families makes these hazards even more problematic. In drawing on Burney, especially her *Camilla*, in *Northanger Abbey*, Austen relates to long-standing views, and therefore debates, on women, childhood, experience, and education.[54]

Alongside patriarchalism and discipline, affection and emotion bonded families together. Parents of all social and religious groups loved their children, and most did not treat them as embodiments of original sin, although many evangelicals still did. Human depravity remained a potent idea, as the writings of Hannah More indicated. However, the inculcation of deference, discipline, and piety by authoritarian parents was not incompatible with affection. In bringing up their children, parents saw the need to teach them basic skills and regarded this, correctly, as for the benefit of children as much as parents. This was particularly the case when children were to follow the occupations of their parents, a tendency made desirable by the nature of inheritance practices across society, by the shortage of capital, and by the limited employment opportunities faced by most people. Furthermore, the absence of state-provided education placed a burden of responsibility on parents and, failing them, other relatives. The same was also true of health, housing, and, to a degree, social welfare.

In addition, there was widespread philanthropy, including from public and ecclesiastical bodies. The social elite were supposed to set an example, and this process can be seen with

Austen's characters, although to a varying extent. Darcy was "a liberal man, and did much good among the poor." Emma has "a charitable visit to pay to a poor sick family," and there is concern about who needs "relief from the parish." Augusta Hawkins finds Jane Fairfax's situation very affecting and urges action on her behalf.[55] In seeking to please Fanny Price, Henry Crawford emphasizes his philanthropy on his estate of Everingham:

> The particular reason of his going into Norfolk at all, at this unusual time of year, was given. It had been real business, relative to the renewal of a lease in which the welfare of a large and (he believed) industrious family was at stake. He had suspected his agent of some underhand dealing—of meaning to bias him against the deserving, and he had determined to go himself, and thoroughly investigate the merits of the case. He had . . . done even more good than he had foreseen . . . he had begun making acquaintance with cottages whose very existence, though on his own estate, had been hitherto unknown to him. . . . To be the friend of the poor and oppressed.[56]

Colonel Brandon characteristically is more to the point: "Regard for a former servant of my own, who had since fallen into misfortune, carried me to visit him in a spunging-house, where he was confined for debt." Brandon also cares for his orphaned niece Eliza after his sister-in-law had been reduced to misfortune by his harsh brother (her husband) and, after divorce, by a seducer. Moreover, once married to the colonel, Marianne Dashwood becomes "the patroness of a village."[57]

Refusal to be liberal was the sign of a harsh personality, as with Sir Walter Elliot, who, characteristically, upbraids Anne for visiting an old schoolfellow who has fallen on hard times:

> "Westgate-buildings!" said he; "and who is Miss Anne Elliot to be visiting in Westgate-buildings?—A Mrs Smith. A widow Mrs Smith,—and who was her husband? One of the five thousand Mr Smiths whose names are to be met with every where. And what is her attraction? That she is old and sickly.—Upon my word, Miss Anne

Elliot, you have the most extraordinary taste! Everything that revolts other people, low company, paltry rooms, foul air, disgusting associations are inviting to you . . . a mere Mrs Smith, an every day Mrs Smith, of . . . all names in the world."[58]

At the same time, there was some state provision, although the 1787 suggestion by John Rolle, MP for Devon, for a national fund for poor relief covered by progressive taxation and compulsory national insurance got nowhere. The Workhouse Test Act of 1723 encouraged parishes to found workhouses to provide the poor with work and accommodation, but too few were founded to deal with the problem, especially as the population rose from mid-century. Gilbert's Act of 1782 gave justices of the peace the power to appoint guardians running Houses of Industry for the elderly and infirm. Workhouses, however, remained less important than "outdoor relief": providing assistance often in kind, and sometimes work, to the poor in their own homes, which had the virtue of flexibility, not least in response to seasonal unemployment. Under the Speenhamland system of outdoor relief introduced in 1795, although never universally applied, both the unemployed and wage laborers received payments reflecting the price of bread and the size of their family. Low wages were added as a legitimate qualification for poor relief, in addition to the traditional criteria, notably age and ill-health. In accordance with social norms, payments to families were made to the male.[59] This system was an aspect of the adaptability of government in the face of the revolutionary crisis of the period.

At the same time, the poor suffered. William Cobbett, a loyalist who became a prominent radical writer, closed his dire account of the diet of the poor in Derby in 1829, "And this is ENGLAND." Food was the largest single item of expenditure for the bulk of the population. With his hostility in the 1800s to the large national debt, Cobbett showed the radical side of Toryism. So also in his opposition to "rotten boroughs"—parliamentary seats with small electorates that were controlled by patrons.

High grain prices tended to increase the incidence of epidemic diseases and death. Climate and weather were also of great significance, particularly in weakening resistance. Most dwellings were neither warm nor dry. Harsh weather was exacerbated by shortages of firewood. Emma and Harriet Smith speak for "some time of what the poor must suffer in winter,"[60] although the distinction between the deserving and undeserving poor remained an issue. The immediacy of an intimidating group of gypsies demanding money leads Harriet Smith and Miss Bickerton to a panic.[61]

Social structures and attitudes were not challenged by the educational system. The majority of children did not attend school, the distribution of schools was uneven, and the curriculum of most was seriously limited. It was generally argued that education should reflect social status and reinforce the status quo and thus that the poor should not be taught to aspire. The educational opportunities for girls were particularly limited.

The degree to which the individual family lived together in close proximity led, in practice, to a need for cooperation and mutual tolerance that necessarily affected the nature of patriarchal authority. The inculcation of deference, discipline, and piety by authoritarian parents was not only not incompatible with affection but was also seen as linked, and the tension between individual preferences and family pressures was scarcely new. So also with husbands. Elizabeth Bennet appreciates Charlotte Collins's (née Lucas) "address in guiding, and composure in bearing with her husband," which, in part, is achieved by her success in encouraging him to work in his garden as much as possible.[62] This is literally an instance of separate spheres, as well as a projection in the household of the difference between individual rooms. Gardening meets Mr. Collins's desire for meritorious behavior, and its private activism accords with his need for some correspondence with his public freneticism.

The basic unit of society was the nuclear family: a married couple and their generally nonadult children. Other than those headed by widows or widowers, there were few one-parent families. Birth, aging, and death ensured that the life cycle of families was continually changing, and it required adaptation when the family altered to include dependents, whether young children or invalid adults. A pattern can be seen. Knightley reflects on the socializing of experience when referring to the Westons' new daughter: "She will be disagreeable in infancy, and correct herself as she grows older."[63] This perspective is probably that of Austen, who wrote in 1814: "One does not care for girls till they are grown up."[64]

At the same time, as Austen makes clear, nuclear families were also nodes within closely connected networks of kin. These networks reflected and were sustained by the normality of cousin marriage, a practice endorsed in *Mansfield Park* and also seen in the royal family. The emphasis in the period was as much on attachments to birth families as to conjugal families, and cousin marriage helped bridge the two.[65] These units and networks reflected the social conventions of the period and could be pressed hard by them. Indeed, this is a setting for Austen's novels, albeit one complicated by the misapplied sentiment and intrigues, both courtship and pecuniary, that underlined the problems posed by these conventions and provided plot development, as with Mr. Collins's pursuit of two successive Bennet cousins. As the novels were comedies, the endings were positive, even joyous, and thus the conclusion was positive. Yet the unspoken possibility of other outcomes acts as an overhang. Indeed, Elizabeth Bennet, summing up the first half of *Pride and Prejudice*, reflects: "The more I see of the world, the more am I dissatisfied with it; and every day confirms my belief of the inconsistency of all human characters, and of the little dependence that can be placed on the appearance of either merit or sense."[66]

NOTES

1. S. Carlile, *Charlotte Lennox: An Independent Mind c. 1729–1804* (Toronto, 2018).

2. R. Phillips, *Putting Asunder: A History of Divorce in Western Society* (Cambridge, 1988).

3. S. Johnson, *The History of Rasselas, Prince of Abissinia* (London, 1759), 26.

4. *MP* III, 7.

5. *MP* I, 3; III, 13.

6. *Sense* III, 2.

7. J. Wiltshire, *Samuel Johnson in the Medical World* (Cambridge, 1991).

8. *Letters*, 49.

9. J. Wiltshire, *Jane Austen and the Body: "The Picture of Health"* (Cambridge, 1992).

10. C. Midgley, *Women against Slavery: The British Campaigns, 1780–1870* (London, 1992).

11. For modern comparisons for the United Kingdom: 108:100 in 1951 and 102:100 for 2011.

12. B. Hill, *Eighteenth-Century Women: An Anthology* (London, 1984).

13. J. Todd, ed., *A Dictionary of British and American Women Writers 1660–1800* (London, 1984).

14. D. Dugaw, *Warrior Women and Popular Balladry 1650–1850* (Cambridge, 1989).

15. E. Spring, *Law, and, and Family: Aristocratic Inheritance in England, 1300 to 1800* (Chapel Hill, NC, 1994).

16. M. Lincoln, *Naval Wives and Mistresses* (London, 2007).

17. H. J. Shroff, *The Eighteenth-Century Novel: The Idea of the Gentleman* (London, 1983).

18. J. Todd, *Women's Friendship in Literature* (New York 1980).

19. *PP* I, 6.

20. *Later Manuscripts*, 81–82.

21. K. Davison, "Occasional Politeness and Gentlemen's Laughter in 18th Century England," *Historical Journal* 52 (2014): 921–45; J. Black, *An Illustrated History of Eighteenth-Century Britain, 1688–1793* (Manchester, UK, 1996), 61–71; H. Berry, "Rethinking Politeness in Eighteenth-Century England: Moll King's Coffee House and the Significance of 'Flash Talk,'" *Transactions of the Royal Historical Society*, ser. 6, 11 (2001): 65–81.

22. J. L. Wood, "Meaner Beauties of the Night," *Factotum* 30 (1989): 12–14.

23. A. Clark, *Women's Silence, Men's Violence: Sexual Assault in England 1770–1845* (London, 1987).

24. E. Mackie, *Rakes, Highwaymen, and Pirates: The Making of the Modern Gentleman in the Eighteenth Century* (Baltimore, MD, 2009).

25. P. D. Garside, "Jane Austen and Subscription Fiction," *British Journal for Eighteenth-Century Studies* 10 (1987): 186.

26. D. Le Faye, "Jane Austen's Friend Mrs Barrett Identified," *Notes and Queries* 244, no. 4 (December 1999): 451–52.

27. *PP* I, 11.

28. C. L. Johnson, *Jane Austen: Women, Politics and the Novel* (Chicago, 1988).

29. H. J. Shroff, *The Eighteenth-Century Novel: The Idea of the Gentleman* (London, 1983).

30. *PP* I, 15.

31. W. Cobbett, *The Parliamentary History of England from the Earliest Period to the Year 1803* (London, 1806), XX:599.

32. Journal du voyage de M. le Cte. de Gisors, Paris, Archives des Affaires Étrangères, Mémoires et Documents Angleterre fols. 25–26.

33. *Sanditon* 3.

34. *Emma* II, 14.

35. *Emma* II, 17.

36. *Emma* II, 16.

37. *Emma* II, 17.

38. *Emma* III, 7.

39. *Juvenilia*, 244

40. *Juvenilia*, 198.

41. *Juvenilia*, 206.

42. *Juvenilia*, 208.

43. *Sanditon* 7.

44. *Letters*, 2. Persian is a plain silk fabric.

45. *Letters*, 108. Susannah Sackree was a nursemaid.

46. B. Hill, *Women Alone: Spinsters in England, 1660–1850* (2001); A. M. Froide, *Never Married: Singlewomen in Early Modern England* (Oxford, 2005); *Emma* I, 10.

47. *The Watsons* from *Later Manuscripts*, 122–23.

48. *Later Manuscripts*, 135.

49. *PP* I, 22.

50. *PP* I, 19.

51. *Persuasion* II, 11.

52. *Sanditon* 1.

53. C. A. Howells, "'The Proper Education of a Female . . . Is Still to Seek': Childhood and Girls' Education in Fanny Burney's Camilla: or, a Picture of Youth," *British Journal for Eighteenth-Century Studies* 7 (1984): 191–98.

54. P. Crown, "Portraits and Fancy Pictures by Gainsborough and Reynolds: Contrasting Images of Childhood," *British Journal for Eighteenth-Century Studies* 7 (1984): 159–68.

55. *PP* III, 2; *Emma* I, 10; III, 8; II, 15.

56. *MP* III, 10.

57. *Sense* III, 14.

58. *Persuasion* II, 5.

59. S. A. Shave, *Pauper Policies: Poor Law Practice in England, 1780–1850* (Manchester, UK, 2018).

60. *Emma* II, 1.

61. *Emma* III, 3.

62. *PP* II, 5.

63. *Emma* III, 17.

64. *Letters*, 276.

65. M. J. Corbett, *Family Likeness: Sex, Marriage, and Incest from Jane Austen to Virginia Woolf* (Ithaca, NY, 2008).

66. *PP* II, 1.

FAITH AND THE CHURCH

Throw down the barriers of religion, law, order, and decency,
and then see what will be the discharge of the relative duties
of life. Can he who is grown hardy enough to fly in the face
of his God be supposed to retain any reverence for a master?

—*British Chronicle or Pugh's Hereford Journal*, July 15, 1779

AUSTEN'S WORLD WAS VERY MUCH defined by religious
belief and practice.[1] To the casual observer of today, her lifetime
may not appear a particularly religious age. Urban building of the
period is not generally recalled for its churches any more than
the painters of the period are usually remembered for religious
works. The eighteenth century is generally presented as a period
of enlightenment, as well as the Enlightenment as a secular movement. Faith is commonly ascribed to superstitious conservatism
or irrational religious enthusiasm. The serious anti-Catholic Gor-
don Riots of 1780, which took place not only in London but also
in provincial centers including Bath, are widely regarded as an
anachronism, and the eventual repeal of legislation discriminat-
ing against Nonconformists and Catholics was considered over-
due as well as necessary. The Church of England was often seen
as moribund.

This account, in practice, has been much eroded by recent scholarship that has demonstrated widespread piety, impressive conduct by most clerics, and, indeed, much more church building than was often assumed.[2] So also with the painting of religious works, notably by Benjamin West, Joshua Reynolds's successor as president of the Royal Academy from 1792 to 1805 and 1806 to 1820. The period saw a remarkable increase in overseas Anglican missionary activity. The records of the Society for the Propagation of the Gospel indicate pious donations from the great and the good as well as ordinary parishioners. Evangelical Anglicanism was closely linked to notions of a spreading civil society.

Moreover, England was a Church-State. The Test and Corporation Acts of 1673 and 1661 respectively remained in force until 1828. They obliged officeholders under the Crown both to take Oaths of Allegiance and Supremacy that accepted the position of the Crown as head of the Church of England and to receive communion in the Church of England. This system was strongly supported by the Tories whereas the Whigs were close to the Dissenters. Moves to repeal the acts were defeated in 1787, 1789, and 1790.

This situation both helped ensure a continued role for Anglican ideology in English national identity and also sustained local tensions. Dissenters (Nonconformists who believed in the Trinity, as well as those who did not) tended to support more radical political positions, because of being outside the established church, and their urban locale ensured that their activism was predominantly middle class and had only limited reference to aristocratic leadership and interests. Whether the Church was in danger or not at the national level, Anglicans felt it necessary to protect it in the localities and in all parishes.

Furthermore, the clergy tended to be particularly aware of competition between the churches. In 1790, the Reverend Thomas Brand wrote to a fellow Anglican cleric, Thomas Wharton, rejoicing in "the defeat of the Dissenters. Their success would have opened a door to every vile set of petitions which ambitious demagogues and disaffected spirits could have invented and the constitution must have been completely destroyed if the votes of Parliament could have been thus influenced by associations from without. Besides what would have become of our tithes, and our prebendal estates, our archdeacons, and our visitations."[3]

Furthermore, in the absence of a modern structure of party organization, ecclesiastical links provided the community and sociability that were so important in the development of political alignments and in the mobilization of political support. They were also important culturally and historically. Indeed, English history was in part contested in ecclesiastical terms. Thus, the misleading imprint of monastic writers on English history was a theme of the *Encyclopaedia Britannica*.[4] Ecclesiastical history and the religious aspects of national history remained political and cultural signifiers throughout Austen's life, which was not surprising given the significance of Catholic emancipation as an issue.

In Oliver Goldsmith's only novel, *The Vicar of Wakefield* (1766), the vicar, in giving his blessing to a would-be officer, an important moment, refers to the cause of the "sacred king" [Charles I] during the English Civil War (1642–46), a classic Tory theme.[5] The title of Austen's *History of England from the Reign of Henry the 4th to the Death of Charles the 1st*, written in 1791, was modeled on Goldsmith's *The History of England, from the Earliest Times to the Death of George II* (1771); more directly, she wrote extensive marginalia on Goldsmith's volumes—indeed, over one hundred marginal comments on her brother James's copy. This marginalia very much reflected the Tory view of history.[6] Family members recalled Austen's strong support for Charles I (r. 1625–49),[7] and her *History* praised him and his loyal supporters. Referred to as "*villains*," his opponents were blamed for the civil wars of the 1640s and associated distresses. She ended the *History*: "As therefore it is not my intention to give any particular account of the

distresses into which this King was involved through the mis-
conduct and cruelty of his Parliament, I shall satisfy myself with
vindicating him from the Reproach of Arbitrary and Tyrannical
Government with which he has often been Charged. This, I feel,
is not difficult to be done, for with one argument I am certain of
satisfying every sensible and well disposed person whose opinions have been properly guided by a good Education—and this
argument is that he was a STUART."[8]

This is not a self-consciously exaggerated teasing. In her marginalia on Goldsmith, Austen made her views clear on the course
of "the Civil War" (the war of 1642–46),[9] and on John Hampden,
a leading Parliamentarian killed in 1643, she noted that it was a
pity that "such virtues should be clouded by Republicanism!"[10]
Oliver Cromwell is a "detestable monster!,"[11] God is called on to
bless those who helped Charles II (r. 1660–85) to escape after his
defeat by Oliver Cromwell at Worcester in 1651,[12] and the selectiv-
ity of historians is noted when the "modest" address of the Anglican bishops against James II's Declaration of Indulgence toward
Catholics and Nonconformists in 1688 attracts her comment,
"*Modest*! It would have been *impudent* had it been from Catholics I suppose."[13] So also with her comment on James's persever-
ance despite his unpopularity: "And if he thought those measures
right, he could not be blamed for persevering in them," a theme to
which she returned.[14] William III (r. 1689–1702), the Whig hero,
is presented as a "villain."[15] The death of Queen Anne in 1714 led
Goldsmith to a critical summary of the Stuarts, which Austen
refuted, going on to a similar difference over the Old Pretender—
"James III," the son of James II and Jacobite claimant from 1701 to
1766—and over the '45, the Jacobite rising of that year.[16]

Austen's was a society in which disagreements over how (not
whether it was) best to worship God and seek salvation, how
to organize the Church, and the relationship between Church
and State were matters of urgent concern, whether collective or
individual, political or not. Moreover, millenarianism became

very strong in the wake of the French Revolution, not least with the self-described religious prophetess, Joanna Southcott (1750–1814), who in 1814 proclaimed that she would be delivered of the new Messiah. Although "politeness" was criticized, notably by Evangelicals, for promoting insincerity, *polite* and *religious* were not mutually incompatible terms. Indeed, religious zeal was not exceptional. The established church was not devoid of energy, and its congregations were not sunk in torpor. The Society for the Reformation of Manners indicated the strength and social awareness of Anglican piety.

The problem of providing for population growth did not become very serious for the Church as a whole until the 1780s. From then, despite the construction of new churches, for example St. Paul's in Bristol (1787), many growing towns, such as Leeds and Hull, lacked sufficient church accommodation. There was a spate of church building by parliamentary grant in 1818 and 1824 in response to the lack of accommodation for worship as the population had grown. The fact that establishing new parishes before 1818 required an Act of Parliament contributed to the perceived shortage, especially in newly populous areas in a rapidly changing country. Concerns also included competition from Nonconformists and what contemporaries called infidelity.

Much recent scholarly work has stressed the dedication and diligence of clergymen and the relative effectiveness of the Church's ministry. This situation can also be seen in Austen's novels. In *Persuasion*, Dr. Shirley, the rector of Uppercross, "for more than forty years had been zealously discharging all the duties of his office."[17] Clerical diaries, for example that of John Skinner of Camerton (1772–1839),[18] indicate faith, an attempt at self-examination, and clerics fulfilling the standards of clerical life, although Skinner himself was a difficult man who fell out with most of his parishioners and eventually committed suicide. Clerical standards included daily attendance at morning and evening prayers, care to find replacement clergy when absent, and concern to provide food for the poor and catechize children. The vigilance of the Anglican hierarchy in supervising clergy promoted pastoral commitment. Popular piety and religious observance were high despite some clerical pluralism, where one parson held two posts, and nonresidence. Moreover, in Hampshire, while pluralism may have been high, nonperformance of services was not because of the supply of curates. The Church of England was anything but moribund. Being raised as a clergyman's daughter in that milieu, as well as being spiritually formed by a more dynamic church than older accounts recognized, shaped Austen.

In general, increasing clerical income helped attract better-educated clergy to the Church, at least in the South. The rise in the social standing of the clergy and in their general educational standard were widely ascribed by contemporaries and historians to a rise in income from livings due to the greater profits from agriculture from mid-century and to opportunities for pluralism.

However, a higher and growing proportion of Anglican clergy in the North were not graduates,[19] as were many in the South, while the socially unsettled state of being a clergyman, primarily as the result of the appointment to livings, is repeatedly suggested by Austen. It can be seen, for example, in the relationship between Lady Catherine de Bourgh and Mr. Collins. The latter praises his patron, a necessary habit, but one he takes to extremes: "She had always spoken to him as she would to any other gentleman; she made not the smallest objection to his joining in the society of the neighbourhood . . . had once paid him a visit in his humble parsonage."[20] Once he is married, he and his wife dine at her house twice a week and are taken back by one of her carriages, instead of having to walk in the dark.[21] This is a courtesy for which he is ostentatiously grateful.

Moreover, Mr. Collins is not alone as an instance of dependence. Darcy's father intended to "provide" for Wickham in the church and left instructions accordingly in his will. Wickham, who made a failure of the law and lived "a life of idleness and dissipation," finally seeks a living—more particularly Kympton, with its "Excellent Parsonage House"—only for Darcy to turn him down. "I knew that Mr Wickham ought not to be a clergyman." This is appropriate behavior on the part of a patron careful of the parishioners but also one that indicates the power of the patron.[22] Patronage has to be considered by all keen on pursuing a career in the church. It is an extension and also accentuation of the more general nature of patronage. This pursuit entails implications not only for oneself but also for relatives as connections are built up. Charlotte Lucas, once married to Mr. Collins, prefers Darcy to Colonel Fitzwilliam for Elizabeth, as the former has "considerable patronage in the church and his cousin could have none at all."[23] Fitzwilliam, in contrast, is a younger son. The assumption is that Elizabeth's spouse will be able to help Mr. Collins, a theme to which he indeed later returns. For Mr. Collins, there is the wish to mesh together his patron, Lady Catherine, and his would-be patron, her nephew Darcy.

Patronage often involved a variety of supports. Charles Hayter, a curate, "has a very fair chance, through the Spicers, of getting something from the Bishop in the course of a year or two."[24] Clerical dependence required a grace on the part of patrons that could be lacking, as when Maria Bertram, contemplating Sotherton, the owner of which she proposes to marry, remarks: "I am glad the church is not so close to the Great House as often happens in old places. The annoyance of the bells must be terrible."[25]

The Church remained a career open to the talent of the humbly born, as was demonstrated by several bishops. Others were from the middling orders; for example, Henry Phillpotts (1778–1869), bishop of Exeter from 1831, whose father, John (1743–1814), kept a tavern, operated a brick and tile factory and was also a land agent. George III very much emphasized merit in his appointments to the bench of bishops, as did Robert, second Earl of Liverpool, prime minister from 1812 to 1827. Nevertheless, connections and patronage generally worked to the benefit of the wellborn, and clerics from a gentry background received a disproportionately high share of the good livings. Shute Barrington (1734–1826), the son of John, first Viscount Barrington, was bishop of Llandaff (1769–82), Salisbury (1782–91), and Durham (1791–1826). His first wife, Lady Diana Beauclerk, was the daughter of a duke, but she died in childbirth with the child stillborn.

In contrast, a large number of ordinands, particularly in the South of England where competition was strongest, could not get a living. Instead, many were limited to the prospects of curates and their low pay.

Lay patronage was a major issue for the clergy. Appointments to 53 percent of parish livings were controlled by private individuals and 10 percent by the Crown. Bishops and the universities of Cambridge and Oxford controlled the bulk of the other livings. In addition, one-third of tithes were held by lay impropriators.

However, clerics who held the tithes, as was true of most livings, benefited directly from rising prices for food. Most benefices tripled in value between 1770 and 1800. Indeed, rising tithe income enabled George Austen to retire from Steventon aged seventy in 1800 and to live in Bath with his wife, whose health required it, and two daughters. He had acquired his own living because of his uncle's purchase of the presentation to it—indeed, of two, so he could give him whichever came up first. Austen's understanding of clerical incomes and prospects, an element in her fiction, was well-grounded, and her family benefited greatly from the agrarian boom of the period. Aside from the value of their tithes, clerics who had no squire in the parish, the situation for Edmund Bertram at Thornton Lacey,[26] could preside socially in the parish.

Clerics were key figures in the English Enlightenment and, thus, in the more bookish side of provincial culture. They were particularly important in education and in publication other than of novels. Thus, in 1799, Henry St. John Bullen, a clerical schoolmaster in Bury St. Edmunds, published his *Elements of Geography, Expressly Designed for the Use of Schools.*

Thanks to the toleration of Dissenters, the Church had to operate effectively to resist competition. Its duty to teach the faith was much emphasized: religious activism for clergy and laity was stressed in Anglican literature, not the soporific complacency of a stagnant establishment. One of the last publications of Francis Blackburne, archdeacon of Cleveland, was *A Short Discourse on the Subject of Preaching* (York, 1785). In no way restricted to the Evangelicals, there was a stress on devotion. Indeed, despite some later suggestions, observance and piety were not necessarily Evangelical.

Moreover, there is copious evidence both of massive lay observance of the formal requirements of the Church and of widespread piety. The formal requirements were crucial to membership in the community. Thus, Austen, having been immediately christened after birth at home by her clergyman father, was taken to Church the following spring for a formal christening, a public affirmation of commitment to the faith.

The religious worldview provided the most effective explanatory model, the best psychological defenses, and the essential note of continuity in an unstable and often harsh world. William Grasing, a Gloucestershire farmer who died in 1798, recorded, in his much-thumbed notebook, charms to be sung to bring health. The charm to stop bleeding was a statement of faith beginning, "I believe Jesus Christ to be the son of God.... This charm must be repeated five times." Pre-Christian customs continued. Edward Wakefield's *Account of Ireland* (1812) recorded many, including swinging children over and driving cattle through fires lit on St John's Eve in order to ensure health and fortune. However, unorthodox providential views could be unacceptable. Richard Brothers, who foretold the apocalypse in 1792, was treated as a criminal lunatic from 1795 after further prophecies.

Sunday schools and devotional literature, such as the chapbooks read by relatively humble people, as well as anniversaries and rites of passage, notably baptism, marriage, and funerals, fostered sanctity, piety, and a strong awareness of salvation. Established religious works that aided popular devotion continued to sell. Thus, 1812 saw the forty-second edition of *The Church Catechism Explained by Way of Question and Answer, and Confirm'd by Scripture Proofs* (1700) by the Kent cleric John Lewis, a keen defender of the Church of England, and 1826 the thirtieth edition of Robert Nelson's *A Companion for Festivals and Fasts of the Church of England* (1704). Sermons and devotional material were the most widely sold books.

Popular piety was also internalized, and there was a high level of introspective or "internalized" faith, some of which was linked to the rise of the Evangelical movement. This internalized faith played a role in the autobiographical spiritual narratives that, as it were, linked biography and novels. Concerns over the frequency of receipt of communion were caused by feelings of unworthiness; one reason for this infrequency was that many people felt unworthy of it. Austen's prayers, probably intended for her family, reflected this piety.

Devotional literature and sermons were extensively purchased, which testifies to the role of religion in ordering peoples' experiences and responses. The Bible was known through listening to it being read or quoted and through reading it. Mary Wollstonecraft might have been a radical, but she also knew her Bible[27] and, unlike Tom Paine, did not hold it up to ridicule. Her feminism had a strong religious basis.[28] This was also the age of Hannah More, a prolific writer on moral and religious topics. More generally, Britain was treated as a new Israel, the "Promised Land," while, for individuals, the risk of the journey to an earthly perdition and a hellish end was extensively rehearsed by commentators.

The public dimension of religion and the spiritual health of the community were each seen as important and as requiring positive action. Linked to this, the Church of England played a major role in education and social welfare. Indeed, religion was regarded as a way to maintain order. In 1815, a school was opened in Warwick by the National Society for the Provision of Education for the Poor, a conservative Anglican body, so that children would learn "habits of industry, submission and economy" and would "contribute to the diminution of crime. . . . And our first aim is religious teaching."[29]

The very nature of established churches that sought to minister to all, in an age when religion was a social obligation, as well as a personal spiritual experience, posed problems for some of those, both clergy and laity, who criticized anything that might compromise the latter. Believers sure of their faith could find the compromises of comprehension abhorrent, but the determination of clerics to ensure standards of religious knowledge and observance meant these compromises were not those of the lowest common denominator. Dissatisfaction, moreover, reflected the importance of, and widespread commitment to, religion, the Church, and the clergy. Indeed, dissatisfaction was a testimony to them. Few believed that they could, or should, be dispensed with or doubted the close relationship of faith and reason, Church and State, clergy and laity, religion and the people, providence and Britain.

As an important part of public commitment, anti-Catholicism remained a powerful force. Indeed, as a central aspect of the Anglican Church-State, Catholics continued to be barred from some aspects of public life until 1829, although the Oaths of Allegiance and Supremacy were amended for Catholics in 1791 after negotiations with the Catholic Committee. When Austen's cousin Eliza Hancock married a French count in 1781, there was concern that she would convert to Catholicism. Yet she did not do so, and her husband was an Anglophile, therefore a more acceptable choice. The novelist Fanny Burney married a French émigré Catholic in 1793. Prime minister from 1783, Pitt the Younger had to resign in 1801 because George III would not accept his more liberal proposals for Catholics, such as Catholic emancipation, a key political issue, which did not come until 1829. Such views were also not accepted elsewhere—for example, by Shute Barrington, who wanted to keep Catholics from political power. In 1807, "No Popery" was the issue that dominated the general election. Spencer Perceval, an Evangelical Tory and the prime minister from 1809–12, stood firm against Catholic emancipation. Nevertheless, there was a spread of open Catholicism, particularly in the shape of the foundation of Catholic chapels.

Although a devout Anglican, Austen herself was not critical of Catholicism. In her *History of England*, she vilified Elizabeth I for her treatment of Mary, Queen of Scots, a Catholic, and drew out the religious element in her positive account of the latter: "She bore it with a most unshaken fortitude; firm in her mind; constant in her religion; and prepared herself to meet the cruel fate to which she was doomed, with a magnanimity that could alone proceed from conscious innocence. And yet could you reader have believed it possible that some hardened and zealous Protestants have even abused her for that steadfastness in the Catholic religion which reflected on her so much credit? But this is a striking proof of *their* narrow souls and prejudicial judgments who accuse her."[30] Subsequently, in her treatment of Mary's Protestant son, James I, Austen voiced criticism of the Gunpowder Plot of 1605 but after the remark wrote: "I am myself partial to the roman catholic religion."[31] This fitted in with her sympathies with the Stuarts. As a context, Anglican ecclesiology was closer to Catholicism than Reformed Protestantism. Many Tories—for example, Samuel Johnson (and later George Canning, Tory officeholder from 1807 to 1809 and 1814 onward and prime minister in 1827)—preferred Catholics to Dissenters, especially so before George III opposed Catholic emancipation.

Protestant Nonconformity was significant. Dissent was affected by a revival from the 1770s that owed much to itinerant and lay preaching. Methodism was a vibrant new force, and its position was entrenched with imposing churches, such as that built in Plymouth in 1813. At the same time, the Church of England remained dominant. Religious tension is difficult to measure because its classic product was not the violence that might attract judicial and possibly political or even military attention but the prejudice that was expressed in endogamy (marriage within the group); discriminatory political, social, economic, and cultural practices; and words and actions of abuse and insult. The role of clergymen and ecclesiastical and religious bodies in education, charity, and social welfare furthered identification with confessional groupings, although, at the same time, different religious groupings were not isolated from one another.

Clerics played a major role in the cultural world of the period, notably in various branches of literature. Among Austen's contemporaries who impressed her, this was especially the case of George Crabbe, a poet and naturalist as well as a cleric. He benefited from the patronage of John, fifth Duke of Rutland, duke from 1787 until 1857, and became his chaplain at Belvoir Castle. During these years, Crabbe published *The Village* (1783), *The Borough* (1810), and *Tales* (1812). Like Austen, he was sincere, pious, self-controlled ,and lacking in arrogance. He later became a rector in Wiltshire.[32]

Pious herself, as the inscription on her gravestone in Winchester Cathedral notes, Austen was a daughter of a rector, and two of her six brothers became clergymen. Moreover, her sister Cassandra became engaged to the Reverend Thomas Fowle in 1795. However, he accompanied his patron, the libidinous William, seventh Lord Craven, to the West Indies as a regimental chaplain and died there in 1797 from yellow fever.

Three of Austen's prayers survive, and she was able to write to Anna in September 1814 about her views on sermons (also a topic when George III met Johnson): "I am very fond of Sherlock's Sermons, prefer them to almost any."[33] This reference to the sermons of Thomas Sherlock (1678–1761), bishop of London

(1748–61), serves as a reminder of the influence of earlier works and ideas, not least through new editions, as with the 1812 edition of Sherlock's sermons. The bishop himself had published his sermons in 1725 and 1754–58.

Austen's piety was the background for her judgment of individuals. Austen had scant time for those clerics who did not meet her standards. The fictional Mr. Collins was in part based on a clerical cousin, Edward Cooper, an Evangelical who, self-centered, sent letters of little comfort. Rector of Hamstall Ridware in Staffordshire, where Austen visited him in 1806, the wealthy Cooper included among his friends William Gilpin (see chap. 11) and Thomas Gisborne (1758–1846). As a reminder of the multiple links of individuals, the latter, an Anglican priest, was author of the censorious and much reprinted *Duties of the Female Sex* (1797), which emphasized subordination to the divinely ordained social order, as well as a critic of circulating libraries, a poet, an active opponent of the slave trade, and an opponent of geology's abandonment of a biblical background.

A facetious Austen refers via Elizabeth Bennet to Mr. Collins's "kind intention of christening, marrying, and burying his parishioners whenever it were required."[34] Collins's interest in accumulating "other family livings" is noted.[35] As far as the antisentiment of *Northanger Abbey* is concerned, Richard Morland, the father of the heroine, is neither neglected nor poor but has two good livings. One, of which he was patron and incumbent, was worth about four hundred pounds yearly. That is what he proposes to give to his son James as soon as he is ready for ordination.[36] Meanwhile, Woodston, a family living of the Tilneys, is held by General Tilney's younger son, Henry, a positive character.[37]

In *Mansfield Park*, a novel with much Evangelical influence, Edmund Bertram, also a positive character and the young son of Sir Thomas, is intended for the Church. He plans to reside in his parish and provides Austen, in the voice of his father Sir Thomas, with an opportunity to denounce pluralism:

I should have been deeply mortified, if any son of mine could reconcile himself to doing less . . . a parish has wants and claims which
can be known only by a clergyman constantly resident, and which
no proxy can be capable of satisfying to the same extent. Edmund
might, in the common phrase, do the duty of Thornton, that is, he
might read prayers and preach, without giving up Mansfield Park; he
might ride over, every Sunday, to a house nominally inhabited, and
go through divine service; he might be the clergyman of Thornton
Lacey every seventh day, for three or four hours, if that would content him. But it will not. He knows that human nature needs more
lessons than a weekly sermon can convey, and that if he does not
live among his parishioners and prove himself by constant attention
their well-wisher and friend, he does very little either for their good
or his own.[38]

Described by Austen as a "little harangue,"[39] this was a deeply
serious account. Far from being solely Evangelical, this view
reflected the strong Anglican commitment of many clerics and
much of the laity both when Austen was writing and over the
previous century. High Churchmen, including Liverpool, dis-
liked pluralism and sought to remedy it within the limited means
available to them.

Mary Crawford, who had designs on Edmund, was startled
by the views of the Bertrams, as she had hoped "to shut out the
church, sink the clergyman, and see only the respectable, elegant,
modernized, and occasional residence of a man of independent
fortune."[40] Her brother also emerges as flawed, not least through
declaring that, if a preacher, he would only wish to preach occasionally. Fanny Price shakes her head.[41]

Pluralism led in the absence of incumbents to curates being
appointed and paid to serve some of the benefices.[42] In 1780,
only about 38 percent of English parishes had resident incumbents, and 36 percent of Anglican clergy were pluralists. Pluralism often arose due to lay impropriation or clerical poverty
arising from major discrepancies in clerical income and the
inadequacy of many livings, but nonresident incumbents

frequently lived nearby, and, in general, there were resident stipendiary curates. The difficulties of their position, not least needing to wait to be able to support a wife until they got a living, are brought out by Austen.[43] Pluralism was more common in areas where many parishes had poor endowments—for example, on the Essex coast—but that would not have been an issue for Mr. Collins.

Mr. Collins has a very harsh response to Lydia's elopement with George Wickham, informing Mr. Bennet: "The death of your daughter would have been a blessing in comparison of this . . . this licentiousness of behaviour in your daughter, has proceeded from a faulty degree of indulgence, . . . this false step in one daughter, will be injurious to the fortunes of all the others . . . throw off your unworthy child from your affection for ever, and leave her to reap the fruits of her own heinous offence."[44] He subsequently writes to Mr. Bennet: "I must not, however, neglect the duties of my station, or refrain from declaring my amazement, at hearing that you received the young couple into your house as soon as they were married. It was an encouragement of vice; . . . You ought certainly to forgive them as a christian, but never to admit them in your sight, or allow their names to be mentioned in your hearing." Mr. Bennet adds: "*That* is his notion of christian forgiveness!"[45] The punctuation makes Austen's attitude clear. Criticism of clerics who did not meet appropriate standards was seen in Austen's correspondence and writing. Writing to Cassandra in April 1805, Austen referred to another cleric, Edward Bather, as a "wretch!" who did not deserve the maid of the woman to whom he had become engaged. Austen herself was criticized by an Irish cleric who liked living in Bath for the comment in *Mansfield Park* about nonresidence.[46] In *Catherine, or the Bower*, Austen presents as a parish clergyman the proud Mr. Dudley, "the younger son of a very noble family," who is "forever quarrelling" about tithes, "and with the principal neighbours themselves concerning the respect and parade, he exacted."[47]

This is a psychological and social dislike on Austen's side, but there was also an ideological and historical side. In her correspondence with Cassandra, Austen felt able to write in January 1809 that she did "not like the Evangelicals." Their enthusiasm and zeal would have reminded her of the Puritans, who were perforce villains due to her views of the civil war.

Thus, the clergy are not necessarily the heroes in Austen's novels or always significantly virtuous. This is particularly the case if one overlooks the young clergy, as they are often the positive clerics. There was no equivalent of Henry Fielding's Parson Adams or the Reverend Arthur Villars in *Evelina* (her careful guardian) or a narrator like the *Vicar of Wakefield*. Collins is less attractive than the dully respectable Mr. Boyer, an unsuccessful suitor, in Hannah Foster's novel *The Coquette* (1797), while the Reverend Norris in *Mansfield Park* is presented as fairly useless and his wife as monstrously selfish. It is appropriate that they would have "carried on the garden wall, and made the plantation to shut out the churchyard," as their successor, the keen-on-the-claret Dr. Grant, does.[48] Offered the patronage of the prince regent, or at least of his librarian, Austen turned down James Stanier Clarke's idea that she write a novel about a clergyman or, as he continued later in 1815, a naval chaplain.

Yet, while there are no Dissenting heroes in her novels, there are clerical ones, notably Edmund Bertram, Henry Tilney, and Edward Ferrars. Elinor Dashwood is able to assure Colonel Brandon that "Edward's principles and disposition" deserved the living of Delaford that he was giving him.[49] Edward indeed shows both good character and humility. Austen condemns characters who are contemptuous of the clergy—for example, Robert Ferrars's attitude toward his elder brother:

> The idea of Edward's being a clergyman, and living in a small parsonage house, diverted him beyond measure;—and when to that was added the fanciful imagery of Edward reading prayers in a white surplice, and publishing the banns of marriage between John Smith and Mary Brown, he could conceive nothing more ridiculous.

> Elinor, while she waited in silence, and immoveable gravity, the conclusion of such folly, could not restrain her eyes from being fixed on him with a look that spoke all the contempt it excited . . . it relieved her own feelings.[50]

Such anticlericalism was associated with Whigs; in Elinor, Austen was very much expressing a Tory clericalism.

Austen expected others to be pious. Her naval brother, Francis, was very much so and was part of a powerful devout tendency in the Royal Navy. In 1809, she responded to the death of General Sir John Moore in battle at Corunna: "I wish Sir John had united something of the Christian with the Hero in his death."[51] This response was an aspect of a wider engagement with the providential character of Britain. In September 1814, with reference to the possibility of continued war with the United States, which, on rational grounds, she viewed with much foreboding,[52] Austen wrote to Martha Lloyd: "I place my hope of better things on a claim to the protection of Heaven, as a Religious Nation, a Nation in spite of much Evil Improving in Religion, which I cannot believe the Americans to possess."[53] There was a higher proportion of Protestant non-Anglicans (non-Episcopalians) in North America than in England.

Austen has little time for the laity who are wanting in piety or, more particularly, behavior. Some faults are minor. Typically self-centered, Lady Bertram, crying herself to sleep "after hearing an affecting sermon," achieved little.[54] Vice receives more attention. Austen is critical of the adulterous elopement of Henry Crawford and Maria Rushworth, and, both in *Lady Susan* and in her correspondence, Austen is hostile toward adultery. Mr. Price remarks, "So many fine ladies were going to the devil now-a-days that way, that there was no answering for anybody." As an instance of observance of the Sabbath, Anne Elliot is critical of Sunday traveling.[55]

The disagreement at Sotherton Court over chapel attendance reflects Austen's values. Mary Crawford jokes, when told that the chapel was formerly in constant use, both morning and evening,

but that the late Mr. Rushworth had stopped this, "Every generation has its improvement." This leads Fanny to respond: "It was a
valuable part of former times. There is something in a chapel and
chaplain so much in character with a great house, with one's ideas
of what such a household should be! A whole family assembling
regularly for the purpose of prayer, is fine!" The immoral and selfish Mary replies, bringing up social control: "It must do the heads
of the family a great deal of good to force all the poor housemaids
and footmen to leave business and pleasure, and say their prayers
here twice a day, while they are inventing excuses themselves for
staying away . . . it is safer to leave people to their own devices on
such subjects." Edmund Bertram ably answers Mary's points, as
he also later does when discussing his sister's elopement with her
brother.[56] Edmund also shows a grasp of human flaws in describing Mrs. Norris not as cruel but as having "faults of principle . . .
and a corrupted, vitiated mind."[57] Such remarks capture Austen's
insights into personality, insights that drew on her experience.
Yet Edmund is able to draw attention to "a spirit of improvement
abroad," both in preaching and among the laity: "It is felt that
distinctness and energy may have weight in recommending the
most solid truths; and, besides, there is more general observation
and taste, a more critical knowledge diffused, than formerly; in
every congregation, there is a larger proportion who know a l little
of the matter, and who can judge and criticise."[58]

In a broader sense, alongside such criticism, Austen's novels are
Anglican works, not least in their faith in human nature and their
desire to be positive: "Let other pens dwell on guilt and misery.
I quit such odious subjects as soon as I can, impatient to restore
everybody, not greatly in fault themselves, to tolerable comfort,
and to have done with all the rest."[59]

The discussion of sin is very much restrained,[60] even in the
somewhat amoral *Lady Susan*. Nevertheless, according to her
brother Henry, Austen objected to what he presented as the low
moral standards in the work of Henry Fielding,[61] whose approach

was certainly very different, while her favor for Richardson was a key indicator of her preference in style and content. Moreover, Austen makes explicit reference to evil in *Emma* and *Persuasion*, and, more potently so in *Sense and Sensibility*, when Elinor's response to John Willoughby's revelations leads her to consider the origins of evil:

> Her thoughts were silently fixed on the irreparable injury which too early an independence and its consequent habits of idleness, dissipation, and luxury, had made in the mind, the character, the happiness, of a man who, to every advantage of person and talents, united a disposition naturally open and honest, and a feeling, affectionate temper. The world had made him extravagant and vain—Extravagance and vanity had made him cold-hearted and selfish. Vanity, while seeking its own guilty triumph at the expense of another, had involved him in a real attachment, which extravagance, or at least its offspring, necessity, had required to be sacrificed. Each faulty propensity in leading him to evil, had led him likewise to punishment.[62]

The religious theme is brought forward melodramatically soon after by Marianne Dashwood, who wishes to have time "for atonement to my God."[63] Sin was generally seen as communal as well as individual, with the former having political consequences, and understandably so, in a world governed by providence. Thus, George III was convinced of the widespread propensity of fallen man, of elite and populace alike, to corruption and factionalism.

If Austen's works rest on a judgmentalism born of Anglican piety, the focus is, as Elizabeth Bennet points out, on "thoughtlessness, want of attention to other people's feelings, and want of resolution,"[64] rather than sin. "Self-denial," paradoxically rather a Whiggish, Low Church attitude, is applauded as part of a God-given desideratum of "a good mind and a sound understanding."[65] Similarly, in *Sense and Sensibility*, Edward Ferrars, a clergyman, his suit for Elinor's hand in marriage accepted, "was not only in the rapturous profession of the lover, but in the reality of reason and truth, one of the happiest of men." He and Colonel Brandon resemble each other "in good principles and good sense."[66] As a result, the moral quality of Austen's work fits into a strong tradition of pragmatic Anglican didacticism.

Worried about the effect on Catherine Morland of her visit to Northanger Abbey, her sensible mother recalled: "There is a very clever Essay in one of the books up stairs upon much such a subject, about young girls that have been spoilt for home by great acquaintance—'The Mirror,' . . . I am sure it will do you good." When Catherine did not improve from her listlessness, Mrs. Morland "hastily left the room to fetch the book in question, anxious to lose no time in attacking so dreadful a malady."[67] Number 12 of the *Mirror*, that of March 6, 1779, included a letter from "John Homespun" on the bad consequences for his daughters of visiting a wealthy lady and acquiring bad habits. The *Mirror* is made superfluous by the unexpected arrival of Henry Tilney. Otherwise, Catherine, to a modern eye, might have had another reason for listlessness, although that would not have captured the attitudes of Austen's contemporaries.

Austen, indeed, takes the didactic tradition forward in a fashion shown as sensible by the trajectories of her characters. In *Mansfield Park*, Sir Thomas Bertram comes to reflect that his daughters' education was flawed because, while "instructed theoretically in their religion," they were "never required to bring it into daily practice," and this is related to the lack of "that sense of duty which can alone suffice" when teaching how to govern "their inclinations and tempers." Thus, he had failed in his wish for "them to be good."[68] At the same time, Austen was cautious about her public stance:

> Miss Austen had on all the subjects of enduring religious feeling the deepest and strongest convictions, but a contact with loud and noisy exponents of the then popular religious phase made her reticent almost to a fault. She had to suffer something in the way of reproach from those who believed she might have used her genius

to greater effect; but her old friend used to say "I think I see her now defending what she thought was the real province of a delineator of life and manners, and declaring her belief that example and not 'direct preaching' was all that a novelist could afford properly to exhibit."[69]

The novelist certainly dissected the social aspect of religious observance, as in a superb chapter introduction: "Mrs Elton was first seen at church: but though devotion might be interrupted, curiosity could not be satisfied by a bride in a pew, and it must be left for the visits in form which were then to be paid, to settle whether she were very pretty indeed, or only rather pretty, or not pretty at all."[70] This was ironic, and accurate, human observation linked to a spirited engagement with life, a life illuminated by spiritual purpose.

NOTES

1. I. Collins, *Jane Austen and the Clergy* (London, 1993) and *Jane Austen: The Parson's Daughter* (London, 2007); M. Griffin, *Jane Austen and Religion: Salvation and Society in Georgian England* (New York, 2002).

2. T. Friedman, *The Eighteenth-Century Church in Britain* (New Haven, CT, 2011).

3. Brand to Wharton, March 12, 1790, Durham University Library, Wharton papers; Thomas Sunderland to Mylord, February 1, 1794, Preston, Lancashire Record Office, Cavendish of Holker papers, DD Ca 22/9/14.

4. *Encyclopaedia Britannica* (Edinburgh, 1815), VIII, 44.

5. Chapter 21.

6. J. J. Sack, *From Jacobite to Conservative: Reaction and Orthodoxy in Britain, c. 1760–1832* (Cambridge, 1993).

7. J. E. Austen-Leigh, *A Memoir of Jane Austen and Other Family Recollections*, ed. K. Sutherland (Oxford, 2002), 71, 173. The references to the displaced household chaplain at Sotherton and to oaks can be linked to the Nonjuring family on Jane's mother's side.

8. *Juvenilia*, 187–89.

9. *Juvenilia*, 319–21.

10. *Juvenilia*, 320.

11. *Juvenilia*, 323.

12. *Juvenilia*, 324.

13. *Juvenilia*, 331.

14. *Juvenilia*, 331, 333.

15. *Juvenilia*, 332.

16. *Juvenilia*, 337, 346, 341, 347–50.

17. *Persuasion* I, 9.

18. H. Coombs and P. Coombs, eds., *Journal of a Somerset Rector, 1803–1834* (Bath, 1971).

19. S. Slinn, *The Education of the Anglican Clergy, 1780–1839* (Woodbridge, 2017).

20. *PP* I, 14.

21. *PP* II, 5.

22. *PP* II, 12; III, 10.

23. *PP* II, 9.

24. *Persuasion* I, 9.

25. *MP* I, 8.

26. *MP* II, 7.

27. S. Tomaselli, "Remembering Mary Wollstonecraft," *British Journal for Eighteenth-Century Studies* 15 (1992): 127.

28. B. Taylor, *Mary Wollstonecraft and the Feminist Imagination* (Cambridge, 2003).

29. D. Fowler, "Reading and Writing in Warwick, 1780s–1830s," *Warwickshire History* 11, no. 2 (winter 1999–2000): 72.

30. *Juvenilia*, 184.

31. *Juvenilia*, 186.

32. T. C. Faulkner, ed., *Selected Letters and Journals of George Crabbe* (Oxford, 1985).

33. *Letters*, 278.

34. *PP* I, 13.

35. *PP* II, 7.

36. *Northanger* II, 1.

37. *Northanger* II, 7.

38. *MP* II, 7.

39. *MP* II, 7.

40. *MP* II, 7.

41. *MP* III, 3.

42. An overly sympathetic account of Collins is offered in I. Morris, *Mr Collins Considered: Approaches to Jane Austen* (London, 1987).

43. *Sense* III, 2.

44. *PP* III, 6.

45. *PP* III, 15.

46. Letter 44; D. Le Faye, "Jane Austen's Friend Mrs Barrett Identified," *Notes and Queries* 244, no. 4 (December 1999): 452.

47. *Juvenilia*, 245.

48. *MP* I, 6.

49. *Sense* III, 3.

50. *Sense* III, v.

51. *Letters*, 173.

52. *Letters*, 273.

53. *Letters*, 274.

54. *MP* III, 16.

55. *MP* III, 15; T. Winnifrith, "Jane Austen's Adulteress," *Notes and Queries* 235, no. 1 (May 1990): 19–22; *Persuasion* II, 5.

56. *MP* I, 9; III, 16.7

57. *MP* III, 16.

58. *MP* III, 3.

59. *MP* III, 17.

60. G. Koppel, *The Religious Dimension of Jane Austen's Novel* (Ann Arbor, MI, 1988).

61. H. Austen, "Biographical Notice of the Author," in the 1818 edition of *Northanger Abbey* and *Persuasion*.

62. *Sense* III, 8.

63. *Sense* III, 10.

64. *PP* II, 1.

65. *Sense* III, 11.

66. *Sense* III, 13.

67. *Northanger* II, 15.

68. *MP* III, 17.

69. Le Faye, "Jane Austen's Friend Mrs Barrett," 452.

70. *Emma* II, 14.

CULTURE, ARTS, AND THE ENLIGHTENMENT

Much could not be hoped from the traffic of even the busiest part of Highbury;—Mr Perry walking hastily by; Mr William Cox letting himself in at the office door, Mr Cole's carriage horses returning from exercise, or a stray letter-boy on an obstinate mule, were the liveliest objects she could presume to expect; and when her eyes fell only on the butcher with his tray, a tidy old woman travelling homewards from shop with her full basket, two curs quarrelling over a dirty bone, and a string of dawdling children round the baker's little bow-window eyeing the gingerbread, she knew she had no reason to complain, and was amused enough; quite enough still to stand at the door. A mind lively and at ease, can do with seeing nothing, and can see nothing that does not answer.

—*Emma*

IN THIS PASSAGE AUSTEN CAPTURED the repetition and boredom of so much provincial life—Highbury not being part of London. Given this repetition, there was the obvious significance of new arrivals, such as Frank Churchill, the Bingleys, and Mr. Darcy, and of being able to visit them. Who they are, what they would say and wear, their connections, deportment, and goals, would be a matter of anticipation and then analysis, with individuals' responses to them carefully cross-calibrated. This process provided a new means of activity, a new course for reflection, and the opportunity to assess and assert values, priorities, and hierarchy. So also with those who are talked about, but never met, such as the Sucklings.[1]

This boredom also helps explain the attempt to add interest by games of chance, and the linked gambling, notably on cards but, in practice, on just about everything.[2] More positively, boredom could be countered by reading. Doing so enabled the reader to enter the imaginary worlds of the writer and those created in response by readers, both the individual reader and those with whom they discussed the book and other books. Most particularly, reading provided knowledge of more characters to inhabit the reader's experience and a narrative to engage and instruct. The narrative appeared under control: control by the author and control by the response of the readers.

The middling orders were fighting boredom, and their activity and patronage was of growing importance in English culture in Austen's lifetime. Unable individually to provide the sustained patronage offered by many members of the elite, they participated through public performances of works and public markets for the arts. Moreover, the major expansion of the middling orders helped provide a public culture that saw itself in terms of openness and reasoned argument. This formed an equivalent to the English self-image of their own religious culture in the shape of the unique Church of England considered in the prior chapter, as well as the Englishness discussed in chapter 12.

Patronage by the middling orders did not always take place in a public context. Instead, there was also a major domestic theme in cultural patronage and consumption. This was especially important for women—and notably so with reading. Within the domestic sphere, women were able to assert independence and self-control—for example, in music making—although this assertiveness was not limited to the domestic sphere. Similarly, religion could be "consumed" privately by reading the Bible and sermons and through individual prayer.

In contrast, the nature and role of the commercial market could lead to concern, which was generally related to perceptions of the political and social situation. An entrepreneurship in which values were allegedly dissolved in money was seen as an unworthy corruption of quality and morality. Indeed, the rise of a modern, commercial, urban, and, increasingly, meritocratic culture, at least in terms of the market and its values, was represented by commentators, who generally were under the influence of traditional civic humanist ideas, as a growth in luxury and effeminacy. The theme of the enervating threat of luxury to taste and, more seriously, to civilization was a weighty motif of anxiety. This theme contributed to caricatures of fashions in prints and prose and was reflected in much of the literature of the period, fictional or not.

Although musical activity centered in London, it was by no means confined to the capital. As in the world of the theater, some provincial towns that nowadays have no live music (other than karaoke in the local pub, a highly derivative process) had regular instrumental concerts and could boast their own amateur musical societies, many of which bought, or subscribed to, all the latest productions of the London music publishers. It was easy for amateurs to participate in instrumental and vocal music, collectively or singly. Thus, choral music flourished in the wake of the Three Choirs Festival held in Gloucester, Hereford, and Worcester from the early eighteenth century. The popularity of glee singing (part songs usually sung unaccompanied) testified to the widespread enthusiasm for performing vocal music. Families, friends, and neighbors all took part in sociable singing, frequently accompanied by other aspects of conviviality, especially food and drink. In London in 1793, John Ley reported to his mother that he had visited relatives in suburban Blackheath: "Monstrous good fun it was, every person in the highest spirits and very much pleased, we danced the most riotous dances we could, Sir Roger de Coverley, Country Bumpkin etc which on account of the party's being select were very pleasant, we had nine couples."[3]

Although private performances were important to her plots, Austen was skeptical about them at times. Of "a small musical party at her house" in London held by Mrs. John Dashwood, Austen noted: "The party, like other musical parties, comprehended a great many people who had real taste for the performance, and a great many more who had none at all; and the performers themselves were, as usual, in their own estimation, and that of their immediate friends, the first private performers in England."[4] Such ironic comments were based on experience and would have resonated with many readers' own experience or imagination.

Chamber and solo works intended for amateurs enjoyed considerable popularity, and instruments, music, and manuals were produced accordingly. In 1785, a French visitor commented that music was cultivated "universally, in London as it is throughout the kingdom." Music teachers came to play a major role, and women were often depicted in paintings and fiction as playing music, as Charlotte Raikes was in her luminous portrait by George Romney. Austen herself sang for her family.[5] In her parody "Plan of a Novel," Austen's heroine is "particularly excelling in Music—her favourite pursuit—and playing equally well on the Piano Forte and Harp." In *Pride and Prejudice*, Miss Bingley applauds Miss Darcy: "Her performance on the piano-forte is exquisite."[6] In *Lady Susan*, the "small pianoforte" is moved at the protagonist's request into her dressing room so her daughter Frederica can practice it,[7] and the gift of a piano in *Emma* invites speculation.

So also at social gatherings. In *Pride and Prejudice*, the Bennet girls vie in singing and playing at a party held at Lucas Lodge. Elizabeth sings first. Then Mary sings Scottish and Irish airs and plays "a long concerto." Marianne does the same in *Sense and Sensibility*.[8] Mary Crawford is very proud of her ability to play the harp while, returning to Mansfield Park, Sir Thomas

Bertram calls for music from his daughters.[9] In contrast, despite initial enthusiasm, the young Catherine Morland, a figure of somewhat uncertain enthusiasms, cannot bear to learn music and soon gives up.[10]

The private world of music provided the demand for expansion in music publication. This benefited the large numbers who played alone and lessened their potential isolation. More generally, self-improvement was important across English culture, from devotional literature to guides on playing music to devices to improve artistic skills. Thus, newspaper advertisements offered tuition in a range of accomplishments, such as learning foreign languages. Reading itself was improving, which made suggestions that it was not so inherently contentious.

Self-improvement was also highly significant to the matrimonial game, as noted by Lady Catherine de Bourgh. Moreover, Miss Bingley pointed out how much young women are expected to achieve in order to have accomplishments and thus make themselves attractive, only for Darcy to trump these accomplishments with reading.[11] This was clearly a frequent conversation in Austen's circle, and Darcy can be assumed to express Austen's view.

Musical instruments were displayed and played in the fine rooms constructed in so many houses during the major rehousing of much of the well-off in both town and countryside that occurred during the eighteenth century. These instruments also helped structure family space and activity. New houses also had more furniture, especially chairs, tables, dressers, clocks, and looking glasses, as well as plastered ceilings, curtains, and fireplaces. Many individuals reflected on the presence, quality, or cost of such items. Thus, in his rectory, Mr. Collins shows off "every article of furniture in the room, from the sideboard to the fender."[12] All provided opportunities and employment for craftsmen, as well as a conversation point for hosts and guests. Economic expansion, consumerism, and material culture were interrelated.

Middle-class patronage was also crucial in the theater, which had shed its immoral and blasphemous reputation and had developed in London but also elsewhere. In response to the use of the stage by opposition writers, including Henry Fielding, the Licensing Act of 1737 gave the lord chamberlain the power to censor plays and made unlicensed theaters illegal. However, although this legislation restricted permission to stage spoken drama in London to two theaters, in practice the situation was more liberal, both there and, even more so, outside London. This was a characteristic aspect of governance in this period—for example, the death penalty was applied less than its extension to cover crimes might suggest. By 1800, there were nearly three hundred theaters in the British Isles, including one in Richmond, Yorkshire, opened in 1788, that can still be visited and that illustrates the close relationship between the actors and the audience.[13] Other theaters continued to open, including the New Theatre Royal in Bath in 1805. Moreover, the Enabling Act of 1788 allowed justices of the peace to issue licenses for performances.

Regional circuits were created out of the routes of strolling players, who increasingly acted in purpose-built playhouses. When, in 1786, the leading theatrical company in East Anglia, the Norwich Comedians or the Duke of Grafton's Servants, ceased to tour smaller towns, it was still able to concentrate its attentions on Norwich, King's Lynn, Great Yarmouth, Barnwell (Cambridge), Bury St. Edmunds, Colchester, and Ipswich. Theatrical productions were extensively discussed in the press.

On the stage, tragedy's service to morality was presented against a variety of backgrounds, both historical and contemporary. In her whimsical *History of England*, Austen criticizes Nicholas Rowe's *The Tragedy of Jane Shore* (1714), which was highly popular at the time, as "a tragedy and therefore not worth reading."[14] Rowe (1674–1718), a Whig placeholder, was made poet laureate in 1715. As a prominent Whig writer, he would have been unpopular to Austen.

Morality was matched by comedy. Whether on the stage, on canvas, or on the printed page, the middling orders watched both themselves and caricatures that reflected the anxieties and drives being depicted and the personality traits debated. Thus, the comedies of the Irish playwright Richard Brinsley Sheridan (1751–1816), namely *The Rivals* (1775), *A Trip to Scarborough* (1777), *The School for Scandal* (1777), and *The Critic* (1779), offered satires on manners that in part captured anxieties over social standing. Mistaken identities played a major role in Sheridan's plays, as well as in Oliver Goldsmith's successful comedy *She Stoops to Conquer* (1773), a play set more than those of Sheridan in the social milieu of Austen's world and in rural England. Austen refers to *The Critic* in her *History of England*, mentioning that it contains anecdotes about Sir Walter Raleigh and his friend Sir Christopher Hatton,[15] which it does in the shape of Mr. Puff's brilliantly comic play-within-the-play, *The Spanish Armada*. Sheridan himself was a Whig MP.

Although, in a long-standing pattern, mistaken identities were exploited to comic effect in the plays of Sheridan, Goldsmith, and others and provided much of the dynamic of the plots, they also captured concern about identity and worries arising from the dangers of misidentification. The latter focused on the ability to deceive as to character. In *The School for Scandal*, the most frequently produced play of Austen's early years, Joseph Surface is menacing in his deceitful self-interest and unctuous hypocrisy, and part of the pleasure of this excellent play derives from seeing him thwarted. Misidentification in this sense is very much the case in Austen's plots, as with George Wickham in *Pride and Prejudice*. Falling in love with the wrong person is a continual danger. Somewhat differently, misidentification, of circumstances and/or intentions, is also a repeated feature of her other novels, including, in particular *Emma*, *Northanger Abbey*, and *Mansfield Park*.

In comedies, tensions could be defused, and social role-playing could be presented with humorous consequences and no long-term difficulties thanks to the plot deployment of a benign fortune. Reversals as plot devices also captured a sense of social fluidity and yet an underlying set of social rules. These were seen across the drama of the age. For example, Isaac Jackman, like Sheridan a transplanted Irishman, produced a series of comic works. His *The Divorce* (1781), an operatic farce about a divorce arranged to ensure publicity, presented, like Sheridan's *The Critic*, a world in which the pressure for artificiality was both strong and open to satirical representation as absurd. This was also seen in the ridicule, notably from the 1770s, of the fashionable, affected men termed *macaronis*, who were concentrated in London. The ridicule was, for some, a way to strike at the capital.

However, although Sheridan lived until 1816, *The Critic* was his last first-rate play, and *Pizaro* (1799) was his last really successful work. The 1800s and 1810s were not great periods of drama, but Austen visited the theater in London, including the Lyceum in 1811 and Drury Lane and Covent Garden in 1814. In *Pride and Prejudice*, Elizabeth Bennet goes to "one of the theatres" when in London en route to Kent, but there is no description of the theater or the production.[16] In *Sense and Sensibility*, John Willoughby runs into Sir John Middleton "in Drury-lane lobby."[17] Neither would be assumed to be particularly interested in the theater, but attendance was a social opportunity, even duty, and notably so for married people on show as a couple. Like the assembly rooms at Bath and elsewhere, theater lobbies were places where people could meet and mingle.

In addition to theaters, there were private productions of plays, as in the Austen household. These could involve the socially prominent. John O'Keeffe's *The Agreeable Surprise* (1781), a comic opera about love eventually successful, was performed at Brandenburg House in 1795, with Albinia, Countess of Buckinghamshire, the wife of the third earl, among the cast.

A private production is the topic of much discussion in *Mansfield Park*, and there is heated disagreement about the allocation of the parts and the appropriateness of the play.[18] There are moral and social issues in young ladies playacting. It is the "moral" characters, Edmund and Fanny, who demur, although Edmund gives in. The more dubious characters, such as Yates and Mary Crawford, support the performance. The return of Sir Thomas Bertram brings the scheme to an abrupt close after much emotion and expense had been invested in it and the related socializing. The productions at Steventon were more orderly, but in *Mansfield Park*, the latent tensions present in drama are ably brought to the fore.

Alongside the moral critique of affectation in much of the writing of the period, and the preference for honesty as an aesthetic as well as a moral choice, is the sense of flux and uncertainty that led to lack of clarity over identity and classification or, at least, a challenge to them. In this situation of flux, performance was the condition of mankind, certainly in the social maelstrom of London and the viewing gallery of Bath. Performance was also a challenge to appropriate conduct and to the social categorization it was supposed to reflect and sustain. In terms of the affirmation, testing, or breaking of norms, the representation of men and women in fiction threw light on the situation in the public sphere. Moreover, this fluidity provided plots and satisfied public interest.

The role of the middling orders was important in the definition of taste. By means of this definition, both conduct and the imagination were organized and encouraged, and culture was developed. Yet a focus on "politeness," consumerism, and the public sphere can lead to an underplaying of the continual role of elite culture and an exaggeration of secularization. There was, in practice, a trickle-down effect from the elite in both form and content. Emulation was crucial, as Austen's novels revealed. This emulation was seen more widely in material culture and manners. Thus, Josiah Wedgwood's pottery was an important instance of emulation: he made elite objects and then cheaper emulative versions for the middling orders. Engravings provided another instance of the same process.

At the same time, difference, even divisions, affected every aspect of life, from style to politics, and that theme is not adequately worked out if the academic stress instead is solely on polite consumerism or a "trickle-down." Austen's work can be located in terms of this tension, which preceded the revolutionary crisis of the 1790s and continued subsequently. Unsurprisingly given her experience, plots, and characterization, Austen has little to say about working-class culture—the culture of the streets—although, very movingly, as so often in their sibling relationship, William Price recalls to Fanny their Portsmouth childhood: "We used to jump about together many a time, did we not? When the hand-organ was in the street?"[19] That culture is difficult to recover.

While sharing the same cultural world as men, women faced important differences in access and presentation. Thus, in conversation pieces—the group portraiture that presented relationships—men took the more prominent roles and commissioned the paintings. Performance, moreover, was dominated by men. Orchestras were male, and, in London, instrumental music was largely an all-male profession, although there were women pianists.

Although there was gradual change, women faced major difficulties. Indeed, it has been argued that assertive women outside their "proper" roles aroused concern. There was certainly a degree of typecasting and condescension, as in Tobias Smollett's popular novel *The Adventure of Roderick Random* (1748), in which Narcissa is presented as an unsuccessful writer "without consistency or capacity" to bring her work to completion but also, extraordinarily, writing not of love, but rather tragedies that did not cover it. There were certainly differences in plots between male and female writers: many male writers posed a choice between duty or love, but female counterparts were apt to unite the two. At the same time, it would be misleading simply to see a contrast in subject or approach.

Like their male counterparts, but often more so, many female writers are obscure. Moreover, writers prominent in their day, such as Jane West (1758–1852), have frequently slipped from attention. This is possibly because the canon of major and second-rank works emphasizes male writers, but much more was involved. West, an industrious writer who was typical in producing across different genres, with novels, plays, and poems, also had a somewhat leaden style. More significantly in terms of taste, West was an insistent moralist who was opposed to what she saw as the troubling radicalism of writers such as Mary Wollstonecraft. West's politics were illustrated by her *Elegy on Edmund Burke* (1793) and her moralism by her novel *The Advantages of Education: or The History of Maria Williams* (1793). Neither will ever challenge Austen's reputation. Male writers with this style also tend to be forgotten.

The canon was, is, and will continue to be fluid—possibly more so than over the last century. Hannah More, another critic of Wollstonecraft, wrote *Percy* (1777), one of the most successful plays of the period, as well as books that at the time greatly outsold Austen's. She was then long overlooked but has recently made a return to the spotlight with the first modern biography and the first to make full use of a correspondence much more extensive than that of Austen.[20] More saw herself as a conservative and (*not* but) also envisaged women playing a prominent role. The implication of her call for female patriotism was that politics in its broadest sense had to involve women, who were responsible for protecting the morality of the country. Morality, indeed, was presented as a patriotic guarantee of the nation. Novels were very much associated with female writers and readers, not least due to the epistolary form that was so important in many novels and much female socializing, notably so as marriage or other factors led female friends to live apart. In Austen's circle, commenting on novels was also prominent in correspondence.

Indeed, novels, like letter writing, in many respects could be seen as an important part of the world of women's activity. However insincere, the promise to write could be a plot enabler. When she leaves the neighborhood, the totally insincere Caroline Bingley presses Jane Bennet for a "very frequent and most unreserved correspondence."[21] That Caroline does so makes the idea of such a relationship between the two itself suspect. For Austen, letter writers were significant to the plot and revealed their character through correspondence, as Lucy Steele did in *Sense and Sensibility*. Letters, in reality, were definitely a form of conversation, which was an important aspect of the leisure of the period, especially for women.[22] At the same time, of course, many epistolary novels were written by men, notably the genre-setter *Pamela*,[23] as well as Sir Walter Scott's *Redgauntlet* (1824).

Less instrumental than correspondence, and personal rather than social, novels could also be presented as a drug. This was done satirically in Sheridan's play *The Rivals*: "Madam, a circulating library in a town is an evergreen tree of diabolical knowledge! It blossoms through the year! And depend on it, Mrs Malaprop, that they who are so fond of handling the leaves, will long for the fruit at last."[24]

At the same time, novels dealt with issues of concern. Most were about courtship or used it as an important plot device. They therefore offered women models of desirable partners and wooing that were different from whatever might be sanctioned by parents and guardians. This was troubling to the latter but proved particularly attractive to many female readers and thus sustained the feminization of the genre. On the whole, marriage for love was very much endorsed in fiction. However, in accordance with conventions of sensibility and practicality, marriage for love was constrained by an emphasis on propriety and filial duty, notably to fathers. These were all aspects of Austen's fictional offering, as when the consent of the unpleasant and manipulative General Tilney has to be sought at the close of *Northanger Abbey*.

Such marriage was often the concluding episode of a story essentially about growing up into society, with a young woman, frequently very young, as with Fanny Price in *Mansfield Park*, usually serving as the protagonist and her trajectory as the dynamic course and chronology of the plot. Adaptation to others and to social conventions was a key theme. In Fanny Burney's first novel, *Evelina: Or, A Young Lady's Entrance into the World* (1778), a novel written in the form of letters, Evelina is shown being brought into the world at the age of seventeen, a course that closes when she marries one of her guides, the sage Lord Orville, a kind of Colonel Brandon from *Sense and Sensibility*. This process of maturation provided opportunity for exciting, but predictable, sensibility. In the preface, Burney explains her plan as "to draw characters from nature, though not from life, and to mark the manners of the times." A far less benign upbringing, with malevolent guardians, a melodramatic descent to insanity, and a touch of the gothic, was offered in Burney's second novel, *Cecilia, or an Heiress* (1782).

The third novel, *Camilla, A Picture of Youth* (1796), was less unsettling and more conventional. Burney presented it to George III and Queen Charlotte, and Austen, who greatly admired Burney's work, was on the subscription list for the novel. The challenges in *Camilla* were more marked than those in *Evelina*. Several of the characters have faults. Edgar Mandlebert, the wealthy hero, is also judgmental, difficult, and overly concerned with appearances. There are elements later seen with Darcy, but there are clear differences. Eugenia, the heroine's younger sister, is crippled as a result of an accident, and she previously suffered from smallpox. Her personality, however, is a demonstration of true beauty. The heroine's older brother, Lionel, is highly mischievous and selfish, and another instance of selfishness is provided by her beautiful, flirtatious cousin, Indiana. Her brother Clermont is harsh to the servants and a bully. Camilla's father, a positive figure, is a cleric. The plot includes Alphonso Bellamy, a fortune hunter, kidnapping Eugenia. She is forced into marriage only for her captor to kill himself accidentally. This provides a gothic dimension.

While not a successful dramatist,[25] Burney was an important and much recognized female novelist at the time Austen developed her style. Alongside the theme of adaptation in Burney's work were the pressures to which women were subject, including violence. As a result, Burney has been depicted as a writer of contradictions, indeed anger.[26] Yet Burney, like Austen later, in part eludes ideological fixing,[27] which qualifies the depiction of Austen as a Tory writer. Moreover, the character of Burney's writing varied by individual novel much more than that of Austen.

Men were also readers, and Austen's father, George, bought novels, which helped ensure their availability to his daughters. In *Northanger Abbey*, Henry Tilney, who was not opposed to fiction, responded to the suggestion that "young men despised novels amazingly": "It is *amazingly*; it may well suggest *amazement* if they do—for they read nearly as many as women. I myself have read hundreds and hundreds. Do not imagine that you can cope with me in a knowledge of Julias and Louisas."[28] So also with Sir Edward Denham in *Sanditon*.

In *Northanger Abbey*, Catherine Morland herself was "left to the luxury of a raised, restless, and frightened imagination over the pages of *Udolpho* [Ann Radcliffe's *The Mysteries of Udolpho*], lost from all worldly concerns of dressing and dinner."[29] However, she discovers that the titular abbey is not a setting from the pages of gothic fiction. Yet, ironically, in *Northanger Abbey*, real life turns out unpleasant, as Catherine is exposed to the ire of the avaricious General Tilney. He bullies his children, creating an atmosphere that is differently unpleasant, and more real and emotionally menacing, than the imagined perils of gothic fiction.

The tendency of women in sentimental novels to lack self-restraint, or what was depicted as self-restraint, was presented as a sign of heightened nerves and emotions. This could also be seen as a lack of maturity. In Wollstonecraft's novel *Wrongs of Woman: or Maria* (1798), overwhelmingly a tale of male cruelty and the oppression of women, there is also a reference to the interacting dangers of female sensibility and fiction. A novel, Rousseau's *La Nouvelle Heloise*, plays a role in an unfortunate love affair.

Heightened nerves were also a commonplace in sentimental plays. The audience was given clear clues. This process was mocked in Sheridan's *The Critic*: "When a heroine goes mad she always goes into white satin" (act 3, scene 1). Novelists could work with these conventions, question them in order to make a point, or both. Often, in characterization or plotting, concerns about female sensibility were heightened, and women were sometimes, as in conduct literature, treated as minors. More positively and realistically, women were also presented as the key figures in family life and its culture of sociability, especially music making. Austen repeatedly makes successful fun of the conventions of sentimental fiction.

Meanwhile, children were treated, increasingly, as a distinctive part of society, with products being designed particularly for them. These included types of children's literature, a massive publishing phenomenon, and a genre in which women writers played an important role. Much of this literature was didactic. Thomas Day's best-selling *History of Sandford and Merton* (1783–89), an exemplary tale for children, presented the meritorious Harry Sandford, the son of a farmer, and Tommy Merton, the lazy son of an affluent gentleman. Morality through comparison, the theme in most novels, looks back to sermons, and secular equivalents such as William Hogarth's 1747 series of engravings "Industry and Idleness" were to the fore in this novel and in the genre as a whole. Yet the depiction of children also became more informal. As in other respects, the conventions changed rapidly. Austen does not devote an enormous amount of attention to children, particularly if young, but her discussion of them—for example, of the young Price children in *Mansfield Park*—is perceptive and successful.

This was also the age of the English Enlightenment. Reason was a goal as well as a method and a system.[30] Contemporaries believed it necessary to use reason to appreciate mankind, society, and the universe and thus improve human circumstances, an objective combining religious faith, utilitarianism, and the search for human happiness. Reason and moderation (rather than the logical sense of reason) were believed to be the distinguishing marks of mankind; correspondingly, the insane were usually regarded as monstrous. Reason was presented as the characteristic of human development and social organization while the savage mind was held to be obsessed by a world of terror in which monstrous anxieties were projected onto nature. In *Emma*, Mr. Knightley, with reference to Frank Churchill, provides an account of maturity in terms of fighting off fears: "I can allow for the fears of the child, but not of the man. As he became rational, he ought to have roused himself and shaken off all that was unworthy in their authority."[31]

As part of the Enlightenment, notions of causation changed greatly, at least for some. In this context, a displacing of providence was particularly apparent in the case of the weather. Instead of demonstrating immediate divine purpose, the weather was increasingly understood as a natural process. Equipment to that end was offered in the form of barometers and thermometers. Moreover, data led to classification. Thus, Luke Howard, in his *On the Modifications of Clouds* (1803), established and named three major categories of clouds: cumulus (heap), stratus (layer), and cirrus (rainy). Knowledge was displayed and enjoyed in the furnishing of houses with clocklike cased barometers. Geography as furniture was also seen with the display of globes and maps as part of a more general use of geographical information to assert and display social and intellectual status.[32] In this context, Fanny Price's complete lack of such knowledge served, unfairly, to castigate her in the eyes of her better-educated cousins.

Knowledge conveyed status in this account, a view that would have surprised Sir Walter Elliot with his emphasis on lineage, which certainly does not guarantee any quality on his part. Indeed, Sir Walter underlined the extent to which, with their foibles, the casts of characters in novels were scarcely a display case for the English Enlightenment. Thus, Austen's characters do not really engage with the provincial aspects of the scientific revolution, such as being a member of a literary and philosophical society, attending scientific lessons, or observing the workings of an orrery, a clockwork machine that showed the workings of the solar system. The topic of one of the best paintings of Joseph Wright of Derby (1734–97), *A Philosopher Lecturing on the Orrery* (1766), displayed Enlightenment values and knowledge, although another, his painting of *An Experiment on a Bird in the Air Pump* (1768), shows a girl distressed at the death of a bird as a result of an experiment. This highlighted an Enlightenment dilemma: how medical knowledge could be reconciled with sentimentalism over animals.

The vogue for geology, linked to interest in the workings of providence, history, the underpinning of physical geography, and tourism, does not feature in Austen's novels other than in the interest in landscape. The work of James Hutton (1726–97), the key figure in the development of geology, was made more readable by John Playfair (1748–1819), notably with his *Illustrations of the Huttonian Theory of the Earth* (1802). Geology was displayed in William Smith's *Delineation of the Strata of England and Wales with Part of Scotland* (1815). This depiction was linked to the evolution of minerology, another aspect of accessible and useful knowledge.

The Enlightenment was not only about science, knowledge, and discovery. It also drew on, but reconceptualized, a general worthiness, and Austen certainly engaged with this. Religion was a major (but today often underappreciated) influence on this worthiness, as in the campaign against the slave trade. Major abolitionist texts were by clerics, such as *Considerations on the Abolition of Slavery and the Slave Trade, Upon Grounds of Natural, Religious, and Political Duty* (1789) by Thomas Burgess, a prebendary of Salisbury Cathedral.

In *Pride and Prejudice*, the arrogant, foolish, and selfish Caroline Bingley suggests that balls were "insufferably tedious. . . . It would surely be much more rational if conversation instead of dancing were made the order of the day."[33] What is being satirized here are not Enlightened views but, instead, her ridiculous attempt to manipulate her way into Darcy's notice by throwing words like *rational* around. She is not enlightened at all: she just imagines that opposing balls in the name of rationality is going to attract Darcy, who, as she knows, has a big library and does not like dancing. Indeed, in contrast to Caroline's intentions and methods, actual enlightened attitudes are promoted by the novel. Crucially, Elizabeth has to learn to judge Darcy and Wickham on the evidence instead of going by her initial, irrational impressions.

Austen, however, does show a degree of skepticism about new intellectual developments, not least concerning their social context. In *Emma*, this skepticism leads to reflections on education: "Mrs Goddard was the mistress of a school—not of a seminary, or an establishment, or any thing which professed, in long sentences of refined nonsense, to combine liberal acquirements with elegant morality upon new principles and new systems—and where young ladies for enormous pay might be screwed out of health and into vanity—but a real, honest, old-fashioned boarding-school, where a reasonable quantity of accomplishments were sold at a reasonable price."[34]

As with politics, there are tensions within intellectual and cultural tendencies, and these tensions affect socializing. This is seen in *Emma* with contrasting ideas of how to enjoy the visit to Mr. Knightley's organized around strawberry collecting.

Mrs. Elton proposes: "A sort of gipsy party.—We are to walk about your gardens, and gather the strawberries ourselves, and under trees,—and whatever else you may like to provide, it is to be all out of door—a table spread in the shade, you know. Every thing as natural and simple as possible. Is not that your idea?" This proposal earns a rejoinder from a more practical Knightley that acts as a clear qualification to enthusiasm: "My idea of the simple and natural will be to have the table spread in the dining-room. The nature and the simplicity of gentlemen and ladies, with their servants and furniture, I think is best observed by meals within doors. When you are tired of eating strawberries in the garden, there shall be cold meat in the house."[35] Like sentiment, reason and the natural could look in different directions. Knightley is also proposing English moderation.

A more pointed critique of the Enlightenment, and of false values in general, comes in *Sanditon* when Mr. Parker, disparaging the rival bathing resort of Brinshore and noting that Mr. Heywood has not heard of it, remarks: "We may apply to Brinshore, the line of the poet William Cowper in his description of the religious cottager, as opposed to Voltaire—'*She*, never heard of half a mile from home.'" In practice, Parker misunderstands Cowper's *Truth* (1782) in which the pious cottager is contrasted with Voltaire: "His the mere tinsel, hers the rich rewards."[36] Austen praised Cowper (1731–1800), the son of a rector. Cowper became an evangelical and was also a prominent hymnodist and an opponent of slavery. Austen had Marianne Dashwood and Fanny Price approve of him. The cottager understands true value, as far as Austen was concerned. Mr. Parker does not.

NOTES

1. *Emma* III, 6.
2. J. E. Mullin, *A Sixpence at Whist: Gaming and the English Middle Classes, 1680–1830* (Woodbridge, 2015).

3. John Ley to his mother, October 19, 1793, Exeter, Devon Record Office, 63/2/11/6.

4. *Sense* II, 14.

5. D. Le Faye, "Three Missing Jane Austen Songs," *Notes and Queries* 244, no. 4 (1999): 454–55; R. Leppert, *Music and Image. Domesticity, Ideology and Socio-Cultural Formation in Eighteenth-Century England* (Cambridge, 1988).

6. *PP* I, 5.

7. *Lady Susan*, letter 17.

8. *PP* I, 6; *Sense and Sensibility* II, 2.

9. *MP* I, 6; II, 2.

10. *Northanger* I, 1.

11. *PP* I, 8.

12. *PP* I, 5.

13. S. Rosenfeld, *The Georgian Theatre of Richmond Yorkshire and Its Circuit* (London, 1984).

14. *Juvenilia*, 179.

15. *Juvenilia*, 187.

16. *PP* II, 4.

17. *Sense* III, 8; P. Gay, *Jane Austen and the Theatre* (Cambridge, 2006); P. Byrne, *Jane Austen and the Theatre* (London, 2007).

18. *MP* I, 13–18.

19. *MP* II, 7.

20. A. Stott, *Hannah More: The First Victorian* (Oxford, 2003).

21. *PP* I, 21.

22. D. Selwyn, *Jane Austen and Leisure* (London, 1999).

23. S. E. Whyman, *The Pen and the People: English Letter Writers 1660–1800* (Oxford, 2009). See also, on provincial culture, her *The Useful Knowledge of William Hutton: Culture and Eighteenth-Century Birmingham* (Oxford, 2018).

24. *The Rivals* I, 2.

25. B. Darby, *Frances Burney, Dramatist: Gender, Performance and the Late-Eighteenth-Century Stage* (Lexington, KY, 1997).

26. J. Epstein, *The Iron Pen: Frances Burney and the Politics of Women's Writing* (Bristol, 1989). For a less combative Burney, M. A. Doody, *Frances Burney: The Life in the Works* (Cambridge, 1988).

27. B. McCrea, *Frances Burney and Narrative Prior to Ideology* (Newark, DE, 2013).

28. *Northanger* I, 14.

29. *Northanger* I, 7.

30. R. Porter, *Enlightenment: Britain and the Creation of the Modern World* (London, 2000); K. Sloan, ed., *Enlightenment: Discovering the World in the Eighteenth Century* (London, 2003); R. G. W. Anderson, M. L. Caygill, A. G. MacGregory, and L. Syson, eds., *Enlightening the British: Knowledge, Discovery and the Museum in the Eighteenth Century* (London, 2004).

31. *Emma* I, 18.

32. J. Golinski, *British Weather and the Climate of Enlightenment* (Chicago, 2007); J. Kington, *The Weather of the 1780s over Europe* (Cambridge, 1988).

33. *PP* I, 11.

34. *Emma* I, 3.

35. *Emma* III, 6.

36. *Sanditon* 1.

LONDON

The Capital of Empire

THE ROLE AND GROWTH OF London were aspects of the changeable and exciting but unstable world in which Austen lived. By 1800, London had a population of more than a million. Five years later, George III, who had a markedly conservative view of social values and structures, referred to "the overgrown metropolis,"[1] a long-standing Tory theme. London, nevertheless, was the center of government, the law, and consumption, and its position in the world of print helped shape news, opinion, and fashion.

Both the role and growth of London were key points in the cultural critique of change that was a long-standing feature in England. It was notably so in conservative, rural, and Anglican circles. Set in Surrey, a county in the shadow of London, Austen's *Emma* very much reflected traditional themes of such criticism, themes that are accentuated by the proximity of London. So also with *Pride and Prejudice*, which is set in Hertfordshire, a county close to London from another direction. From a greater geographical distance, this critique of change was also the key issue in *Mansfield Park*.

London's role and growth focus the more general pressure on established conventions and assumptions and practices of politeness. The equivalent disruption in *Pride and Prejudice* was the war and the resulting military preparations. The self-confidence of Londoners was reflected in *Pride and Prejudice*, when Bingley's sisters, in response to Jane Bennet's poor health, opposed the idea of local medical attendance and, "convinced that no country advice could be of any service, recommended an express to town for one of the most eminent physicians." Both Bingley and Jane Bennet rejected this advice,[2] which was not in the event required. Physicians congregated in London and Bath, whereas country apothecaries were trained only by apprenticeship.

The comparison of town and country is a frequent theme, especially in *Pride and Prejudice*. The following morning, a somewhat different cast return to the theme. Darcy declares, "In a country neighbourhood you move in a very confined and unvarying society." Elizabeth Bennet refers to people changing so much that there is something new to be observed in them forever. Mrs. Bennet then states that there "is quite as much of *that* going on in the country as in town.... I cannot see that London has any great advantage over the country for my part, except the shops and public places. The country is a vast deal pleasanter." Appealed to, the emollient but honest Bingley, possibly reflecting Jane's views, reflects: "When I am in the country, I never wish to leave it; and when I am in town it is pretty much the same. They have each their advantages, and I can be equally happy in either," earning the justified assessment, "That is because you have the right disposition."[3]

In *Emma*, Mr. Woodhouse, a fussy and self-obsessed valetudinarian, and thus unwitting source of humor, is repeatedly concerned about one of his two daughters, who lives in London. This concern leads to a dialogue that presumably reflects the views of many in the period, albeit with his characteristic fretful commitment to self-centered complaint:

"Ah! my poor dear child, the truth is, that in London it is always a sickly season. Nobody is healthy in London, nobody can be. It is a dreadful thing to have you forced to live there!—so far off!—and the air is bad!"

"No, indeed—*we* are not at all in a bad air. Our part of London is so very superior to most others!—You must not confound us with London in general, my dear sir. The neighbourhood of Brunswick Square is very different from almost all the rest. We are so very airy! I should be unwilling, I own, to live in any other part of the town;—there is hardly any other that I could be satisfied to have my children in:—but *we* are so remarkably airy! . . .

". . . but after you have been a week at Hartfield, you are all of your different creatures; you do not look like the same."[4]

Air, indeed, is a theme. Thus, Sir William Lucas thinks of moving to London: "For I am fond of superior society; but I do not feel quite certain that the air of London would agree with Lady Lucas."[5] In this and other cases, *air* stands literally for air quality but also for a range of less obvious issues about suitability, including sanitation. Mr. Woodhouse's concerns were differently expressed by the London-based Society for Bettering the Condition of the Poor, which noted in 1805

> that many of the inhabitants of the more crowded parts of the Metropolis suffer very severely under infectious fever . . . that in many parts of the habitations of the poor are never free from the febrile infection; there being not only courts and alleys, but some public buildings, in which it has continued for upwards of 30 years past;—and that, by means of the constant and unavoidable communication which exists between the different classes of the inhabitants of the Metropolis, and between the Metropolis and other parts of the kingdom, this dreadful disease has frequently been communicated from the London poor to country places, and to some of the more opulent families in the Metropolis.[6]

Nevertheless, for those who could afford it, medical expertise was present more in London than elsewhere in England. In *Sanditon*, Mr. Heywood has to explain to a skeptical visiting Londoner that there is no surgeon in Willingden. In *Emma*, Harriet Smith goes to London to consult a dentist and, while there, visits Astley's

Amphitheatre, a performance venue opened in 1773, in which overtly patriotic shows and the circus were held,[7] thus enjoying the variety of the city.

Austen knew of London before she visited it. The fashionable world of the capital was very much part of the conversation of her cousin Eliza, who visited in December 1776. Eliza was brought up in London but then married a French count, and she and her mother had rented a house close to Portman Square in the fashionable West End and went to Almack's, the very fashionable assembly rooms.

Austen herself subsequently visited London on numerous occasions. She stayed there en route between Kent and Hampshire from 1788 on and also stayed in London with her brother Henry, a London banker, whom she liked. Henry was important to her coping with the world of publishing and printing, as she stayed with him when she went to London to have her books edited and proofread. At the same time, Austen liked to visit London for social reasons and to have a break from the constant predictability of rural society. Henry was successful in banking (for a while), and he moved from Brompton, where Austen visited him in 1808, to the more spacious 64 Sloane Street, where Austen visited in 1811 and 1813, enjoying the city and moving her novels forward.[8] London was very much the center of the publishing world, and it was not simply a contrivance of the plot in *Joseph Adams* (1742) that had Henry Fielding send Parson Adams to London to get his sermons published. In 1814, after the death of his wife, Eliza, the previous year, Henry moved to accommodation over his bank on Henrietta Street in Covent Garden, and Austen stayed with him there that spring. Later that year, Henry moved to a house at 23 Hans Place, Knightsbridge, which Austen liked when she visited in 1814 and 1815. The house had a garden where Austen liked to walk while working.

As a result of the failure of his bank, Henry moved to become curate at Chawton in 1816, and it is not known that Austen visited

London again. This was typical of the closing in of options that financial difficulties caused dependents. Closing in was a theme in many novels and affects many of Austen's characters—for example, the Dashwoods and, in prospect, the Bennets.

Many of Austen's characters visited London, notably the fashionable West End. Bond Street is mentioned in *Emma* and in *Sense and Sensibility*; in the latter, Marianne stays in Berkeley Street. In *Mansfield Park*, Julia Bertram stays with cousins near Bedford Square and her sister Maria in Wimpole Street, from which she abandons her husband and elopes with Henry Crawford.[9] In *Sense and Sensibility*, the Palmers live in Hanover Square while Mrs. Jennings spends each winter near Portman Square in Berkeley Street, the Dashwoods stay in Harley Street, and Edward Ferrars lodges in Pall Mall and John Willoughby in Bond Street.[10] The Middletons stay in Conduit Street. Their less "grand" relations, the Miss Steeles, stay in a cousin's house in Bartletts Buildings, Holborn, off Fetter Lane,[11] in the in-between world between the city and the West End.

In *Pride and Prejudice*, the Bingleys stay in Grosvenor Street, which is central to the West End, and Miss Bingley disparages Elizabeth Bennet for having an uncle "somewhere near Cheapside"— in other words, in trade. Geographically, Cheapside is outside the West End. Both Elizabeth and Jane had "frequently" stayed with their uncle, but it is "so different a part of town, all our connections are so different" to those of the Bingleys.[12] In contrast to the Bingleys, the fallen Wickham and Lydia hide outside the West End: in St. Clement's—St. Clement's Eastcheap or St. Clement Danes.[13] Indeed, *Pride and Prejudice* sharpens the social distinctions that London engages: "Mr Darcy may have *heard* of a place called Gracechurch Street, but he would hardly think a month's ablution enough to cleanse him from its impurities."[14]

In *Mansfield Park*, Maria Bertram is ready to accept marriage with the wealthy Mr. Rushworth as it would "ensure her the house in town, which was now a prime object." Planning marriage to

Rushworth, Maria feels that "the preparations of new carriages and furniture might wait for London and spring, when her taste could have fairer play." In turn, as Henry Crawford has "been much in London," he is deemed attractive. Considering whether he could be a preacher, Henry notes: "I must have a London audience. I could not preach, but to the educated; to those who were capable of estimating my composition."[15] London also threatens downward social mobility. In *Northanger Abbey*, Isabella Thorpe's father was a lawyer, and the family who live at Putney are not very wealthy. Due to her "want of consequence and fortune," her engagement to Captain Tilney is not welcomed by his father.[16]

As the center of fashion,[17] London was a place to visit for those from elsewhere in England. Facilities for and patterns of social activity responded to the example of London, which was presented as the benchmark for habits elsewhere. Traveling from London to the Bennets in nearby Hertfordshire, Mrs. Gardiner has "to describe the newest fashions . . . long sleeves."[18] Lady Catherine tells Elizabeth Bennet, "Your mother should have taken you to town every spring for the benefit of masters," which would have taught her skills.[19] In *Persuasion*, Sir Walter Elliot, pressed to save money, complains about being unable to visit London. In *Emma*, Miss Bates hears that Mrs. Ford, the shopkeeper, has "a charming collection of new ribbons from town,"[20] which always means London, and certainly so in nearby Surrey. Edward Ferrars suggests that if Elinor and Marianne Dashwood had been wealthy, London's "booksellers, music sellers, and printshops" would have thrived.[21] So also for politics. Returning from London at Hartfield, Mr. Weston at dinner "spread abroad what public news he had heard" before "proceeding to a family communication."[22] The "public news" is not specified, which helps ensure the book did not date.

London was crucial to the economy of England, indeed all of Britain, including in publication, an economic as well as cultural activity. John Tisdal, a Belfast printer who, in 1782, published

Flora's Banquet, a collection of Irish poems he had edited, stated, "It does not follow, that works of merit can *only* originate in the metropolis of England; and that, unless a book is distinguished by a *London* title page, and character in the review, it is beneath the notice of the curious." However, the London publishers were dominant.

The city was presented by some as a site of liberty, trade, and progress; others viewed it in terms of moral, political, and economic disorder and decay, Edward Gibbon referring to "crowds without company and dissipation without pleasure."[23] Provincial self-consciousness helped focus unease about London. The city was certainly very different in all physical forms, as it was crowded, dirty, noisy, and more colorful. The smoke and dust of a coal-burning city were part of a physical assault that included the sight and smell of filth from large numbers of people. This was very different from country life. The filth provided work for bootblacks and also increased the pressure on servants to keep clothes clean.

Concern about public morality in London helped lead to George III's 1787 proclamation "For the Encouragement of Piety and Virtue, and for the Preventing and Punishing of Vice, Profaneness and Immorality" and to the activities of the related Proclamation Society. The role of London as a center of pointless conspicuous consumption is shown in Robert Ferrars's lengthy purchase of an expensive toothpick case in *Sense and Sensibility*.[24] The city is the counterpoint to "the happy privilege of country liberty, of wandering from place to place in free and luxurious solitude," as enjoyed by Marianne Dashwood at Cleveland in distant Somerset.[25]

Alongside the critique of London was another approach that was also an important background for the assumptions of Austen and her readers. This was a strong theme of criticism of the "people of fashion" from London commentators who argued they set a poor model for ordinary citizens. Indeed, Henry Fielding presented London in terms of a corrupt court and aristocracy at its West End, with their commerce in vice, contrasted to the more acceptable commercial metropolis. The interplay between the two was a major theme in literature. London, generally understood as the West End, was a setting for villainy, notably aristocratic vice,[26] for many artists and writers, such as the snares that bedevil William Booth in Fielding's novel *Amelia* (1751). In Fielding's *Joseph Andrews*, the lascivious Lady Booby returns to London to devote herself to "a young Captain of dragoons, together with eternal parties at cards."[27] Wickham, no aristocrat but someone who has based himself on an aristocratic model, fits into this pattern: "His intrigues, all honoured with the title of seduction, had been extended into every tradesman's family."[28] In Oliver Goldsmith's play *She Stoops to Conquer*, the countryside residents are more honest and balanced than their London counterparts. In 1785, London was described by a visitor of two years earlier as the only place in England where condoms were sold publicly.[29]

The distorting role of show in London—its denial of true pleasure—is shown by Austen in Lady Middleton's opposition to her husband's decision to hold a ball: "In the country, an unpremeditated dance was very allowable; but in London, where the reputation of elegance was more important and less easily attained, it was risking too much for the gratification of a few girls, to have it known that Lady Middleton had given a small dance of eight or nine couple, with two violins, and a mere side-board collation."[30] Yet hostility to London is satirized in *Northanger Abbey* when Isabella Thorpe remarks: "For my own part, my wishes are so moderate, that the smallest income in nature would be enough for me. Where people are really attached, poverty itself is wealth: grandeur I detest: I would not settle in London for the universe. A cottage in some retired village would be ecstasy. There are some charming little villas about Richmond [an expensive area]."[31] In fact, she lives in less costly Putney.

In *Mansfield Park*, the color is more somber and the tone harsher, as it generally is in that novel. Mary Crawford complains of the difficulties of hiring a cart to move her harp, which, as Edmund Bertram points out, is unsurprising given her determination to ignore the timing of the hay harvest. He appreciates the importance of getting in the grass, but she juxtaposes town and country: "Coming down with the true London maxim, that every thing is to be got with money, I was a little embarrassed at first by the sturdy independence of your country customs."[32] Subsequently, Edmund Bertram disagrees when Mary argues that "the metropolis . . . is a pretty fair sample of the rest." He replies, "Not, I should hope, of the proportion of virtue to vice throughout the kingdom. We do not look in great cities for our best morality. It is not there, that respectable people of any denomination can do most good; and it certainly is not there, that the influence of the clergy can be most felt."[33]

Edmund adds a key point about the importance of the everyday setting of example, not the public show of the grand occasion: "A fine preacher is followed and admired; but it is not in fine preaching only that a good clergyman will be useful in his parish and his neighbourhood, where the parish and neighbourhood are of a size capable of knowing his private character, and observing his general conduct, which in London can rarely be the case. The clergy are lost there in the crowds of their parishioners. They are known to the largest part only as preachers."[34] Thus, the London clergy had audiences rather than congregations with whom they could have personal and appropriate relations as spiritual counselors. Edmund continues by explaining true example, a theme more generally the case with Austen's novels:

> And with regard to their influencing public manners, Miss Crawford must not misunderstand me, or suppose I mean to call them the arbiters of good breeding, the regulators of refinement and courtesy, the masters of the ceremonies of life. The *manners* I speak of might rather be called *conduct*, perhaps, the result of good principles; the

effect, in short, of those doctrines which it is their duty to teach and recommend; and it will, I believe, be every where found that as the clergy are, or are not what they ought to be, so are the rest of the nation.[35]

London helped mold a national economic space, although it is clear that specialization for the London market was accompanied by the persistence of more local economic patterns. Most of the food for London's growing population came from within Britain, and even more so within England itself, far more so than today, and the prices in London were printed in provincial newspapers. The prime agricultural market for all aspects of Austen's rural world was London. Animals for the London market, such as turkeys from Norfolk, were "driven"—in other words, walked—across southern England. Similarly, beef cattle were driven from Scotland, Wales, and northern England.

Moreover, London finance was important to the rest of the country. An interregional credit structure based on London was established, ensuring that local economies were very much linked to the situation in London, as well as to each other via London. In 1775, the establishment of a bank clearinghouse in Lombard Street in the city led to a great improvement: banks were allowed to balance credits and withdrawals by a ticket system. London-based insurance companies operated across the country through agents. Mr. Heywood goes to London twice yearly in order to receive his dividends.[36] Proximity to the capital was a key element in appeal, with Mr. Parker praising *Sanditon* as a bathing place for having "the most desirable distance from London"—it was a mile closer than Eastbourne. In practice, each was in competition with Brighton as a Sussex resort. The wealth of the city is captured in Lucy Steele's description of Mr. Richardson: "He makes a monstrous deal of money."[37]

London publications spread designs while London craftsmen were in demand across the country. Bright provincials such as Thomas Sheraton went to London and had their ideas and talents validated there. The literary equivalent included works such as Charles Vyse's *New London Spelling Book* (1776). The norms of the language were set in London by these and other methods and books, which, in turn, were advertised in provincial newspapers. Talented foreigners also visited London. Josef Haydn went there in 1791 and 1794 to give very successful public concerts for which he wrote his London symphonies.

Metropolitan influence, however, did not prevent autonomous developments elsewhere in Britain. Thus, provincial silversmiths, such as those in Exeter, were influenced by London designs but also produced works with unique features. The provinces had the capacity both to preserve local practices and take initiative. At the same time, this was most pronounced at a distance from London—for example, in Newcastle—and least so nearer in, which was where Austen lived and where her novels were set.[38] Hertfordshire and Surrey were very much in the shadow of the capital; for example, both were reliant on London newspapers.

London's influence also owed much to the extent that the social basis of its development—a major expansion in the middling orders and a growing practice by the rural elite of spending part of the year there—was matched in regional capitals, such as Norwich and Nottingham; in county centers, such as Warwick; and in established developing entertainment towns, such as Bath, Buxton, and Tunbridge Wells.[39] London's role and image were made more prominent by the greater importance of provincial towns within their particular regions, as the city was seen to exemplify a national trend. The pleasure gardens were showpieces for all kinds of art and music, and they, and the walks and assembly rooms of London, were emulated in other cities and towns.

As in other cities, such as Leeds,[40] there was both growth and social differentiation. London changed physically during Austen's lifetime. The street plan of the West End was filled in and also spread. Thus, Fitzroy Square, in the angle between the

Tottenham Court Road and the New Road (now the Euston Road), was begun in the 1790s to a design by Robert Adam. At that stage, there was little development to the north of the New Road. Indeed, on the other side of the road could be found Kendal's Farm, and to the east of the Tottenham Court Road were still empty fields in the 1790s. In *Emma*, the protagonist's sister lives on the edge of the expanding city. Further south, in contrast, in the West End, the grand houses reaffirmed the aristocratic stamp on that part of the city.

London and Londoners were affected by the abrupt political changes of the period. The American Revolutionary War (1775–83) divided opinion, with much initial support for the revolutionary cause but also considerable anger and opposition to it. Moreover, there was periodic pressure from Londoners for radical political changes. The Westminster Association pressed for universal manhood suffrage, annual elections, the secret ballot, and equal constituencies in 1780. The first female-only abolitionist society met in London in 1788.

The French Revolution saw an upsurge in radicalism, with the London Corresponding Society, a radical body, founded in 1792. However, there was also a rise in loyalism. The Seditious Meetings Act of 1795 made agitation for reform more difficult, and the membership of the London Corresponding Society declined. It suffered from its opponents smearing the cause of radicalism as extremist and un-English. *Northanger Abbey* was written probably from 1798–99, and Austen has Catherine Morland, a character prone to alarmism, warn that "something very shocking indeed, will soon come out in London."[41] The joke is that Catherine just means a new gothic novel but Eleanor misunderstands and thinks she means riots. Radicalism focused on London in the 1800s and 1810s. However, this does not affect the content or tone of Austen's treatment of London in the novels.

Alongside criticism of London, the rapidly developing cult for nature—and, more particularly, "sublime" landscape—encouraged a repositioning of the appeal of London and cities as a whole. Earlier, London was frequently presented as the key site of liberty, trade, progress, and sociability. Its pleasure gardens and assembly rooms, like "politeness" itself, served to further the ideal of a free yet ordered city in which people mixed in an orderly fashion. As a result, these contrived spaces helped both challenge the belief that linked circulation of luxury commodities with social dislocation and tame the fears and concerns surrounding the commercial expansion of the metropolis.[42]

Nevertheless, criticism of London developed during Austen's lifetime. William Wordsworth's preface to his *Lyrical Ballads* (1798) asserted the pernicious consequences of the move to the cities. Four years earlier, the London poet and painter William Blake (1757–1827) published a bleak poem entitled "London":

> I wander through each chartered street,
> Near where the chartered Thames does flow,
> And mark in every face I meet,
> Marks of weakness, marks of woe.
>
> In every cry of every man,
> In every infant's cry of fear,
> In every voice, in every ban,
> the mind-forged manacles I hear.
>
> How the chimney-sweeper's cry
> Every blackening church appals,
> And the hapless soldier's sigh
> Runs in block down palace-walls.
>
> But most, through midnight streets I hear
> How the youthful harlot's curse
> Blasts the new-born infant's tear,
> And blights with plagues the marriage-hearse.

Blake could see clearly behind the facades and marble vistas of the Georgian city. For him, London contained throngs of poor or disadvantaged human beings who understood only too well—and had come to accept—the life of misery, hardship, and hopelessness that was their lot. Although the setting is Portsmouth, Fanny Price's reflection on the difference between town and country also relates to London and is a powerful piece of writing: "The sun's rays falling strongly into the parlour, instead of cheering, made her still more melancholy; for sun-shine appeared to her a totally different thing in a town and in the country. Here, its power was only a glare, a stifling, sickly glare, serving but to bring forward stains and dirt that might otherwise have slept. There was neither health nor gaiety in sunshine in a town. She sat in a blaze of oppressive heat, in a cloud of moving dust."[43]

NOTES

1. George to Lord Hawkesbury, 3 February 1805, BL. Loan Manuscripts 72/1, fol. 135.
2. *PP* I, 8.
3. *PP* I, 9.
4. *Emma* I, 12.
5. *PP* I, 6.
6. Paper from the Society for Bettering the Condition of the Poor, January 1, 1805, BL. Add. 35645 fol. 143.
7. *Emma* III, 16, 18.
8. E. Clery, *Jane Austen: The Banker's Sister* (London, 2017).
9. *MP* III, 14.
10. *Sense* I, 20; II, 3, 5; III, 2, 8.
11. *Sense* II, 10, 12.
12. *PP* II, 2; N. Pevsner, "The Architectural Setting of Jane Austen's Novels," *Journal of the Warburg and Courtauld Institutes* 31 (1968): 404–22.
13. *PP* III, 9.
14. *PP* II, 2.
15. *MP* I, 4–5; II, 3; III, 3.
16. *Northanger* II, 10–11.
17. H. Greig, *The Beau Monde: Fashionable Society in Georgian London* (Oxford, 2013).
18. *PP* II, 2.
19. *PP* II, 6.

20. *Emma* II, 9.

21. *Sense* I, 17.

22. *Emma* II, 17.

23. John Holroyd, ed., *Miscellaneous Works of Edward Gibbon*, vol. 1 (London, 1796), 81.

24. *Sense* II, 11.

25. *Sense* III, 6.

26. D. T. Andrew, *Aristocratic Vice: The Attack on Duelling, Suicide, Adultery, and Gambling in Eighteenth-Century England* (New Haven, CT, 2013).

27. H. Fielding, *Joseph Andrews*, chapter 16.

28. *PP* III, 6.

29. J. L. Wood, "Bladder Policies," *Factotum* 38 (February 1994): 10.

30. *Sense* II, 5.

31. *Northanger* I, 15.

32. *MP* I, 6.

33. *MP* I, 9.

34. *MP* I, 9.

35. *MP* I, 9.

36. *Sanditon* 2.

37. *Sense* III, 2.

38. D. Wahrman, "National Society, Communal Culture: An Argument about the Recent Historiography of Eighteenth-Century Britain," *Social History* 17 (1992): 43–72; P. Borsay, "The London Connection: Cultural Diffusion and the Eighteenth-Century Provincial Town," *London Journal* 19 (1994): 21–35; H. Berry, "Promoting Taste in the Provincial Press: National and Local Culture in Eighteenth-Century Newcastle upon Tyne," *British Journal of Eighteenth-Century Studies* 25 (2002): 1–17.

39. P. Borsay, *The English Urban Renaissance: Culture and Society in the Provincial Town, 1660–1770* (Oxford, 1989).

40. M. Beresford, *East End, West End: The Face of Leeds During Urbanisation, 1684–1842* (Leeds, 1988).

41. *Northanger* I, 14.

42. J. Conlin, "Vauxhall on the Boulevard: Pleasure Gardens in London and Paris, 1764–1784," *Urban History* 35 (2008): 24–47, esp. 46.

43. *MP* III, 15.

EIGHT

—ᴍ—

BATH

The Capital of Leisure

BATH WAS A SETTING FOR many novelists, with Austen and Tobias Smollett making particularly good use of the
city—Austen in *Northanger Abbey* and *Persuasion* and Smollett
in the very funny *The Expedition of Humphry Clinker* (1771). The
city's appearance in novels reflected the appeal of the new, the
attraction of leisure, and its significance in social life. Bath was
far from new as a settlement, going back to pre-Roman days, but
it was new as an eighteenth-century experience, both as a place
of leisure—indeed, the place of leisure—and as a new townscape
made dramatic by its rise up an impressive hill. By 1800, Bath had
a population of about thirty-three thousand and was about the
tenth largest town in England and Wales, although the numbers
there fluctuated with visitors and therefore the season.

Bath was scarcely unique as a fashionable spa; the town itself,
as well as its waters, were a commodity to be visited and an image
to be consumed. Thirty-four new spas were founded in England
between 1700 and 1750 and even more in the second half of the
century. Thus, Southampton, where Austen moved in 1806 and
originally not associated with a spa, had its Chaleybeate spa.
Moreover, among the spas, Tunbridge Wells had a major advantage over Bath due to its proximity to London. It was the spa

visited by Austen's cousin Eliza in 1787, and, in Austen's *Lesley Castle*, Tunbridge Wells, along with London and Bath, is where Margaret Lesley and Charlotte Lutterell might meet in 1792.[1] But for having fourteen children, the Heywoods in *Sanditon* would have been able to afford "an occasional month at Tunbridge Wells . . . and a winter at Bath,"[2] the combination indicating that spas could be complementary resorts as well as rivals. In *Pride and Prejudice*, Georgiana Darcy's friends go to Scarborough. For a spa resort, Mrs. Elton suggests Bath or Clifton.[3] If not London, the spas of Tunbridge Wells and Cheltenham are not "the country," as Edmund Bertram notes.[4]

Nevertheless, Bath became the great spa where there was most to do and where you should be seen. When Lady Anson visited Buxton in 1751, in contrast, she was bored and dissatisfied.[5] Bath set out to make certain its visitors were neither. Although already successful, the development of Bath as a city of orderly leisure, and therefore a respectable and safe place to visit, owed much to Richard "Beau" Nash (1674–1761), who, in 1705, succeeded Captain Webster as the city's second master of ceremonies. Nash's "Rules" for the behavior of visitors to Bath were first published in 1707. This was part of the process by which the codification of social propriety was expressed and debated, explicitly or implicitly, in print. Novels were another aspect of this process,[6] and the two combined in that, in fact and in fiction.

Health might be the basis of the resort, but Bath was often a destination for those seeking marriage, and this goal attracted visitors of all ages. This was the case for men and women of all ages wishing to marry and for the parents acting as chaperones for the young women. Once rejected by Emma, Philip Elton promptly sets off for Bath, where he goes to a full master of ceremonies ball,[7] where prospective partners are introduced.[8] The process works as intended, for his progress to an engagement with Augusta Hawkins is rapid: "the first hour of introduction had been so very soon followed by distinguishing notice . . .

the rise and progress of the affair was so glorious—the steps so quick, from the accidental rencontre, the dinner at Mr Green's, and the party at Mrs Brown's—smiles and blushes rising in importance."[9]

Elton is a clergyman who stays at the White Hart, a large coaching inn, when in Bath.[10] There was a strong clerical presence in the city, as it was the center of Lady Huntington's evangelical "connexion" based on propriety chapels into which she placed Anglican chaplains. Augusta, once established in Surrey as Elton's wife, recommends Bath's waters to Mr. Woodhouse, only to be told that he had tried them without success. In a condescending manner toward Emma, Augusta goes on to draw attention to the city's other, more social and matrimonial, attractions: "It is so cheerful a place, that it could not fail of being of use to Mr Woodhouse's spirits, which, I understand, are sometimes much depressed.... As to its recommendations to *you* ... the advantages of Bath to the young are pretty generally understood. It would be a charming introduction for you, who have lived so secluded a life."[11] Emma was not impressed, but then Augusta is a caricature of misunderstanding and social solecism, indeed repeatedly so. Subsequently, Frank Churchill, with reference to the Eltons, comments on the misleading social show of Bath: "How well they suit one another!—Very lucky—marrying as they did, upon an acquaintance formed only in a public place!—They only knew each other, I think, a few weeks in Bath! Peculiarly lucky!—for as to any real knowledge of a person's disposition that Bath, or any public place, can give—it is all nothing; there can be no knowledge. It is only by seeing women in their own homes, among their own set, just as they always are, that you can form any just judgment. Short of that, it is all guess and luck—and will generally be ill-luck."[12] Very different in the outcome, but also reflecting the role of show, Eliza Williams is seduced at Bath and made pregnant by John Willoughby, who then abandons her. This leads Colonel Brandon to fight a duel with him.[13]

The first Pump Room at Bath was built in 1706, followed in 1708 by Harrison's Assembly Rooms and in 1730 by additional rooms in the Palladian style by John Wood the Elder. Both sets of rooms—Harrison's and Lindsey's—ran in parallel until the later eighteenth century. The suburbs laid out to the north of the old core of Bath, in large part for the benefit of visitors, were influential for the establishment of urban forms. Circles, even if not the invention of John Wood the Elder, were first used on any scale by him in Bath. Wood began the King's Circus in 1754, the design and decoration reflecting his masonic and druidical beliefs. His son began the Royal Crescent in 1767.

Palladianism greatly influenced the extension of Bath. This was most famously so with the Circus (1754–64) and the Royal Crescent (1767–74). It was also so with John Wood the Elder's Queen Square (1728–34) and Assembly Rooms (1730), his son's Assembly Rooms (1769–71), and the Palladian Bridge created in the nearby gardens of Prior Park. Other buildings included new churches, notably St. Michael (1734–42) and St. James's (1768–69), as well as Robert Adam's Pulteney Bridge. "The white glare of Bath," which makes "the possible heats of September" there unwelcome to Anne Elliot,[14] was a product of its being built largely of stone in the fashion of the eighteenth century and, in its case, of a light yellow oolitic limestone. Austen's mother's great-uncle, James, first Duke of Chandos, had been one of the financial backers of the city's development and had commissioned the development of the Hospital of St. John the Baptist, Chapel Court, and Chandos Buildings in 1727 by Wood, his first major work in Bath.

The walks at Bath were major social attractions. By midcentury, Bath had a series of walks and gardens: the Gravel Walks and the Grove, Harrison's walks and gardens, the Terrace Walk, the Parades, and the Spring Gardens. They were lined with luxury shops, assembly rooms, and socially acceptable accommodation.[15]

Alongside its development as a fashionable resort, the effects of such construction and activity helped make Bath an attractive topic and space for the descriptive poetry, prose, and painting of the period, as in Mary Chandler's poem *A Description of Bath* (1733). Novels joined this trend.

Yet Bath also attracted moral panic, as did so many of the different aspects and sites of urban life in this far-from-secure age. As reflected in the fate of Eliza Williams, the city focused concerns about conduct and misrepresentation, both of which centered on the marriage market and thus sex. Countering perceptions of the city as a place for vice, notably gambling and sex, and the depiction of the worrying problems of luxury,[16] the life of Bath was based on the fusion of gentility and equality. The assurance of the former made it possible, in theory, for the company to set aside status and act as equals, sidelining the concerns about social fluidity that played such a corrosive role in mixing and were actively encouraged by Beau Nash and later, in 1987, contributed to Bath being declared a UNESCO World Heritage site. At the time, these concerns—particularly that of self-serving hypocrisy—were reiterated in society and in fiction. Indeed, social mixing played a large role in real and fictional dramas about seduction and misalliances.

The challenges to honor that led to duels represented another threat to appropriate social relationships and were recorded fictionally, as in Sheridan's play *The Rivals*, which was set in Bath, and Tobias Smollett's novels *Roderick Random, Humphry Clinker*, and *Peregrine Pickle*. First produced in 1775, *The Rivals* was also staged in 1784 at the Steventon barn by Austen's family and friends, with her brother Henry delivering a prologue by her brother James.

However threatening, social mixing, in practice, had its limits. Indeed, the organization of space—both within towns and in individual sites such as buildings—excluded the bulk of the population in the cause of what was an uneasy mix of hierarchy, status, and profit. So also did the norms of behavior that were encouraged.

Like the West End of London, Bath became normative as a setting for the urban play of the social elite through their repetition in novels, plays, and paintings. The town also had a rich cultural life, notably in music, and, in this respect, was more advanced than most other cities. Nevertheless, a poem printed in *Swinney's Birmingham and Stafford Chronicle* on May 23, 1776, included criticism of a concert audience in Bath for not concentrating on the music, especially condemning a peer who talked during an excellent chorus. A purpose-built theater opened in 1705, followed by the Orchard Street Theatre in 1750, which, in 1767, was the first outside London granted a royal license. The *Bath and Bristol Magazine*, which included poetry and literary reviews, began publication in 1776—an instance of spas being part of the cultural infrastructure. So also with Sanditon, where Mr. Parker is "anxiously willing to support" the library,[17] the juxtaposition of anxiety and willingness ably characterizing his personality and language.

Popularized by the visits of Queen Anne in 1702–3 and developed in part by the Bath stone mined by the city's postmaster, Ralph Allen (1693–1764),[18] Bath became a city where it was fashionable to be seen. The social elite went, as did politicians and painters. Aside from Austen, Bath attracted a number of writers, including, among women, Fanny Burney, Catharine Macaulay, and Hannah More. Cassandra, Austen's mother, had gone with her sister, another Austen, to Bath with her parents when her father, Thomas Leigh, retired from his parish, Harpsden, but he died soon after. Austen's parents had married at St. Swithin, Walcot in Bath in 1764, and her father was buried there in 1805.

Austen, unsurprisingly, did not particularly enjoy her time in Bath. It was the city where her father, George, retired and where he died. Judging from her correspondence, her time there with her family in 1801 to 1804 was filled with visits and concerns about conversation and clothes. Thus, in April 1805, she noted the cape she wore and "a monstrous deal of stupid quizzing, and common-place nonsense, but scarcely any wit."[19] The Austens moved to Green Park Buildings in October 1804 when the (short) lease at 4 Sydney Park expired. George Austen died the following January, and the family left Green Park Buildings on March 25, 1805, and moved into 25 Gay Street. Mrs. Austen had always liked Gay Street, which was closer to her brother in the Paragon.

Austen was very familiar with the city, and she walked long distances to neighboring villages, now suburbs. Austen had previously visited Bath in 1797, and the city had played a role in her juvenilia. Envy leads to Lucy being poisoned in Bath in Austen's *Jack and Alice*. In *Amelia Webster*, the protagonist is seen by George Hervey en route to Bath, and he proposes to her. In *The Three Sisters*, Mary Stanhope demands a string of unreasonable requests, including an annual timetable, from her intended: "You must let me spend every winter in Bath, every spring in town [London]." In *Love and Freindship*, a censorious woman warns her daughter to "beware of the unmeaning luxuries of Bath."[20]

"Unmeaning luxuries" play a role in the major novels while visits are usually the consequence of particular circumstances and plans. In *Persuasion*, Sir Walter Elliot needs to leave Kellynch and is persuaded that he should move to Bath, not London, in part on the grounds that he would lose neither consequence nor enjoyment by settling there. Lady Russell spends part of every winter in Bath and likes its noisy activity.[21] A key element is the role of Sir Walter's friend Mr. Shepherd, a lawyer, who felt Sir Walter could not be trusted in London. It is claimed that Sir Walter's daughter Anne would benefit from the "larger society" of Bath compared to where she lived.[22]

In *Persuasion*, Austen places her characters at addresses suited to their income and social status. The part of Bath in which visitors stay is important to those keen to maintain status in their visits, such as Sir Walter Elliot.[23] Alongside those who visit and thus provide variety of a sort are those who go there to retire, as

George Austen had done. The cost of lodgings was part of the city's social nuances. Fashionability and cost were related to position on the hills.

In *Mansfield Park*, Henry Crawford leaves to meet his uncle at Bath; although early, "it is about my uncle's usual time."[24] Also in that novel, Mrs. Rushworth, the widowed mother of the current owner of Sotherton Court, leaves that house to make way for his bride: "[She] removed herself, her maid, her footman, and her chariot with true dowager propriety to Bath—there to parade over the wonders of Sotherton in her evening parties—enjoying them as thoroughly perhaps in the animation of a card table as she had ever done on the spot."[25]

Bath had maintained its prominence because the Continental Grand Tour was stopped by war for most of the period from 1793 to 1815. In previous wars, British tourists had not been interned by the French, but this one was different. At the same time, Bath faced growing competition from Cheltenham and sea bathing. The city was no longer considered as fashionable as before. The cult of landscape was a particular threat to Bath. Catherine Morland is so impressed by Henry Tilney's introduction to the fashionable views of William Gilpin that "she voluntarily rejected the whole city of Bath, as unworthy to make part of a landscape."[26] This is the overenthusiastic response of a not very bright young girl to a half-understood lecture from the young man she fancies. At the same time, her response captured the growing fashion for landscape over townscape.

Separately, the fashionability of parts of Bath changed so that the young Musgroves, in going to Bath, do not wish to go to Queen Square in the center of the city,[27] where Austen herself had stayed in 1799. There was a determined effort, nevertheless, to keep Bath attractive. The Bath Improvement Act of 1789 gave the city extensive powers of purchase and demolition, which it used to rebuild the old part of the town. The city surveyor, Thomas Baldwin, was responsible for the new, broad, and colonnaded

Bath Street (1791–94). Isabella Thorpe complains that, at Bath, "the dust is beyond any thing."[28] Many of the new developments were on low-lying damp ground, and, in 1801, the Austens had to spend some time to find acceptable lodgings. At the same time, the northern heights continued to see new building, notably Camden Place, where Sir Walter Elliot stays in *Persuasion*.

Unavailable in Bath, sea bathing became fashionable during Austen's lifetime and was a reason to travel for those who could afford it. "A little sea-bathing would set me up for ever," the ostensible reason for a visit to Brighton, reflected the advice of doctors. George III popularized the idea at Weymouth from 1789 to 1805. In 1803 and 1804, the Austen family took seaside holidays in Lyme Regis, where "the young people are all wild" to go in *Persuasion*.[29] Cassandra Austen visited Weymouth in 1804, and Austen's characters go there—for example, Frank Churchill in *Emma* and Mrs. Palmer (and her uncle) in *Sense and Sensibility*. Going on, as well as into, the water was a pastime at Weymouth, but both were dangerous as knowledge of how to swim was very limited. In *Emma*, Mr. Dixon saves the day: "The service he rendered Jane [Fairfax] at Weymouth, when they were out in that party on the water, and she, by the sudden whirling round of something or other among the sails, would have been dashed into the sea at once, and actually was all but gone, if he had not, with the greatest presence of mind, caught hold of her habit."[30]

By July 22, 1754, the *Salisbury Journal* had listed eighteen "persons of distinction" who had arrived at Lymington in Hampshire "to drink the sea water and take the diversion of the place," while the issue of September 2, 1754, named a further thirteen. Resorts developed in the late eighteenth century, not only Ramsgate, Margate, Brighton, and Weymouth but also, on the coast of Devon, at Sidmouth, Dawlish, Torquay, Exmouth, and Teignmouth. Fortfield Terrace, Sidmouth was begun in 1792, and there were also efforts to provide genteel housing in Exmouth and Torbay in the 1790s. Assembly rooms opened in Exmouth in 1801, with Dawlish following in 1811. The first guidebook for part of Cornwall was published in 1815.

Despite George III's patronage, the reputation of coastal resorts was problematic. Indeed, in 1783, John, second Earl of Buckinghamshire, a rakish (and married) former diplomat, admired the scantily clad bathing beauties at Weymouth:

> There is a peculiar gentility in Weymouth which softens even the Eastern and Northern Blasts. It is to this warmth we owe the semblance of living in a state of primeval innocence. Wherever you turn your eyes nakedness greets them without fig leaves or blushes. It seems indeed. . . .
>
> That e'en as you list you may stick in your T
>
> To a Jolly Brown (or a Lilly White) A[31]

Weymouth's reputation was changed to a degree by royal patronage, but Brighton was another newly fashionable resort, and its patronage was more questionable than that of Weymouth. From 1783, George, Prince of Wales, spent summers there; needing a residence, he had a house transformed into a villa by 1787. Subsequently, this house, the Brighton Pavilion, became an oriental-style pleasure palace. In 1807, the Theatre Royal was founded at Brighton under the prince's patronage.

Austen did not go to Brighton, which was really a resort for the fashionable of London. She has the ridiculous Margaret Lesley prefer to spend her time there in *Lesley Castle*, and it is referred to as one of her "favourite haunts of Dissipation."[32] Elizabeth Bennet is worried about the exposure of her sister Lydia to "the temptations" at Brighton, and, as the plot shows, her fears are well-founded, for the consequences of these temptations not only threaten Lydia with calamity but also have potential serious results for her family, affecting its reputation and the marital chances of her sisters.[33] For their honeymoon, the Rushworths go to Brighton "to take a house there for some weeks. Every public place was new to Maria, and Brighton is almost as gay in winter as in summer. When the novelty of amusement there was over, it would be time for the wider range of London."[34]

Austen had visited Sidmouth (1801), Dawlish (1802), Teignmouth (1802), Lyme Regis (1803), Ramsgate (1803), and Worthing (1805). Her perception of them is possibly reflected in Mr. Knightley's judgment that Weymouth and similar places are the "idlest haunts in the kingdom."[35] However, as ever, Austen's concern is with the subtleties of character and behavior because everything Knightley says in relation to Frank Churchill is infected by his unconscious jealousy. The resorts play a role in her plots. Jane Fairfax and Frank Churchill secretly become engaged at Weymouth: Mr. Knightley reflects that Frank had met Jane "at a watering-place" and gained her affection.[36] In *Mansfield Park*, the extravagant Tom Bertram spends time at Weymouth, meeting the Honorable John Yates, another useless individual.[37] The Sneyds spend time at Ramsgate, where Mrs. Sneyd is "surrounded by men," and, keeping in character, the visiting Henry Crawford tries to make himself agreeable to the younger daughter.[38] Visitors are not simply motivated by pleasure. In *Emma*, John Knightley and his wife, Isabella, take their children sea bathing at Southend, particularly "for the weakness in little Bella's throat,—both sea air and bathing."[39] Austen's brother Charles and his family had visited Southend in 1813.

The significance of report to reputation, and thus the contrasting, indeed contested, character of reality, is captured at the outset of *Sanditon*, when Mr. Parker, having been overturned in his coach, states that Willingden must have a surgeon despite the views of the resident, Mr. Heywood:

> "I can bring proof of your having a surgeon in the parish—whether you may know it or not. Here Sir —" (taking out his pocket book —) "if you will do me the favour of casting your eye over these advertisements, which I cut out myself from the *Morning Post* and the *Kentish Gazette*, only yesterday morning in London—I think you

will be convinced that I am not speaking at random. You will find it an advertisement sir, of the dissolution of a partnership in the medical line—in your own parish—extensive business—undeniable character—respectable references—wishing to form a separate establishment—you will find it at full length sir—" offering him the two little oblong extracts.

"Sir"—said Mr Heywood with a good humoured smile—"if you were to show me all the newspapers that are printed in one week throughout the kingdom, you would not persuade me of there being a surgeon in Willingden,—for having lived here ever since I was born, man and boy fifty-seven years, I think I must have *known* of such a person. . . . To be sure, if gentlemen were to be often attempting this lane in post-chaises, it might not be a bad speculation for a surgeon to get a house at the top of the hill."[40]

Parker is wrong. The issue of quality is linked to reputation and the contrasts it offers. Here, again, reputation played a role, as when Parker contrasted Sanditon and Brinshore. The former is extolled by Parker:

Nature had marked it out—had spoken in most intelligible characters—The finest, purest sea breeze on the coast—acknowledged to be so—excellent bathing—fine hard sand—deep water ten yards from the shore—no mud—no weeds—no slimy rocks—Never was there a place more palpably designed by nature for the resort of the invalid. . . .

The attempts of two or three speculating people about Brinshore, this last year, to raise that paltry hamlet, lying as it does between a stagnant marsh, a bleak moor and the constant effluvia of a ridge of putrefying sea weed, can end in nothing but their own disappointment. . . . A most insalubrious air—roads proverbially detestable—water brackish beyond impossible, impossible to get a good dish of tea within three miles of the place—and as for the soil—it is so cold and ungrateful that it can hardly be made to yield a cabbage.[41]

The emphasis on nature is ironic as Parker's focus is on manmade intervention, with himself as a creator who is unrealistic about his creation. Throughout, he is a focus for ironic comment.

NOTES

1. *Juvenilia*, 145.
2. *Sanditon* 2.
3. *Emma* II, 18.
4. *MP* II, 3.
5. Stafford, Staffordshire County Record Office, D615/PCS 1/1/40A-B.
6. R. S. Neale, *Bath: 1680–1850: A Social History, Or, A Valley of Pleasure, Yet a Sink of Iniquity* (London, 1981).
7. *Emma* II, 1.
8. *Northanger* I, 3.
9. *Emma* II, 4.
10. *Emma* II, 5.
11. *Emma* II, 14.
12. *Emma* III, 7.
13. *Sense* II, 9.
14. *Persuasion* I, 5.
15. P. Borsay, "The Rise of the Promenade: The Social and Cultural Use of Space in the English Provincial Town *c.* 1660–1800," *British Journal for Eighteenth-Century Studies* 9 (1986): 127–29.
16. P. Borsay, "Image and Counter-image in Georgian Bath," *British Journal for Eighteenth-Century Studies* 17 (1994): 165–79.
17. *Sanditon* 2.
18. B. Boyce, *The Benevolent Man: A Life of Ralph Allen of Bath* (Cambridge, MA, 1967).
19. *Letters*, 103–4; M. Lane, *A Charming Place: Bath in the Life and Novels of Jane Austen* (Bath, 2000).
20. *Juvenilia*, 31, 59, 83, 105.
21. *Persuasion* I, 2; II, 2.
22. *Persuasion* I, 2.
23. *Persuasion* II, 6.
24. *MP* II, 2.
25. *MP* II, 3.
26. *Northanger* I, 14.
27. *Persuasion* I, 6.
28. *Northanger* II, 12.
29. *Persuasion* I, 11.
30. *Emma* II, 1.

31. Buckinghamshire to Sir Charles Hotham, July 12, 1783, Hull, University Library, Hotham papers, 4/22.

32. *Juvenilia*, 155.

33. *PP* II, 18.

34. *MP* II, 3.

35. *Emma* I, 18.

36. *Emma* III, 10, 13.

37. *MP* I, 12, 13.

38. *MP* I, 5.

39. *Emma* I, 11–12; *The Guide to All the Watering and Sea-Bathing Places* (London, 1815); J. K. Walton, *The English Seaside Resort: A Social History, 1750–1914* (Leicester, 1983); G. Shaw and A. Williams, eds., *The Rise and Fall of British Coastal Resorts* (London, 1997).

40. *Sanditon* 1.

41. *Sanditon* 1.

NINE

—꽈—

TRANSPORT AND INDUSTRY

It is much to be lamented that the lower orders
of manufacturers [workers] betray on every
occasion such a propensity to fly in the faces of
their employers, whenever any improvements are
attempted in the manufactures of this country.

—*Salisbury and Winchester Journal*, June 7, 1790

THE KEY METHOD OF TRANSPORT throughout the period
was walking. Although some contemporaries wrote about it,[1]
including in London, where there is a subset of picaresque and
other accounts of walks,[2] walking is largely ignored in scholarly works on transportation in the period. These works focus,
instead, on turnpike roads, canals, and the early signs of railways.
Unlike hot-air balloons, which made their appearance in Austen's
lifetime but on which she did not comment, these, notably the
first two, were important.

Nevertheless, although "respectable" people were not expected
to walk long distances, as Karl Philipp Moritz discovered en route
from London to Oxford in 1782,[3] most people walked at the start
of Austen's life and the same at the close. Alongside change in
transport facilities, there was much continuity—notably so at

the local level, unlike the revolution in transportation that subsequently followed the development of the motor car. Trampsmen (peddlers, some of whom were women) expected to walk twenty miles per day.

Most journeys, moreover, were not only done by walking but also were very local, whether daily journeys to work or weekly journeys to market, which, for many, were also a journey to work. The significance of walking as the sole or major option for many people was that socializing very much took place in the local context. This had an immediate effect on the possibilities for matrimony. Moreover, with walking, it was easy to move, meet others, and talk with them while moving.

Walking was eased by the density of long-established tracks and paths, which was denser than in the more regulated modern world of public footpaths and linked all settlements. Many tracks and paths, however, were scarcely easy routes. Instead, they closely reflected the nature of the local terrain, in particular the topography, drainage, and soil type. In areas with a high water table, such as the heavy clay of the Midlands, south Essex, and the Vale of Berkeley, rainfall turned tracks into impassable quagmires, not least as water ran off the fields. The same is still the case in much of the West Country.

Hilly and mountainous terrain made the situation far more difficult. Even in lowland areas, a small hill affected journeys. Moreover, steep climbs were hard. However, once a hill was ascended, walking downland was relatively easy because it was well drained and far drier than the valley floor, where, as Edward Ferrars points out, there was "dirt," or mud, notably in winter.[4] Downland also provided prospects.

No one went far in winter if they could avoid it. Aside from difficulties with the weather, roads and ferries were also more difficult, and it was light for less of the day. Emma finds a late December in which the ground is "covered with snow, and the atmosphere in that unsettled state between frost and thaw, which is of all others the most unfriendly for exercise, every morning beginning in rain or snow, and every evening setting in to freeze," such that "she was for many days a most honourable prisoner." In *Persuasion*, dreadful weather means the Musgroves have no callers in the second half of January apart from the unwelcome curate,[5] a local figure without connections who was dependent on the hospitality of neighbors.

Snowmelt, moreover, ensured that the early months of the year could be very difficult. In February 1776, the thaw led to floods in Hampshire, which helped keep Austen's mother in the house. In contrast, a fair April meant that in 1805, as Austen wrote, "We do nothing but walk about."[6] Local knowledge was very important in terms of the particular vulnerabilities of tracks to weather conditions.

Some of the problems of walking are referred to in *A Collection of Letters*. Austen portrays the unpleasant Lady Greville telling Maria, whom she dislikes, "There will be no occasion for your being very fine for I shant send the Carriage—If it rains you may take an umbrella . . . you are used to be blown about by the wind Miss Maria and that is what has made your complexion so ruddy and coarse. You young Ladies who cannot often ride in a Carriage never mind what weather you trudge in, or how the wind shews your legs. . . . There will be no Moon—and You will have an horrid walk home."[7]Austen's characters frequently walk, as Elizabeth does in *Pride and Prejudice*, Anne in *Persuasion*, and Jane Fairfax in *Emma*. Indeed, it can be an aspect of their integrity and purpose, as with Elizabeth. In contrast to her sister Jane, she is "no horse-woman" and, instead, walks the three miles to Netherfield despite her mother commenting on "the dirt." She jumps over stiles, springs over puddles, and arrives "with weary ankles, dirty stockings, and a face glowing with the warmth of exercise," to the incredulity of the Bingley women. The walk makes her truly distinctive. Darcy admires "the brilliancy which exercise had given to her complexion," but Miss Bingley finds it "an abominable sort of conceited independence, a most country-town indifference to decorum."[8]

The clash is more generally true in the novels. Elizabeth also walks for pleasure, rather than simply to reach a destination, notably doing so rather than call on Lady Catherine at Rosings.[9] Elizabeth's sisters Catherine and Lydia usually walk the mile to the nearby town of Meryton (and the mile back): "When nothing better offered, a walk to Meryton was necessary to amuse their morning hours and furnish conversation for the evening."[10] So also with other characters. Thus, Catherine Morland walks up Beechen cliff, and Emma Woodhouse walks back from the Westons.

The difficulty of much walking is underplayed in Austen's novels, but, in *Pride and Prejudice*, the anticipation of the ball counters the dreariness of a patch of bad weather that prevents going out: "From the day of the invitation, to the day of the ball, there was such a succession of rain as prevented their walking to Meryton once."[11] Rain is a major problem for walkers, particularly for women given their clothes and expectations as to their appearance. Fanny Price is caught by a heavy shower en route to the village and is brought into the parsonage to dry. The walks and plans of Elinor and Marianne Dashwood are affected by rain.[12]

Walking certainly provides an opportunity for plot development, especially as each walk offers the options of company from the outset or the transition from solitary status to company or a mixture of the two. Thus, in her juvenilia—in *Frederic and Elfrida*, Austen's mock romance—her protagonists and Charlotte swiftly go on a walk, where they meet two others, thus moving the plot forward. In *Jack and Alice*, the plot walk is also mocked: "Lady Williams called on Miss Johnson to propose a walk in a Citron [citrus] Grove which led from her Ladyship's pigstye to Charles Adams's Horsepond. Alice was too sensible of Lady Williams's kindness in proposing such a walk and too much pleased with the prospect of seeing at the end of it, a Horsepond of Charles's, not to accept it with visible delight."[13] In *The Three Sisters*, Mary Stanhope walks to the village of Stoneham, her conversation entirely consisting "in abusing the man she is soon to marry and in longing for a blue chaise [carriage] spotted with silver."[14]

Walking is also important in Austen's mature novels. In *Emma*, the first conversation is interrupted by Mr. Knightley walking the mile to Highbury, where Emma tells him that she and the new Mrs. Weston had met Mr. Weston "in Broadway-Lane, when, because it began to mizzle [light rain], he darted away with so much gallantry, and borrowed two umbrellas for us from Farmer Mitchell's." Meeting while walking provides opportunities for sociability with less formal conventions than otherwise, including for private conversations that are not closely observed. This is seen in the artifice noted in *Pride and Prejudice*, when "Miss Lucas perceived him [Mr. Collins] from an upper window as he walked towards the house, and instantly set out to meet him accidently in the lane,"[15] which led to their engagement. The pompous Collins does not understand that he is being played, which is an aspect of both his character and the plot.

Walking was also very important in cities, particularly where pavements were planned and used, such as in many spas and notably in Bath. In London, distances encouraged the use of carriages, but walking was important in the West End—notably so if visiting a series of shops.

After walking, the next most significant form of local travel was horseback, which also faced many of the problems already outlined, including the impacts of weather, terrain, and drainage. Moreover, there was a gender dimension. Women and girls were not generally expected to ride horses, but men and boys did. For example, Harriet Smith's suitor, the honest and industrious farmer Mr. Martin, rides through every week on his way to the local market town, Kingston,[16] which Austen herself went through on her way between Chawton and Kent. In going to Box Hill for their outing in *Emma*, the gentlemen go on horseback and the women by carriage.[17] The problem of transport for women leads Augusta Hawkins to comment: "I wish we had a donkey. The thing would be for us all to come on donkies. . . . I really must talk to him about purchasing a donkey. In a country life I conceive it to be a sort of necessary; for, let a women have ever so many resources, it is not possible for her to be always shut up at home;—and very long walks, you know—in summer there is dust, and in winter there is dirt."[18]

However, in *Pride and Prejudice*, Mrs. Bennet, with her usual open eagerness to make arrangements, suggests to Jane that, when she goes to the Bingleys at Netherfield for dinner, she should not take the carriage, but rather "go on horseback, because it seems likely to rain; and then you must stay all night,"[19] which would develop the desired social links. Jane indeed goes on horseback, getting wet through. The links develop, and Mrs. Bennet is vindicated, although that success is not matched with her other matchmaking.

In *Mansfield Park*, Fanny Price has a "dear old grey pony," the riding of which is good for her health, and Edmund gets her another horse when it dies.[20] The opportunistic Mary Crawford learns to ride on this horse. In *Persuasion*, Mrs. Croft is a safer driver of their gig than her husband, the Admiral. In *A Collection of Letters*, in the juvenilia, riding is advised on medical grounds, and the "Young Lady crossed in Love" notes, "We have delightful Rides round us, I have a Charming horse, am uncommonly fond of the Amusement. . . . I ride a great deal," only for "Miss Jane," who was about thirty-five, to reveal that she has not ridden since she married.[21] However, Austen's poem "To the Memory of Mrs Lefroy" was a response to the death of her friend Anne Lefroy, wife of a rector near Steventon, in December 1804, four years earlier, which was caused by the horse bolting and Anne falling on hard ground. In the poem, Austen praises Anne's "Christian spirit."

Horses could readily follow paths and tracks, but carriages had to be used on roads. The state of the latter was therefore important—notably the ability and determination of local communities to keep them in good repair—because, under the Statute for Mending of Highways of 1555, each parish was responsible for road upkeep. However, as the resistance of the surface, usually loose and rough, to bad weather or heavy use was limited, there was a need for frequent repair. Expensive in money and manpower, as it could not be mechanized, this duty was generally not adequately carried out. Only the largest holes were usually filled. Nevertheless, landlords could improve roads near their seats, as did Mr. Rushworth near Sotherton Court.[22]

Although local road systems were extensive, there were many problems that encouraged interest in improvement. In his play *She Stoops to Conquer* (1773), Oliver Goldsmith wrote of a rural journey: "It is a damned long, dark, boggy, dirty, dangerous way" (act 1, scene 2). In December 1782, Jeremy Lister wrote from Gainsborough: "The roads are exceeding bad, the road towards Lincoln being the only one that is anything tolerable, and that in general is through very deep sand."[23] In *The Watsons*, Austen refers to the Watsons splashing along a "dirty lane,"[24] and the arrogant Robert Watson complains to his sister: "Your road through the village is infamous . . . worse than ever it was. By heaven! I would endite it if I lived near you. Who is the surveyor now?"[25] In *Mansfield Park*, Lady Bertram has "to go through ten miles of indifferent road, to pay a morning visit" on Mrs. Rushworth, and the problems of rural travel are a theme in the novel. Display, as well as comfort, are affected for narrow lanes can scratch the varnish off the carriage, while she continues: "If you had seen the state of the roads *that* day! I thought we should never have got through them, though we had the four horses of course . . . when we got into the rough lanes about Stoke, where what with frost and snow upon beds of stones, it was worse than any thing you can imagine. . . . And then the poor horses too!—To see them straining away! . . . when we got to the bottom of Sandcroft Hill . . . I got out and walked up."[26] En route from Willingden to Sanditon, conversation in the carriage serves "to lighten the tediousness of a long hill, or a heavy bit of road."[27] Austen herself had her journey from Kent to Steventon in 1798 affected by bad weather. That journey, at least, greatly benefitted from turnpikes. In contrast, there were no turnpikes in many areas—for example, in parts of Devon, where, although there were twenty turnpike trusts by 1772, by 1800 there were still no turnpikes between Bideford and Launceston and from Ilfracombe to Lynton, and the district of the South Hams was poorly served.

Carriages were an expression of social position and were seen in that light. "All the grandeur of the connection" of Mr. Elton with Augusta Hawkins "seemed dependent on the elder sister, who was *very well married,* to a gentleman in a *great way,* near Bristol, who kept two carriages!" This implied ownership of a carriage house and the relevant horses, grooms, drivers, and so on. Henry Crawford has a barouche, as does Mrs. Palmer, which Julia Bertram prefers for the visit to Sotherton over the smaller family post chaise. She competes successfully with her sister Maria to sit next to Henry in a social grasp for position that would have been well recognized. In turn, Maria proposes to get new carriages in London when married to Mr. Rushworth. Lucy Steele confides of her friends the Richardsons: "They are very genteel people. He makes a monstrous deal of money, and they keep their own coach."[28] Mrs. Perry wants her medical husband to get a carriage, which would be seen as a sign that he can afford one.[29] Mrs. Norris is able to borrow Lady Bertram's carriage and thus can mix "in society without having horses to hire."[30] Ambitious for her brother, Edward Ferrars, the unpleasant Mrs. John Dashwood wants to see him driving a barouche.[31] In *Persuasion,* the endlessly complaining Mary Musgrove whines: "It is so very uncomfortable, not having a carriage of one's own. Mr and Mrs Musgrove took me, and we were so crowded! They are both so very large, and take up so much room!"[32] Miss Denham "was immediately gnawed by the want of a handsomer equipage than the simple gig in which they travelled."[33]

Austen was well aware of the issue of expense in the case of carriages and thus the cost of status. Having started maintaining a carriage the previous winter, George Austen has to give it up in late 1798 because he discovered he could not afford to keep it. He never took it up again.

There was danger as well as expenditure in travel. Carriages were affected by deficiencies in the road surface such that moonlight, when the surface could more readily be seen at night, ensured there were more social engagements.[34] Carriages were also affected by springs snapping and horses bolting. Going up and down steep hills could be particularly difficult and dangerous, and being on the roof of a coach was especially risky. *Sanditon* starts with a carriage overturning on a very rough lane, leading its owner, Mr. Parker, to determine to turn back to the turnpike,"[35] while the jovial Admiral and Mrs. Croft in *Persuasion* overturn their gig "very often," although they do not mind.[36]

Overturning, however, could be fatal. In Austen's early and satirical story *Love and Freindship*, Edward and Augustus die as a result of a carriage overturning. Indeed, there was a craze for driving fast in the 1780s and 1790s. Even when not fast or fatal, there were accidents: in October 1812, Austen referred to the carriage from Alton in Hampshire overturned en route to London.[37] This was not the sole type of accident. In *Emma*, a lame carriage horse delays the planned trip to Box Hill.[38]

Much improvement was brought by Turnpike Trusts, bodies established by groups of local businessmen and landowners who obtained individual Acts of Parliament as authorization to raise capital to repair and improve a road or network of local roads and charge tolls to those ends. Improvement was a key theme. Many turnpikes improved road maintenance and widened roads so they could take wheeled vehicles rapidly, which led to the spread of such traffic.[39] In contrast, walkers turned to "turnpike tracks" in order to bypass the tolls, but that was essentially the recourse of the poor and was not a choice or experience that interested novelists, including Austen. Although trusts reflected local initiatives, the definition of necessary and profitable links ensured that a national system was established. By Austen's birth, most of England was within twelve miles of a turnpike, and during her lifetime, a series of often quite small-scale changes expanded and improved the system. Thus, the replacement of poor routes by smoother, more level, and wider roads made travel easier. In east Devon, where Elinor and Marianne Dashwood move with their mother, the Honiton and Ilminster Turnpike Trust constructed a new road from Yarde to near Ilminster from 1807 to 1812, and the Cullompton Turnpike Trust constructed another from near Broadclyst to near Cullompton from 1813 to 1816. Turnpiked roads enabled coach times to improve and become more predictable.

Turnpikes were very much an aspect of Austen's world. She visited Edward Austen frequently, and the Ashford to Faversham turnpike ran alongside his seat, Godmersham in Kent, just as there was a turnpike close to Lady Catherine's park at Rosings. Austen's great-uncle, Francis Austen, was an original trustee of the Westerham and Edenbridge Turnpike Trust. Moreover, the turnpike from Kingston in Surrey to Portsmouth, completed in 1749, speeded travelers between London and Hampshire and was used by George III when he visited Portsmouth in 1773. As a reminder of the multiple links of people and places, it is instructive to note Sir Joshua Reynolds's report on George's return from his review of the fleet there, a route that took him through Hampshire and Surrey:

> The King is exceeding delighted with his reception at Portsmouth. He said to a person about that he was convinced he was not so unpopular as the newspapers would represent him to be. The acclamations of the people were indeed prodigious. On his return all the country assembled in the towns where he changed horses. At Godalming every man had a branch of a tree in his hand and every woman a

nosegay which they presented to the King (the horses moving as slow as possible) till he was up to the knees in flowers, and they all singing in a tumultuous manner, God Save the King. The King was so affected that he could not refrain shedding abundance of tears, and even joined in the chorus.[40]

Godalming is not far from where *Emma* is set. Thanks to such roads, there was a growing sense of ease and improvement. This is reflected in Austen's novels. When Charlotte Lucas moves to Kent, she finds the roads "to her taste,"[41] and Darcy, responding to Elizabeth Bennet's observation that Hunsford was nearly fifty miles from Longbourn and therefore not "an easy distance," observed, "And what is fifty miles of good road? Little more than half a day's journey. Yes, I call it a *very* easy distance."[42] Indeed, Augusta Elton asks: "What is distance, Mr Weston, to people of large fortune?—You would be amazed to hear how my brother, Mr Suckling, sometimes flies about. You will hardly believe me—but twice in one week he and Mr Bragge went to London and back again with four horses."[43] Wealth combined with good roads had shrunk distance.

In *Love and Freindship*, there is a turnpike near Macdonald Hall, the Scottish setting of part of the action. In *Sense and Sensibility*, Mrs. Jennings praises Colonel Brandon's seat at Delaford in part because it is "only a quarter of a mile from the turnpike-road," although that leads to an unexpected advantage: "So 'tis never dull, for if you only go and sit up in an old yew arbour behind the house, you may see all the carriages that pass along."[44]

Travel certainly became more predictable. Despite the concerns of Eleanor Tilney, the young Catherine Morland is able to travel safely without a servant from Northanger Abbey, via Salisbury, to her home at Fullerton, a journey of seventy miles: "Salisbury she had known to be her point on leaving Northanger; but after the first stage she had been indebted to the post-masters for the names of the places which were then to conduct her to it; so great had been her ignorance of her route. She met with nothing, however, to distress or frighten her. Her youth, civil manners and liberal pay, procured her all the attention that a traveller like herself could require; and stopping only to change horses, she travelled on for about eleven hours without accident or alarm."[45]

In the 1780s, John McAdam began experiments on improving road surfaces by consolidating a layer of small, broken, hard stone to form a very hard surface with a camber for drainage, although McAdam did not publish his major works on the subject until 1819–20. Macadam was used on the Exeter to Exmouth turnpike in 1819. More immediately, the system was enhanced by the building of bridges, a skill to which John Metcalf (1717–1810), and, more prominently, Thomas Telford (1757–1834) brought improvements. Stone bridges replaced wooden ones and ferries, improving the load-bearing capability and reliability of the system. Existing bridges were widened, and new and wider bridges with large spans were erected. For example, in 1774, the opening of the Countess Wear bridge provided a crossing point over the River Exe below Exeter. This process, however, was not free from contention. For example, in 1789–90, the proposal for a bridge over the River Ouse near Selby led to a general meeting at York, as those opposed feared it would affect the navigation of the river, and a request to Francis, fifth Duke of Leeds, the foreign secretary, to oppose the measure.

Better links were used to transport both people and goods, and it became easier to move between major centers. Travel was made quicker by the crossbreeding of fast Arab horses while further improvements came from replacing leather straps with steel coach springs.

Travel was also made easier by improving facilities. Across the country, alehouses or inns, such as The Three Jolly Pigeons in Goldsmith's play *She Stoops to Conquer*, provided hospitality to travelers. During Austen's lifetime, many old inns were rebuilt or extended, and new inns were built. Robert Ferrars and his new wife, Lucy, stop "in a chaise" at the New London Inn in Exeter en route from London to Dawlish.[46] However, questionable conditions in many inns deterred some from sleeping there and, indeed, led the fictional Selina Suckling in *Emma* to travel with her own sheets.[47] Traveling certainly could involve delays, far more so than today, as Catherine Morland discovered en route from Bath to Northanger Abbey, when she had to wait at a posting stage where the horses were fed: "The tediousness of a two hours' bait at Petty-France, in which there was nothing to be done but to eat without being hungry, and loiter about without any thing to see, next followed—and her admiration of the style in which they travelled, of the fashionable chaise-and-four—postilions handsomely liveried, rising so regularly in their stirrups, and numerous out-riders properly mounted, sunk a little under this consequent inconvenience."[48]

However, en route to Portsmouth, Fanny and William Price stop at Newbury and have a comfortable meal. Their uneventful journey advances by regular stages. On the return, nevertheless, Fanny, with her sister Susan and Edmund Bertram, go in one day from Portsmouth to Oxford, which is tiring: "their journey occupied a long day, and brought them almost knocked up, to Oxford." Separately, Mrs. Jennings and the Dashwood girls are "glad to be released . . . from the confinement of a carriage" at the end of their three-day journey to London.[49]

Journeys became more regular as well as quicker. By 1783, there were twenty-five departures a week from Norwich to London. The following year, John Palmer's prospectus for employing his stagecoaches to carry the post was vindicated when the Bristol-to-London journey was carried out in under sixteen hours. The use of stagecoaches for the post greatly improved services for the public as a whole. By 1788, the time required for a journey from London to Manchester had fallen to twenty-eight hours and from Exeter to London to thirty-two, and average speeds between London and Birmingham had risen to fifteen miles an hour. Colonel Brandon rides from Barton Park to Honiton and then goes post to London on the major road from the Southwest.[50]

Some routes, however, were slower. In 1787, the coach journey from Exeter to Barnstaple took over twelve hours. There was also a degree of unpredictability. John Lee, en route from London to Oxford in 1806, noted another issue with carriages: "Having in this stage from Hounslow to Slough two leaders very unequal to each other, their traces were observed to be crossed and the coachman informed us that they by that means *would* enable the horses to draw better together. I doubt it much." Pressing on from Oxford to Worcester, he found the coach slower. Leaving Oxford at seven in the morning, he did not arrive in Worcester until a quarter to six in the evening.[51]

Journeys could be affected by a willingness to "travel earlier, later, and quicker," which was the case with Frank Churchill.[52] In practice this tended to be a male prerogative. Leaving London at eight in the morning, John Willoughby, with his carriage drawn by four rather than two horses, is able to reach Cleveland in Somerset by eight at night: "The only ten minutes I have spent out of my chaise . . . procured me a noonchine [light meal] at Marlborough" of cold beef and beer.[53] In a more leisurely fashion, also in *Sense and Sensibility*, Mrs. Jennings takes three days to go from Barton (a fictional place, probably the village of Upton Pyne) near Exeter to London in her own carriage.[54]

Life and etiquette in stagecoaches became a more prominent theme that was picked up by writers. The narrator in *Love and Freindship* has to put up with a snoring Sir Edward in a stagecoach. Stage coaches, moreover, could be crowded.[55] So also with private carriages, such as that of the Musgroves in *Persuasion*. Young women riding unchaperoned in open carriages driven by young men is an issue in *Northanger Abbey*.[56]

As another aspect of etiquette, space was an issue, even in the barouche, a large carriage, that Lady Catherine is willing to use to take Elizabeth Bennet to London. At the same time, Lady Catherine characteristically makes a point about superiority; by preference, she will convey Elizabeth on a box seat near the driver, the usual seat of a servant,[57] rather than give her the status of riding within. Yet such seats also offered privacy for flirting on the trip to Sotherton Court in *Mansfield Park* when Julia Bertram sits next to Henry Crawford. She thus thwarts her sister Maria, but that seating also pleases Mr. Rushworth, her lackluster intended: "He was certainly better pleased to hand her into the barouche than to assist her in ascending the box."[58]

Status is asserted and demonstrated through the type of carriage owned and used, notably a barouche, as well as the seating arrangements. The type, a very public show, provides a ready way for Austen to expose pride and condescension, as with Augusta Elton and her brother-in-law's oft-cited barouche-landau, a new type of four-seater, and Sir Walter Elliot wanting to know if the Crofts traveled with four horses.[59] Traveling in a post chaise was regarded as better than in a stagecoach and was chosen by Mrs. Jennings and led Lucy Steele to congratulate herself accordingly.[60]

Travel was significant not only to Austen personally but also as an important aspect of her plots. Indeed, travel played a particularly key role in *Pride and Prejudice*. In this, as so often, Austen built on well-established conventions. Her use of travel was essentially instrumental, being designed to forward the plot. Elizabeth Bennet accompanies the Gardiners not, as originally intended, to the Lake District but to Derbyshire via Oxford, Blenheim, Warwick, Kenilworth, and Birmingham, which enables her to visit Pemberley and, to her surprise, see Darcy.

In this itinerary, the pursuit of an engagement with landscape, as well as freedom from the home, is important. Austen's novels did not use itineraries as variously seen with Daniel Defoe, Henry Fielding, Laurence Sterne, Tobias Smollett, and their emulators, who demonstrated the literary value of travel. Their use of itineraries underlined satirical purpose. In contrast, Austen offered a more grounded, almost prosaic, account of travel in her novels. She does not focus on the religious and psychological dimensions of travel—the individual soul or spirit and, subsequently, the particular sensibility.[61] Indeed, the most pronounced instance of the latter is both more "domestic" and satirized—namely, the journey within the house in *Northanger Abbey*.

In her juvenilia, however, travel can be somewhat wider. Thus, in *Love and Freindship*, Edward sets off from Bedfordshire for Middlesex, and "though I flatter myself with being a tolerable proficient in Geography, I know not how it happened, but I found myself entering this beautiful Vale which I find is in South Wales,[62] when I had expected to have reached my Aunts" in Middlesex.[63]

A lack of geographical knowledge is also seen elsewhere in Austen's work. Harriet Smith asks, "Will Mr Frank Churchill pass through Bath as well as Oxford?" a question that shows she does not know the route from Yorkshire to Surrey.[64] He sleeps two nights on the journey.[65] The younger Fanny Price "cannot put the map of Europe together . . . cannot tell the principal rivers in Russia . . . never heard of Asia Minor . . . we asked her last night, which way she would go to get to Ireland; and she said, she should cross to the Isle of Wight."[66] In practice, there were many books and maps for real and armchair travelers, as well as board games focused on an itinerary, as in John Wallis's Tour through England and Wales (1794) and Tour of Europe (1794).[67]

The role of the narrator in itineraries captured the extent to which there was a crossover between fact and fiction, as well as observation and comment. So also with letters, which were frequently a type of itinerary as they recorded journeys—for example, Edmund Bertram's account of his visit to London.[68] There was no need to write letters if people had face-to-face contact, which was the normal form of interaction. Letters recorded the journeys of real people, directly or indirectly, as well as of their fictional counterparts. Each category offered geographies that helped shape itineraries and responses for others. Letters, like itineraries, both fictional and factual, provided opportunities for the psychological response that narrative offered. In novels, they also varied the voice and tone.

The nature of letters changed markedly with the improvement in the postal system. The length of a letter could be determined by how much time was available to the writer before the letter had to be finished as the post was collected, a point to which correspondents referred. The departure and arrival of letters became more predictable, both in timing and in reliability, which increased the habit and also encouraged a desire for news: "Everybody at all addicted to letter writing, without having much to say, which will include a large proportion of the female world at least,"[69] a reflection of Austen's, was a somewhat flippant response to the isolation and loneliness overcome by the post. However, its target, Lady Bertram, is an idle and selfish woman whose use of the post, it is suggested, is encouraged by the franking privileges of free postage enjoyed by her husband, an MP.

Letter writers were aware that much of their correspondence was sequential and also made regular reference to letters from others. Understandably, after Lydia Bennet fled: "Every day at Longbourn was now a day of anxiety, but the most anxious part of each was when the post was expected. The arrival of letters was the first grand object of every morning's impatience. Through letters, whatever of good or bad was to be told would be communicated, and every succeeding day was expected to bring some news of importance."[70]

Less urgently, Jane Fairfax, who regularly goes to the post office in order to get letters, and thus remain in touch with friends, is most impressed by the postal system: "A wonderful establishment. . . . The regularity and dispatch of it! If one thinks of all that it has to do, and all that it does so well, it is really astonishing! . . . So seldom that any negligence or blunder appears! So seldom that a letter, among the thousands that are constantly passing about the kingdom, is even carried wrong—and not one in a million, I suppose, actually lost! And when one considers the variety of hands, and of bad hands too, that are to be deciphered, it increases the wonder!"[71]

This was very much a comment on a recent development. The system of fast mail coaches started in 1784 was operating effectively by the time Austen wrote *Emma*. It benefited from the turnpikes and was linked to more ad hoc processes of delivering letters to houses from local post offices. Many of the latter were based at inns where the mail coaches stopped. This was an integrated system in which localities were linked to each other as part of a well-regulated national system. The dour John Knightley offered Emma a financial explanation that was more generally valid: "It is certainly very well regulated. . . . The clerks grow expert from habit.—They must begin with some quickness of sight and hand, and exercise improves them. If you want any further explanation . . . they are paid for it. That is the key to a great deal of capacity. The public pays and must be served well."[72] For much of the population, the experience of travel and the outside world was very limited, even though there were no such constraints on the range of the imagination. Many were fit but essentially lived a life constrained by the limits of the local market town or fair. However, there were tales about the wider world that were retold and thus part of family and communal memories. There was also the world as repeated through the Church. In addition, market towns were destinations for strangers and often the base of printers who produced newspapers.

Travel within a relatively small area was common for seasonal agricultural employment. Many across society—notably, but not only, male society—traveled far more widely, generally for work. This highly varied category included recruits for the army, the navy, and the merchant marine; those droving animals; would-be servants seeking employment; other servants accompanying masters; and so on. Patrick Colquhoun referred to the "inconceivable" number of those "who with their families, find their way to the Metropolis [London], from the most remote quarters of Great Britain and Ireland."[73] In a numerical sense these travels were far more significant than those of the affluent, but the travel of the affluent dominated attention. This was an aspect of geography as consumerism that was especially present through publications, including novels.

Horse-drawn wagon services, which improved with the turnpike system and with entrepreneurial organization, speeded freight,[74] as did the developing canal system, which was seen as a way to integrate producers and markets.[75] Indeed, a canal craze hit much of England in the 1790s, although it was not to the fore in Austen's rural area, conceived of as Wiltshire, Hampshire, and Kent. Instead, canal building focused in the North and Midlands. In the South, the most significant link, the Kennett-Avon canal, was to the north of Austen's stamping ground, although on her travels she would have crossed canals, as did George III, who visited the Stroudwater Canal in 1788, seeing the impressive tunnel driven through the scarp of the Cotswolds.[76] Moreover, London and Bath were linked to the canal network, and there were plans for other canals in Austen's heartland. In the March 16 and April 6, 1789, issues, the *Salisbury and Winchester Journal* praised the plans for a British-London canal via Salisbury, before adding on April 13: "We are happy to hear that most of the gentlemen of rank and fortune in the neighbourhood of the proposed Great Western Canal intended to support the undertaking with all their weight and influence, not only as an object of private emolument, but on the noble and patriotic principle of public good."

Unlike in the Low Countries, France, and northern Italy, where there were regular services for paying passengers, canals did not really carry passengers, concentrating instead on freight. However, passengers, not freight, were Austen's subject.

So also with railways. Wagonways had existed for many years, with horses drawing wagons along rails, especially from collieries to coal-loading quays. The Surrey Iron Railway Company, the world's first railway company and public railway, operated from Wandsworth to Croydon from 1803. Self-propelled steam locomotives soon began to change the situation, not least by making long-distance movement possible. In 1804, Roger Hopkins built a tram road between Pen-y-darren and Abercynon in South Wales upon which Richard Trevithick tried the first steam railway locomotive engine, essentially a mobile beam engine. The development of the locomotive steam engine from the stationary type provided the technology for the railway revolution, and industrialization supplied the necessary demand, capital, and skills. George Stephenson opened the Hetton Railway in 1822, with the more famous Stockton and Darlington following in 1825.

Improved transport helped trade, and this commerce was linked to the spread of what would now be termed consumerism. Publications presented news of new and established products and fashions, including groceries, such as sugar and tobacco, and caffeine drinks like tea, coffee, and chocolate.[77] Consumerism related to material objects as well as stimulants. Tea and coffee had to be prepared and drunk from utensils, such as teapots. The fashionable consumerism of the elite was very apparent in General Tilney's satisfied comment on his elegant breakfast set at Northanger Abbey that Catherine Morland had praised. She was thus a dutiful guest, even if in her case a spontaneous one, which makes her truly charming as well as naive. The general "confessed it to be neat and simple, thought it right to encourage the manufacture of his country; and for his part to his uncritical palate, the tea was as well flavoured from the clay of Staffordshire, as from that of Dresden or Sève. But this was quite an old set, purchased two years ago. The manufacture was much improved since that time; he had seen some beautiful specimens when last in town, and had he not been perfectly without vanity of that kind, might have been tempted to order a new set."[78] The idea of an "old set" being but two years old and the general considering

a replacement was very much consumerism. Austen can be caus-
tic about the world of goods, as in *Sanditon* when she refers to
the library as also selling "all the useless things in the world that
could not be done without."[79] More generally, as the use of new
goods grew, so did concern with novelty and fashion. Robert Ferrars is able to give "a lecture on toothpick-cases,"[80] which helps
make him appear ridiculous.

Demand for goods interacted with the development of shops
and provided the latter with crucial profit margins. The growth
of a retail infrastructure changed the nature of both the domestic market and townscapes. Shops complemented, competed
with, and to a degree replaced the older commercial world markets, peddlers, chapmen, and private dealings in inns.[81] However, all these continued to have a role, albeit not one Austen
tackled—demonstrating the gap between the range of rural society and the perspective of an individual novelist. Thus, the number of licensed peddlers remained at several thousand before
rising in the first quarter of the nineteenth century, in part due
to procedural streamlining by the Hawkers and Pedlars Office.[82]

As a result of the development of shops, towns were increasingly
differentiated from what would become villages. Mrs. Rider's, the
haberdashery in Basingstoke, was where Jane bought items to
add to her hat to make it more attractive and enhance the variety
of appearance it offered. In *Emma*, there is an equivalent: Ford's
in Highbury, "the principal woollen-draper, linen-draper, and
haberdasher's shop united; the shop first in size and fashion in
the place."[83] Frank Churchill and Emma go shopping at Ford's
for hats and gloves (the gloves for the former) "Men's Beavers"
and "York Tan."[84] Also at Ford's, Emma tries to convince Harriet
Smith "that if she wanted plain muslin it was of no use to look
at figured; and that a blue ribbon, be it ever so beautiful, would
still never match her yellow pattern."[85] Shopping was very much
becoming a leisure activity and a social pastime where people
could meet without introduction and on a basis of equality.

Advertising reflected and sustained a pattern of changing retail patterns, as well as underwriting the prosperity of newspapers, while trade directories provided information. Edmund Bertram, taking up a newspaper in order to draw back from a conversation, finds "various advertisements of 'a most desirable estate in South Wales'—'To Parents and Guardians'—and a 'Capital season'd Hunter,'" the last a horse for hunting.[86]

Critics insisted upon the enervating and corrupting effects of luxury. There were certainly more material goods, a rising demand for all types of goods, and a slowly changing material fabric of life. This was most obvious in the cities, but itinerant retailers also took goods throughout the country. Clothes reflected this "consumer revolution," and so Lucy Steele sets out to guess the number of Marianne Dashwood's gowns.[87] The number of gowns indeed would have proved a topic of conversation for young ladies, one that was more interesting than Ferrars on toothpick cases. The cotton fabrics imported by the East India Company were both attractive and could be used to provide for a mass market the styles that were otherwise restricted to more expensive silks and brocades. The Indiamen, the ships of the company, were based in Portsmouth, enhancing the importance and glamour of that port, and one of Fanny Price's brothers is a midshipman on one.

Consumerism was wide-ranging and multifaceted. Wallpaper became fashionable, carpets more common, and furniture more plentiful. People consumed more medicaments, a process encouraged by longer average lifespans and the advertising of these goods. Furniture more directly reflected social changes, including the rise of "politeness" and sedentary activities such as card playing and drinking tea. When Mr. Collins visits, it is necessary to use separate tables in the drawing room so the separate activities could be followed. In *Emma*, the clock strikes as Emma passes through the hall at Hartfield en route to meet Frank Churchill in the parlor.[88]

Production and sale of furniture were due to the entrepreneurial character of the period. Much furniture was fairly simple and was designed for those who were not particularly affluent. It was produced in the neighborhood out of local wood and used alongside inherited pieces. At the same time, the more affluent consumed furniture, as part of a fashionable world in which designs changed and were popularized by fashion books, exotic woods such as mahogany were imported, decoration was greatly enhanced by inlaid woods and veneers, and pieces (such as paintings) were commissioned to complement each other and other items in the room. The entire effect was of a carefully created living environment and a completeness linking material culture and aesthetic values, as when Tom Musgrave finds "Miss Watson sitting at the best Pembroke table, with the best tea things before her."[89] On each side of a Pembroke table is a hinged drop-leaf.

Austen very much comments on the "consumer revolution." To a considerable degree, however, she rather left out the industrial revolution, the world of coal and iron, and its related new means of communication—the canal system. This was understandable because the spread of coal-based industry on and near the coalfields, and the regional specialization greatly fostered by cheaper and more reliable transport, benefited Lancashire, Yorkshire, and the West Midlands. The statistics of change were accompanied by technological innovation and the development of particular sites. Wood required bulk for calorific value and produced barely controllable heat, making it a poor basis for many industrial processes. In contrast, coal, a readily transportable and controllable fuel with high calorific value, was very useful for manufacturing. Coal could be mined throughout the year whereas water mills were affected by ice, flooding, and summertime falls in water flow. Britain was a key center of this technological change. By 1750 coal provided 61 percent of all the energy used in England and produced energy equivalent to that from 4.3 million acres of woodland.[90]

Coal was important to the development of particular industries, especially the iron industry. Henry Cort's method of puddling and rolling, adopted in the 1790s, produced malleable iron with coal more cheaply than by using charcoal. In South Wales there were 25 furnaces by 1796 and 148 by 1811. Merthyr Tydfil, a Welsh hamlet, became, by 1801, the world's leading center of iron production. Coal output in England rose from 8.8 million tons in 1775 to 15 million by 1800. By 1821, Manchester, which, like Sheffield, was relatively close to Chatsworth, had over five thousand power looms.

Far from being removed in their stately homes, the elite were part of this process, notably providing land, mineral rights, and investment. In Staffordshire, which Austen visited in 1806, Granville, Earl Gower, the first Marquess of Stafford (1721–1803), a major landowner, was actively involved in coal, lime, and iron stone extraction and the development of canals and mineral railroads.

However, industrial growth was accompanied by considerable deindustrialization in traditional centers. In the key industry, textiles, such long-established centers as Colchester, Exeter, Taunton, and Worcester, saw a decline in production. For example, poor transport, lack of coal, competition from within England, distance from markets, the development of ports elsewhere, and wartime disruption contributed to a marked decline in Devon's textile industry. The export of pieces of cloth from Exeter fell from 390,000 in 1777 to 8,126 in 1800. The elite in the South of England lacked the opportunities enjoyed by Gower, a Midlands landowner.

Instead, the southern elite pursued profit through agricultural improvement, government office, and more eclectic entrepreneurship. Developing the bathing resort of Sanditon was the recourse of Mr. Parker and Lady Denham. In practice, later in the century, the development of nearby Eastbourne was to bring profit to the dukes of Devonshire: the titles of peerages were not necessarily related to the location of landholdings. William, the seventh duke and the landowner responsible, was the successor to the sixth duke, on whom Mr. Darcy was possibly modeled. Chatsworth, the seat of the Devonshires, was possibly the basis for Pemberley.

By the 1790s, industrial change had a clear regional pattern that was reflected in indicators such as expenditure on poor relief per head of population. In 1801, the average figure for England and Wales was nine shillings one penny (forty-five pence), but in the industrial counties, it was far lower. In contrast, counties with hardly any industry, such as Sussex, or with declining industries, such as Essex, Norfolk, and Suffolk, had to pay more than the average. Thus, there were major regional variations in experience. Slow or nonexistent growth in some regions accompanied rapid change in others.[91]

The industrial revolution was a regional, not a national, phenomenon, which helps explain Austen's lack of coverage. She wrote from experience. Moreover, that regional character made the success of agricultural development more significant for the South of England. The fascination of many of Austen's characters with clothes was facilitated in part by industrialization and its consequences. Generally, Austen does not supply enough information about the provenance of clothes, but their greater availability was the product of trade and industry. Austen herself frequently comments on muslin, a finely woven cotton, as in *Northanger Abbey*. Moreover, after running away, Lydia Bennet is concerned that a servant "mend a great slit in my worked muslin gown."[92]

Elizabeth Bennet visits Birmingham, as did William Gilpin, Thomas Jefferson, and the La Rochefoucaulds. The factory of Matthew Boulton and James Boulton at Soho in Birmingham was a major and much-visited site that was described in print,[93] but Austen does not comment on what Elizabeth saw. Complaining about social upstarts, Mrs. Elton notes that her sister and brother-in-law are greatly annoyed accordingly: "People of the name of Tupman, very lately settled there, and encumbered with many low connections, but giving themselves immense airs, and expecting to be on a footing with the old established families . . . how they got their fortune nobody knows. They came from Birmingham, which is not a place to promise much, you know, Mr Weston. One has not great hopes from Birmingham."[94] Ironically, Suckling, her brother-in-law, had only been a resident at his seat of Maple Grove for eleven years and had made his money from trade. Birmingham's electoral weight led to a dramatic triumph in the Warwickshire county contest during the 1774 general election.

Other aspects of the social dimension are not discussed. Thus, the threat to jobs posed by John Heathcoat's patented bobbin net machines led to rioters destroying his Loughborough factory in 1816. Luddite protests against new machinery were seen across much of the North and the Midlands in the 1810s and led to the deployment of large numbers of troops. In Charlotte Brontë's novel *Shirley* (1849), which is set in 1811–12, the new labor-saving machinery is destroyed by rioters.

Heathcoat moved his machines to a disused Tiverton cotton mill, but production from this factory hit traditional lace making in East Devon. The densely inhabited working-class neighborhood that developed in Tiverton was more typical of northern than southern England. In Lancaster, back gardens were turned into houses, with access through doors and arches on main roads but lacking water supplies, sewerage, or lighting. Similarly, the growth of more than 10 percent in Nottingham's population in 1780–81 was met by back-to-back-to-back housing in courts with access to streets via narrow tunnels through the houses on the street frontages. So also in naval cities. The Price household in Portsmouth has small rooms and a narrow passage and staircase.[95] Presented differently, Portsmouth was the base of naval glory while Lancaster had a mail coach service from London in

1786. From crowded housing, people went daily to long hours of arduous work. Even after the 1833 Factories Act prevented the employment of children under nine, nine- and ten-year-olds could still work nine-hour days and eleven- to seventeen-year-olds twelve-hours days.

Arduous and poorly paid work was an aspect of both long-standing agricultural and industrial toil and the economic transformation of this period. At the same time, a relatively stable political system; legal conventions that were favorable to the free utilization of capital, especially secure property and contracting rights; a social system that could accommodate the consequences of economic change; and an increasing degree of integration and interdependence were all fundamental factors. Belief in the stability of the political and economic arrangements encouraged the long-term investment that was crucial in many spheres, including transport. Taxes on manufacturing industry and transport were low or nonexistent.[96]

Economic growth and more general prosperity were also seen in the expansion of the professions, which play a major role in Austen's novels. The clergy have already been mentioned (see chap. 5). Medicine was more divided: there were significant professional differences, as well as differences within professions. There were also varied relations with patients. The theme of earning money, often by style rather than substance, was frequent. Austen covers all these points.

So also with the law. Criticism could broaden into a more general social critique that focused on "professionals by relation," notably wives, as well as the professionals themselves: "Robert Watson was an attorney at Croydon, in a good way of business; very well satisfied with himself for the same, and for having married the only daughter of the attorney to whom he had been clerk, with a fortune of six thousand pounds.—Mrs Robert was not less pleased with herself for having had that six thousand pounds, and for being now in possession of a very smart house in Croydon, where she gave genteel parties, and wore fine clothes.—In her person there was nothing remarkable; her manners were pert and conceited."[97] Robert proves inconsiderate to his sister.

Society was definitely in flux, much to the regret of many of the characters, some sympathetic but others not. Speaking of the new settlement of Sanditon, and bewailing the lack of a visiting heiress, Lady Denham complains: "Families come after families, but as far as I can learn, it is not one in an hundred of them that have any real property, landed or funded.—An income perhaps, but no property. Clergymen may be, or lawyers from town, or half pay officers, or widows with only a jointure. And what good can such people do anybody?"[98]

There was also uncertainty, and at times there were economic slumps. Indeed, Austen was hit hard by an economic downturn after the Napoleonic Wars that contributed to the failure of Henry Austen's banking partnership on March 15, 1816. Austen herself lost twenty-six pounds two shillings, money from *Mansfield Park* and *Sense and Sensibility*, and her brothers also lost money. This could scarcely have encouraged optimism on her part. However, unlike Charles Dickens with Mr. Merdle in *Little Dorrit* or Anthony Trollope with Augustus Melmotte in *The Way We Live Now*, her writings did not focus on the drama of a crash or, indeed, on the consequences. The difficulties of those years are handled far more elliptically.

In Austen's novels, people are commodified in terms of the marriage market, as was the practice of the age. Novels reflected this. The economics of expectations are seen in John Thorpe's misleading General Tilney over the expectations of Catherine Morland so as to exalt his own consequence in hoping to win her:

> The expectations of his friend Morland, therefore, from the first over-rated, had ever since his introduction to Isabella, been gradually increasing; and by merely adding twice as much for the grandeur of the moment, by doubling what he chose to think the amount of Mr Morland's preferment, trebling his private fortune, bestowing

a rich aunt, and sinking half the children, he was able to represent the whole family to the General in a most respectable light. For Catherine, however, the peculiar object of the General's curiosity, and his own speculations, he had yet something more in reserve, and the ten or fifteen thousand pounds which her father could give her, would be a pretty addition to Mr Allen's estate. Her intimacy there had made him seriously determine on her being handsomely legacied hereafter; and to speak of her therefore as the almost acknowledged future heiress of Fullerton naturally followed.[99]

NOTES

1. W. Thom, *Pedestrianism; or, an Account of the Performances of Celebrated Pedestrians during the Last and Present Century* (Aberdeen, UK, 1813).

2. J. Wallis, *The Stranger's Guide through London and Westminster* (London, 1786); T. Walton, *Picturesque Tour through the Cities of London and Westminster* (London, 1792).

3. Citing C. P. Moritz, *Reisen eines jungen Deutschen in England im Jahr 1782*, G. Jefcoate, "Spreading the Word," *Factotum* 31 (April 1990): 22.

4. *Sense* I, 16.

5. *Emma* I, 16; *Persuasion* II, 6.

6. *Letters*, 99.

7. *Juvenilia*, 201–2.

8. *PP* I, 7–8.

9. *PP* II, 7.

10. *PP* I, 7.

11. *PP* I, 17.

12. *Emma* II, 3; *MP* II, 4; *Sense* I, 9, 20.

13. *Juvenilia*, 20.

14. *Juvenilia*, 85.

15. *Emma* I, 1; *PP* I, 22.

16. *Emma* I, 28.

17. *Emma* III, 7.

18. *Emma* III, 6.

19. *PP* I, 7.

20. *MP* I, 3–4.

21. *Persuasion* I, 10; *Juvenilia*, 195.

22. *MP* I, 8.

23. Halifax, Calderdale Archives, SH7/JL/25.

24. *Later Manuscripts*, 79.

25. *Later Manuscripts*, 120.

26. *MP* I, 4, 8; II, 2.

27. *Sanditon* 3.

28. *MP* I, 8; II, 3; *Sense* III, 2.

29. *Emma* II, 4; III, 5.

30. *MP* I, 4.

31. *Sense* I, 3.

32. *Persuasion* I, 5.

33. *Sanditon* 7.

34. *Sense* I, 7.

35. *Sanditon* 1.

36. *Sanditon* 1; *Later Manuscripts*, 137; *Persuasion* I, 10.

37. D. Le Faye, "Jane Austen: Appearance of Three Missing Letters," *Notes and Queries* 263 (2018): 348.

38. *Emma* III, 6.

39. W. Albert, *The Turnpike Road System in England 1663–1840* (Cambridge, 1972); E. Pawson, *Transport and Economy: The Turnpike Roads of Eighteenth-Century Britain* (London, 1977).

40. Reynolds to John, first Earl of Grantham, July 20, 1773, Bedford, Bedfordshire County Record Office, Lucas papers 30/14/326/2. I am grateful to Lady Lucas for permission to consult and quote from these papers.

41. *PP* II, 3.

42. *PP* II, 9.

43. *Emma* II, 18. In total, they went about 470 miles.

44. *Sense* II, 8.

45. *Northanger* II, 14.

46. *Sense* III, 11.

47. *Emma* II, 18.

48. *Northanger* II, 5.

49. *MP* III, 7, 15; *Sense* II, 4.

50. *Sense* I, 13.

51. A. Byrne, ed., *A Scientific, Antiquarian and Picturesque Tour: John (Fiott) Lee in Ireland, England and Wales, 1806–1807* (London, 2018), 35, 42.

52. *Emma* II, 5.

53. *Sense* III, 7–8.

54. *Sense* II, 4.

55. *Juvenilia*, 136.

56. *Northanger* I, 13.

57. *PP* II, 14.

58. *MP* I, 10.

59. *Emma* II, 14; *Persuasion* II, 180.

60. *Sense* II, 3, 10.

61. J.-P. Forster, *Eighteenth-Century Geography and Representations of Space in English Fiction and Poetry* (Oxford, 2013).

62. The Usk valley.

63. *Juvenilia*, 108–9.

64. *Emma* II, 5.

65. *Emma* II, 5.

66. *MP* I, 2.

67. J. Dove, "Geographical Board Game: Promoting Tourism and Travel in Georgian England and Wales," *Journal of Tourism Research* 8 (2016):1–18.

68. *MP* III, 13.

69. *MP* III, 13.

70. *PP* III, 6.

71. *Emma* II, 16.

72. *Emma* II, 16.

73. P. Colquhoun, *The State of Indigence and the Situation of the Casual Poor in the Metropolis Explained* (London, 1799), 5.

74. D. Gerhold, *Carriers and Coachmasters: Trade and Travel before the Turnpikes* (Chichester, UK, 2005).

75. James Bland Burges to Reverend Lloyd, October 16, 1792, Oxford, Bodleian Library, Bland Burges papers vol. 48 fol. 152.

76. W. S. Baddeley, *History of Cirencester* (Cirencester, UK, 1924), 274.

77. J. Walvin, *Fruits of Empire: Exotic Produce and British Trade, 1660–1800* (Basingstoke, UK, 1997); J. Brewer, *The Pleasures of the Imagination: English Culture in the Eighteenth Century* (London, 1997).

78. *Northanger* II, 7.

79. *Sanditon* 6.

80. *Sense* II, 14.

81. H. Berry, "Polite Consumption: Shopping in Eighteenth-Century England," *Transactions of the Royal Historical Society*, ser. 6, 12 (2002): 375–94.

82. I am grateful to Henry Clark for his advice.

83. *Emma* II, 3.

84. *Emma* II, 6.

85. *Emma* II, 9.

86. *MP* III, 3.

87. *Sense* II, 14.

88. *Emma* II, 5.

89. *The Watsons*, in *Later Manuscripts*, 127; C. D. Edwards, *Eighteenth-Century Furniture* (Manchester, UK, 1996).

90. E. A. Wrigley, *Energy and the English Industrial Revolution* (Cambridge, 2010), 94.

91. P. Hudson, *Regions and Industries: A Perspective on the Industrial Revolution in Britain* (Cambridge, 1989).

92. *Northanger* I, 3; *PP* III, 5, 7.

93. E. Hopkins, *Birmingham: The First Manufacturing Town in the World, 1760–1840* (London, 1989); S. Whyman, *The Useful Knowledge of William Hutton: Culture and Industry in Eighteenth-Century Birmingham* (Oxford, 2018).

94. *Emma* II, 18.

95. *MP* III, 7.

96. J. Mokyr, *The Enlightened Economy: An Economic History of Britain, 1700–1850* (New Haven, CT, 2009).

97. *The Watsons*, in *Later Manuscripts*, 119.

98. *Sanditon* 7.

99. *Northanger* II, 15.

TEN

—ᘐᘐ—

A STATE AT WAR

ANXIETIES CENTERED ON NEW MONEY—or, indeed, on money itself—stretched back centuries. As such, these worries are found across much of literature. More specifically in England in the eighteenth century, these anxieties, especially about the cost of war and government projects and the corrupting poten-tial of a moneyed interest, were a key part in the Tory critique of Whiggery, as presented early in the century by such writers as Alexander Pope, Jonathan Swift, and Samuel Johnson. Linked to this critique, but separate to it, the monetary values of mat-rimonial options, and their denial of choice and romance, were not a new issue.

Austen's politics are a matter for debate.[1] She was scarcely an uncomplicated Tory, but then Toryism was not uncomplicated. Instead, it incorporated, or drew on, many different ideas, trends, and interests. The social location of anxiety was particularly problematic for Tories. There was hostility to new money and commerce but also concern about the attitudes of the greater aristocracy, who, in this period, were often Whigs. The chal-lenge of these interests was matched by worries about the habits, manners, and characteristics of both new money and aristocratic Whigs. Austen addresses these in her novels.

Her novels are not morality tales, however. They contain a real moral seriousness within their comedy, but she laughed at works in which any aesthetic merit is subordinated to didactic intent, such as Mary Brunton's *Self Control* (1811), which Austen mocked, in her *Plan of a Novel* (written in 1816), as a very well-meant, moral, improving tale "without anything of nature or probability in it." Instead, the inconsistencies, indeed hypocrisies, lanced by Austen, often with great humor, provide her with the principal means of critique.

Austen pursues a middle approach in terms of money and values that itself is part of the Tory self-image. For Austen, politeness and good behavior could smooth the disruption of money, as they could the hauteur of class. The latter is exposed to much criticism by Austen and provides an opportunity for moral points and personal development. Thus, Darcy in *Pride and Prejudice* has to learn to put his hauteur aside, as his aunt and the Bingley sisters fail to do.

Yet, drawing on the Tory approach, social hierarchy is not the root of these problems, even if stately homes are shown as a context for poor behavior, notably selfishness. Instead, commerce is the cause, for money itself is a challenge to social norms and therefore hierarchy. Moreover, money can threaten the consideration and considerations that underline good behavior, notably when assessing marital prospects. Austen addresses this issue repeatedly, and each novel offers contingent circumstances through which the solution can be pursued.

There is a superb, albeit early, source for Austen's political views. In her marginalia on Oliver Goldsmith's *History of England*, Austen repeatedly, and without equivocation, revealed herself as a Tory and frequent references the terms *Tory* and *Whig*. These marginalia were the prelude to her own brief *History of England*, written in late 1791, early in her life, but there is little cause to believe she would have changed her views subsequently. There was no reason for her to do so, not least because the personal context that gave rise to her Toryism, notably her Anglican piety, did not change at all. Theophilus Leigh (1691–1785), a great-uncle, was a prominent Tory Anglican. Elected master of Balliol College, Oxford, in 1726, through the influence of James, first Duke of Chandos, Leigh was vice-chancellor of Oxford from 1738 until 1741, as well as holding a rural living. As a result of graduating from Oxford, then one of only two universities in England, many clerics would have been well aware of him. Moreover, as another reason for a probable consistency in her views, the direction of English political culture during Austen's maturity was toward an accentuation and strengthening of Toryism. This was both in response to the French Revolution, which broke out in 1789, and with reference to the domestic radicalism, although that term was not used, this was thought to encourage. For many, this crisis was a reiteration of the English Civil War (1642–46), with the radicals in a direct line from the Puritans, and Austen closely associated herself with the cause of Charles I (r. 1625–49) during that conflict. Her marginal comments on Goldsmith went on to criticize anti-Catholicism during the Popish Plot, praise James II (r. 1685–88) and Queen Anne (r. 1702–14) but criticize the Whig hero William III (r. 1689–1702), and comment on the course of politics.

Some of the comments were very much those of the Jacobite Tories of the early eighteenth century. For example, when Goldsmith wrote: "Through the course of the English history, France seems to have been the peculiar object of the hatred of the Whigs; and a constitutional war with that country, seems to have been their aim," Austen added after "Whigs" the phrase "and without any reason," a reference to the commitment of William III, and the Whigs under Anne, to such a conflict.[2] "Of Henry Sidney [a prominent supporter of William of Orange in 1688], brother to Algernon [a participant in the Rye House Plot against James II], and uncle to the earl of Sunderland," she added, "Bad Breed,"[3] a characteristic response in a dynastic age. The Dutch and Sir

Richard Steele, a Whig, are criticized for their opposition to Queen Anne's Tory ministry.[4]

For the reign of George I (r. 1714–27), Henry, Viscount Bolingbroke, a major Tory writer and politician, is praised; in contrast, Thomas, Lord Coningsby, an ardent Whig, is criticized. Coningsby was a key mover in the impeachment for high treason in 1715 of Robert, Earl of Oxford, formerly Robert Harley, the chief minister in Anne's 1710–14 Tory government and also his local rival in Herefordshire. In addition, the habit of linking Tories with irrationality is mocked,[5] and Whig and Tory positions are counterpointed. Of Goldsmith's passage, which reflected its author's Irish background, "The Whigs governed the senate and the court; whom they could, they oppressed; bound the lower orders of people with severe laws, and kept them at a distance by vile distinctions; and then taught them to call this—liberty," Austen added, "Yes, This is always the Liberty of Whigs and Republicans." She had already observed of his treatment of the Jacobites and "James III," "Oh Dr Goldsmith Thou art as partial an Historian as myself!"[6] That was a reflection pertinent to the Tory critique of the Whigs in Austen's lifetime.

The close of Oxford's speech in his defense in the House of Lords, when impeached by the new Whig government under George I, is given by Goldsmith: "I shall lay down my life with pleasure, in a cause favoured by my late dear royal mistress [Queen Anne]. And when I consider that I am to be judged by the justice, honour, and virtue of my peers, I shall acquiesce, and retire with great content. And, my lords, God's will be done." Austen added, "Nobly said! Spoken like a Tory!"[7] This was also the language of Jacobites on the scaffold. Austen commented on Goldsmith's reflection that the Whigs, the party that had always called for freedom, were passing restrictive laws, "I have lived long enough in the World to know that it is always so!"[8] In the end, Oxford was acquitted.

Austen finds it surprising that Sir Robert Walpole, a Whig who was the leading minister from 1720 to 1742, helped sort out the mess after the financial crisis of the South Sea Bubble. With regard to the Atterbury Plot of 1722, she emphasizes not the treasonable plot on behalf of the Stuarts that certainly existed but, rather, the harsh and bullying way the government conducted the case.[9] Austen approved of the comment in the House of Lords by Allen, Lord Bathurst, a leading Tory, that the government's representation of correspondence as if it was treasonable meant that the Tories, thus under threat, should "retire to their country houses and there if possible, quietly to enjoy their estate, within their own families,"[10] a form of Tory quietism also seen with nonjuror clergy. Christopher Layer, who was convicted in 1722 and executed in 1723 for treason for his role in the Atterbury Plot, is twice described as a "Poor Man."[11] In addition, Goldsmith's reflection that the Whig government was "sometimes" corrupt is changed to "always," the opposition's aversion to "continental connexions" is described as very sensible, and a case of suicide by an impoverished family earns the rejoinder, "How much are the Poor to be pitied, and the Rich to be blamed!"[12] The moral worth of money is not to the fore in such comments.

Austen looks back to praise the Peace of Utrecht of 1713, a key achievement of Queen Anne's Tory government, and, in contrast, condemns the Whigs' Treaty of Aix-la-Chapelle of 1748.[13] Apart from her reiterated support for the Jacobite cause, Austen also expresses her commitment to continuity. Referring to the government's ban on the wearing of Highland dress and the bearing of arms in the aftermath of the suppression of the 1745 Jacobite rising, Austen added: "I do not like This—Every ancient custom ought to be sacred unless prejudicial to Happiness."[14]

These comments are very striking. There is nothing subsequent on this scale to indicate how far Austen's views changed. Those of 1791 are significant because history, notably that of the seventeenth century, was a key frame of reference for the response to the then present day,[15] indeed much more so than in modern Britain. Moreover, in response to the French Revolution, Toryism was very much to the fore, and Tory views were neither dangerous nor unpatriotic. Austen herself in 1791 offers the brash, exaggerated Toryism of a sixteen-year-old enthusiast. In her *History of England* she refers to herself, with very self-aware self-mockery, a "partial, prejudiced, and ignorant historian."

Critics have ably drawn attention to the evolution of Austen's literary style and to changes between early writings and the later novels, notably *Mansfield Park*. Yet those changes do not demonstrate any comparable alteration in her wider politics—indeed, far from it. There is no reason to think Austen later discarded Tory ideals, although in the mature work, her conservatism is a kind of understated backdrop. Arguably, the novels do their ideological work exactly by presenting a certain conservative Englishness as natural and unideological. In the novels, Austen comes across as an impartial, unprejudiced, wise narrator who assumes a similarly wise reader will share her broadly conservative views. In the absence of any other evidence, it is safer to present Austen as a Tory writer.

There are certainly indications to this effect, although they can be contextualized—indeed posed, even poised—with irony. In *Emma*, Austen uses the phrase "female right" in an ironic fashion, not least through being linked to refinement and Emma's snobbery.[16] Emma's notion of "female right" is not to do with the "rights of woman" in the sense used by Mary Wollstonecraft. Rather, this notion is to do with the gender-specific right of a beautiful young woman (Harriet) to be "refined" in her choice, pick and choose among suitors, and demand that anyone she accepts be a gentleman: the right of a beautiful woman to find upward mobility through marriage. It is this romantic-fiction notion of female privilege for which Emma is being mocked in this passage. Wollstonecraft herself objected to women's gaining power over men through sexual attraction. In conjunction with Emma's assertion that a pretty girl did not need brains and Mr. Knightley's preference for intelligence and sense in a woman (a view with which Wollstonecraft would have agreed), the content and tone display purpose and seriousness. This can be variously located ideologically, as it is as much religious and moral as political.

Subsequently, Mrs. Weston's proposal that the ball she was planning have "merely sandwiches, etc set out in the little room … was scouted as a wretched suggestion. A private dance, without sitting down to supper, was pronounced an infamous fraud upon the rights of men and women."[17] The ironic placement of these terms invites treating them with ridicule, and it is unclear how far radicalism is separated from the more mundane and widespread faults of being "pert and familiar."[18]

Austen certainly does not treat these terms seriously. At the same time, it is striking how lightly "the rights of men and women," which had recently been political dynamite, is being tossed around by the narrator and her characters. The mockery, a gentle mockery indeed, is being directed at these privileged young people who made their arguments for a proper ball and a proper supper with all the energy and indignation one would associate with urgent political demands. By 1814, these "rights" do not seem threatening anymore and can be invoked facetiously.

There are signs of Tory attitudes in Austen's other novels. In *Persuasion*, favor is shown to the Musgroves of the older generation: "The father and mother were in the old English style, and the young people in the new. Mr and Mrs Musgrove were a very good sort of people; friendly and hospitable, not much educated and not at all elegant. Their children had more modern minds and manners." The latter, in short, exemplified "alteration"— indeed, "improvement"—which Austen did not favor.[19] In the same novel, the villainous William Elliot is depicted as morally corrupted by, and through, his dominating and manipulative love for money. In part, this is a matter of marrying for money, but more is involved: "All the honour of the family he held as cheap as dirt. I have often heard him declare that if baronetcies were saleable, anybody should have his for fifty pounds, arms and motto, name and livery included," a dramatic rejection of the past and continuity. A letter of his, dated "as far back as July 1803," is cited: "My first visit to Kellynch will be with a surveyor, to tell me how to bring it with best advantage to the hammer."[20]

In *Sense and Sensibility*, Colonel Brandon, a hero, is presented as an appropriate improver, but the totally unimpressive John Dashwood is only concerned with his self-interest. Dashwood's monetarization of everything is shown most clearly in his attitude to the living of Delaford, which Brandon awards to Edward Ferrars on merit, rather than selling. Dashwood remarks: "I wonder he should be so improvident in a point of such common, such natural, concern!"[21] This comment underlines the complexity of the idea of "natural" behavior. *Sanditon* is conservative in that it presents the distortion of a traditional place and community by speculation on behalf of rootless people, which was very much a Tory position.

Given the current intellectual hostility in Britain to the Tory tradition, it is possibly as well for Austen's reputation in fashionable circles if that element of her beliefs is downplayed. This is ironic as the individual character of her Toryism, while different from those of, say, Alexander Pope, Jonathan Swift, Tobias Smollett, Samuel Johnson, or Benjamin Disraeli, serves as a reminder of the broad nature of that tradition and its ability to speak to many aspects of Englishness. Thus, in *Catherine, or the Bower* (1792), Austen has Catherine, her protagonist, disagree with her aunt, Mrs. Percival, an ultra-Tory, over what threatens "to overthrow the establishment of the kingdom." The unsympathetic and unreasonable aunt castigates Catherine's conduct: "The welfare of every nation depends upon the virtue of its individuals, and any one who offends in so gross a manner against decorum and propriety, is certainly hastening its ruin." Catherine contradicts her.[22] Austen here seems to be laughing at the extreme reactions to the French Revolution that see any kind of individual moral failing as leading straight to revolution.

Only hostile critics can treat Toryism, or indeed Englishness, or capitalism, or social change, as a monolith. Indeed, the political and social intimations of Austen's works can be regarded as symptomatic of tensions within the Toryism of that time and, to a major degree, as a debate about it. These tensions, in part, drew on the range of possible challenges to stability and continuity. The threat posed by the French Revolution and its English radical supporters is most apparent.

Yet there were also more long-standing issues. In particular, the dissolving character of money and commercial values, a Tory theme from the seventeenth century, had been joined, from the early eighteenth, to criticism of much of the higher aristocracy as Whig. That remained an issue in Austen's day. Indeed, given that Darcy might have been modeled on William, sixth Duke of Devonshire, a member of a leading Whig house and a close friend of the prince regent, the future George IV, this is directly pertinent in *Pride and Prejudice*. In actuality, any political focus there on Darcy and his linkage to a real person is not pushed forward. Darcy is presented as an excellent landlord with basic good principles. All he needs to do is modify his pride.

George III (r. 1760–1820) offered a different politics to that of the Whigs, not least in his sensitivity to the views of formerly Jacobite families, such as the Ailesburys. On his way back from Weymouth in 1789, George stayed with Thomas, first Earl of Ailesbury, a friend and also lord chamberlain to Queen Charlotte. This was at Tottenham Park, which was not far from Steventon, the rectory of Austen's father. George played cribbage, drove in an open chaise around Savernake Forest (George himself driving), and received a loyal address from the mayor and corporation of Marlborough.[23] In 1789, he also received such an address from

Devizes, another nearby town, and in 1801 and 1804 from South-ampton, one of Hampshire's leading cities.

These were important aspects of George's public politics, with popular loyalty and royal graciousness displayed in an interactive pageant. These occasions were extensively covered in the local press and would have been much commented on by the locals. Thus, in 1789, George also visited Lord Digby's seat of Sherborne Castle and was applauded by vast crowds in the park. George stayed to dinner. The trip also took him to Redlynch, the seat of the Earl of Ilchester; Longleat, the seat of Thomas, first Marquess of Bath; and Stourhead. None of these was far from where Austen lived.

The popular responses to the king were aspects of the strong loyalism already apparent prior to the French Revolution—for example, in the success of the government in the 1784 general election, which was a very clear endorsement of George's removal of the Fox-North ministry the previous December. Pitt the Younger's ministry won a strong endorsement at the election, and he was prime minister for much of Austen's life, from 1783–1801 and 1804–6. Female loyalism was significant throughout this period and was seen with literary figures such as Fanny Burney. Austen lived against the background of this varied loyalism and was part of it.

In the words of Adam Smith in his essay "Of Publick Debts," published in his transformative *An Inquiry into the Nature and Causes of the Wealth of Nations* (1776), a book that appeared a year after Austen's birth and that influenced both William Pitt the Younger and Robert, second Earl of Liverpool, prime minister from 1812 to 1827: "In great empires the people who live in the capital, and in provinces remote from the scene of action, feel many of them scarce any inconveniency from the war; but enjoy, at their ease, the amusement of reading in the newspapers the exploits of their own fleets and armies. To them this amusement compensates the small difference between the taxes which they pay on account of the war, and those which they had been accustomed to pay in time of peace."[24]

Such an interpretation might seem to be backed by the world depicted in Austen's novels, but only if that reading is superficial. Indeed, as recent research has emphasized, although there was nothing to match the engagement with economics of Daniel Defoe, a journalist as well as a novelist,[25] her novels make frequent reference to military matters. In *Persuasion*, Captain Wentworth talks about how he was in a sloop (small warship) that later "broke up" and how he might have been a "gallant Captain Wentworth" in a newspaper report—in other words, a dead one. Anne shudders silently at the thought. We get a sense of the effects of war on noncombatants rather different than that conveyed by Adam Smith.

Readers, moreover, were expected to understand matters such as prize money from captured ships. Moreover, readers were widely affected by the precarious world of credit and debt, which was greatly dependent on international developments. More particularly, the urban economy heavily relied on trade, including international trade and related industrial and financial activity, while its rural counterpart, influenced by the impact of war on food imports, was affected by high wartime taxation. Privateering, impressment, and recruitment hit the national economy and bore down upon the economies of individual families and communities.

Irrespective of their ideological position, the fate of the Continent therefore engaged the attention of the British during the French Revolutionary and Napoleonic Wars, indeed far more so than in recent wars. After 1741, French advances into central Europe during the War of the Austrian Succession (1740–8) had been checked; in that war, the French had taken several years to conquer the Austrian Netherlands (modern Belgium) and invade the United Provinces (modern Netherlands). In the Seven Years' War (1756–63), there had been no fighting in the Low Countries, and the French had been less than successful in their German operations and had been defeated by the British at Minden in 1759. In the American Revolutionary War (1775–83), once it had broadened to include conflict with the French and Spaniards from 1778 and 1779 respectively, there had been no campaigns on the Continent, except for the lengthy, but unsuccessful, Spanish siege of Gibraltar.

In contrast, the French overran much of Europe in the years from 1792, and their rapid conquest of the whole of the Austrian Netherlands that November was but the first of their dramatic advances. How Britain, then at peace, would respond was initially unclear. A self-contained and somewhat distant political attitude toward the Continent was advocated by the MP and experienced diplomat William, Lord Auckland, who wrote to the prime minister, William Pitt the Younger, in 1790: "Whatever may be the course of circumstances, my political creed turns on the expediency of avoiding wars abroad and innovations at home: nothing else is wanting to confirm for a long period the elevated point on which we stand above all the nations of the world either in present times or in history."[26]

It was not to be. British policy changed dramatically as a result of the French Revolution. Although many of the revolutionaries initially looked to British institutions for inspiration while, much to the dismay of Edmund Burke, Britain did not join Austria and Prussia in attacking Revolutionary France in 1792, war with France broke out the following February. With two brief gaps in 1802–3 and 1814, it lasted until 1815.

As a result of the revolutionary crisis, a similar process occurred in Britain and France in the early 1790s: the definition of a political perspective in which foreign and domestic challenges were closely linked and in which it seemed crucial to mobilize mass support for a struggle with an insidious, but also all-too-apparent, enemy—an obvious foreign rival supporting domestic conspiracy and insurrection. This is a singularly modern theme, although, in fact, it goes back to antiquity. A language of nationalism, to which paranoia contributed, therefore developed. In France, revolution was the cause and consequence of this struggle. In contrast, in Britain, the challenge of domestic radicalism and Revolutionary France led to widespread rallying to Country, Crown, and Church that was violently expressed in Church and Crown riots from 1791 and sustained thereafter, albeit with difficulties. This paralleled similar loyalist movements elsewhere in Europe.

Britain was also involved more closely with the Continent than earlier in the eighteenth century thanks to her major and very lengthy role in the struggle with Revolutionary, and then Napoleonic, France. This process culminated in the leading part taken by Britain at the Congress of Vienna (1814–15) and on the battlefield of Waterloo (1815), both of which were key episodes for Austen's contemporaries. The French Revolution thus both focused British political concern on the Continent and introduced a marked ideological slant to British political culture in which domestic cultural and political preferences were clearly matched to, and given opposing force by, differing responses to the situation on the Continent. British society was mobilized for war—not on a scale to compare with Revolutionary France, where there was conscription, and still less with modern "total war," but nevertheless to an extent that was far greater than in other conflicts of the time.

Austen's life found Britain at war, or close to war, and she published her first two novels in wartime and wrote others then. The headline conflicts were the American Revolutionary War, followed by war with France, first Revolutionary and then Napoleonic. This war, which broke out in 1793, lasted until Napoleon's total defeat at Waterloo, with two brief intervals in 1802–3 and 1814–15. There was also the War of 1812, in fact from 1812–15, with the United States, which included three unsuccessful US invasions of Canada, as well as US naval action across the globe.

In addition, there were many other wars and threats of war. The former were particularly the case in India, where there were large-scale conflicts with the Marathas or Mysore in 1775–82, 1790–92, 1799, 1803–5, and 1817–18, as well as smaller-scale conflicts. Threats of war included with France in 1787 in the Dutch crisis, with France and Spain in 1790 in the Nootka Sound crisis, and with Russia in 1791 in the Ochakov crisis, although none involved Britain in war. So also during the French Revolutionary and Napoleonic Wars, including periods of serious confrontation with Russia and Turkey, notably (but not only) in 1800 and 1807 respectively.

Thus, war, or at least the risk of war, was to the fore for much of Austen's life, although she was not a military child, as was the novelist Charlotte Lennox. As a result, Charlotte was born in Gibraltar and grew up in part in North America. There were references in Austen's work to Britain's wars. In her *A Collection of Letters*, written in 1791 or 1792, "Miss Jane," secretly married to Captain Dashwood, cries because "he fell while fighting for his country in America,"[27] a reference to the American Revolutionary War of 1775–83. That collection shows the social prominence of the military, as other characters include Colonel Seaton, "Miss Jane's" father, the late admiral Annesley, and the colonel who adores Henrietta Hatton and proposes to her. So also with *A Letter from a Young Lady*, in which Anna Parker is to marry Colonel Martin of the Horseguards, an elite regiment, in thanks for her lying in court to enable him to set aside his father's will and do down his older brother. This is a prelude to her going on to murder her sister in what is a deliberately lurid tale.[28] In *Emma*, there is Colonel Campbell; his friend Lieutenant Fairfax has died in action abroad, with his wife following soon after, leaving Jane Fairfax an orphan.[29] Less positively, in *Persuasion*, the useless Richard Musgrove had died while a midshipman.[30]

Southern England, more particularly the area where Austen lived much of her life, played a crucial role in the mobilization and movement of troops. Those going abroad generally embarked via nearby Portsmouth. In contrast, Plymouth in Devon was difficult to access by land while shipping from London meant having to work around Kent and through the Straits of Dover, which was difficult against the prevailing westerly winds. Instead, Portsmouth, where Austen's brother Francis entered the tough, and fee-charging, Royal Navy Academy in 1786, was the key port for the navy, the East India Company, and troops going abroad. Indeed, expensive proposed government measures for its defense created a parliamentary storm in 1786 and led to a rare parliamentary defeat for William Pitt the Younger.

In wartime, the roads of Hampshire were thronged with troop movements. So also with wagons carrying supplies for the forces and live animals being driven to Portsmouth for use on ships. Portsmouth, indeed, was a growing market for Hampshire's grain and livestock, in large part thanks to its military role. For the farmers, this was very profitable. Hampshire was also a county that produced a disproportionate number of naval officers, as did Kent and the Southwest, both areas of interest to Austen.

Hampshire's naval busyness became even more apparent when invasion was feared. This was particularly so in 1779 when France and Spain planned a joint invasion to be launched against Portsmouth. However, the invasion preparations were thwarted by the consequences of delay, including the outbreak of disease among the assembled troops. As another aspect of national strengthening during such crises, the clergy were instructed to organize national prayer and fast days, which was very much encouraged by George III.

After peace for Britain in Europe for a decade (for 1783–93), the military situation became acute in the 1790s. Britain entered war with France in 1793, with the support of the other major naval powers—the Dutch and Spain, as well as Austria, Prussia, and Savoy-Piedmont—only for the Dutch to be overrun by French forces in 1795 and Spain, having been defeated and negotiated peace in 1795, to join France against Britain in 1796. Prussia had also left the war with France in 1795. As a result, Britain, its forces driven with serious losses from the Continent, was both outnumbered at sea and vulnerable to invasion. Indeed, French forces were landed in Wales in 1797 and, far more seriously, in Ireland in 1798, although both expeditions were defeated. So also with Dutch, French, and Spanish fleets in 1797–98 in the battles of Camperdown (1797), the Nile (1798), and Cape St. Vincent (1797) respectively. These naval victories were valuable boosts to Britain's fortunes and morale and greatly compensated for earlier naval setbacks. The sole earlier victory of scale, at the battle of the Glorious First of June (1794), had only a limited impact on French fortunes.

The seemingly perpetual threat of invasion made British success at sea crucial, indeed apparently providential. That was the theme of sermons, such as those of Edward Nares, who is mentioned later in the chapter, and also of *Naucratia: or Naval Dominion* (1798), by the lackluster poet laureate, Henry Pye. It was only Horatio Nelson's major naval victory at Trafalgar on October 21, 1805, that made invasion appear far less of a threat. Frank Austen was unlucky to miss action in that battle as involvement was a source of much glory.

Despite Trafalgar, Napoleon continued to build up his naval strength, notably at Antwerp, the target of the unsuccessful Walcheren expedition in 1809, and, in its continual vigilance of blockade, the British navy remained the key line of defense against French forces. Austen's brothers were part of the unprecedented mobilization of the nation.

Naval power not only provided protection but also permitted Britain to dominate the European transoceanic world during the French Revolutionary and Napoleonic Wars. Naval victories left Britain free to execute amphibious attacks against the now-isolated centers of other European empires, such as Dutch-ruled Batavia (Djakarta). Thus, British naval power helped make French control of Louisiana redundant. Indeed, Napoleon's sale of territory to the United States in 1803 was an apt symbol of the Eurocentrism that, despite interest in the Caribbean, was a leading feature of French policy after the failure of the Egyptian expedition as a result of Nelson's victory at the battle of the Nile (1798), although Napoleon also hoped, with reason, that the sale would harm Anglo-American relations to the advantage of France.

British success owed much to her naval power but more to her insular status. Of the islands lying off the European mainland, only Britain was both independent and a major power. This allowed, indeed required, her to concentrate on her naval forces. This was unlike her Continental counterparts, which devoted major resources to their armies, even those, like France and Spain, that were also maritime powers.

Despite Britain's naval power and successes, the Revolutionary and Napoleonic Wars with France were an extremely difficult as well as lengthy struggle, and it was by no means clear that French domination of western Europe would be short-lived. The defeat and overthrow of Napoleon in 1812–14 owed much to Austria, Prussia, and Russia. It would have been impossible for Britain alone to have overthrown his Continental empire. In practice, final British success in Spain in 1813, won under the command of the Duke of Wellington, in part depended on the concentration of French forces in Germany. The British also played a crucial role in Napoleon's eventual defeat in 1815, and, during the war, about thirty thousand men joined the army annually. This commitment was not separate from British history in the nineteenth century but rather was important to British society and a formative experience for the British nation over the following century.

In defensive terms, the Royal Navy was backed up by a large-scale mobilization of national manhood while the repeated threat of French invasion drove defensive precautions. Thus, in August 1792, prior to the war spreading to involve Britain but with conflict already on the other side of the English Channel, there was a large militia encampment on Bagshot Heath that was inspected by George III and much reported in the press, including in the *Reading Mercury*, which was read in Steventon Rectory. Many traveled to see the encampment, including some from the Steventon area. Moreover, the sounds of the practice volleys would have been heard.

In the winters of 1793–94 and 1794–95, the South Devon Militia was posted to Hampshire, where the naval base at Portsmouth was a source of particular vulnerability. They were quartered at Basingstoke, near Steventon. In the summers of 1793 and 1794, there were militia camps at Brighton, to protect the Sussex coast, and they are mentioned in *Pride and Prejudice*.[31] At the same time, concern about domestic radicalism led to the construction of new barracks from 1792—for example, in Norwich (1792–93) and Coventry (1793).

The attraction of the military in such camps had implications for the frustrations of rural dullness in *Pride and Prejudice*, as well as for female sexuality. The appeal of regimentals, which were only worn by men, is a significant theme in that novel, and indeed uniforms were impressive, tickled vanity, and were "a splendid piece of propaganda."[32] A ball takes on added value if officers are present. More generally, there was the dangerous link between the license to kill and the energy of seduction that was taken even further with the rakish seducer Major Sanford in Hannah Foster's novel *The Coquette* (1797). A soldier committed to seduction but promising marriage was the central danger in *The History of Susan Gray* (1815), the novel that made Mary Sherwood, another daughter of a cleric, successful. She had attended the same school at Reading as Austen.

Of the 162,300 effective rank-and-file troops in Britain in 1798, only 47,700 were regulars, with the rest militia and volunteer units. The latter showed the deep-rooted patriotism of the period. Moreover, these units underlined the need for the state to cooperate with local interests in obtaining resources at the same time as reinforcing the hierarchical structure. Indeed, militia colonels regarded their regiments as patronage fiefs that were immensely valuable to them as county magnates and public men for both patronage and prestige. As a result, important changes in the militia laws had to be negotiated with the colonels, and even the practice of regular drafts into the army was carefully conducted to protect their interest.[33]

Austen's social options were affected by the militarization of society possibly more than she knew. Austen may have attended the winter assembly balls in Basingstoke that were frequented by the officers of the South Devon Militia. In Kent in August 1805, a year of justified invasion panic, Austen was invited to a grand ball at Deal where "no gentlemen but of the garrison are invited,"[34] only for the ball to be canceled due to the death of William, Duke of Gloucester, the king's brother. Court mourning was an important religious and social obligation and would have been particularly significant for the army. Invasion fears that year were only quietened (later) by Trafalgar, and Kent would have been in the front line of any invasion. It was assumed that French troops, having landed on the coast closest to France, would march across the county en route to London.

Meanwhile, the cost and economic disruption of the war years, which indeed contributed to the rapidly rising production costs of books, were linked to serious pressures on living standards. Average real wages stagnated, and there was widespread hardship, especially in the near-famine years of 1795–96 and 1799–1801.[35] In his first *Essay on the Principle of Population* (1798), Thomas Malthus (1766–1834), a clergyman then living in rural Surrey, the setting for *Emma*, wrote: "The sons of labourers are very apt to be stunted in their growth and are a long while arriving at maturity. Boys that you would guess to be fourteen or fifteen are . . . frequently found to be eighteen or nineteen . . . a want either of proper or sufficient nourishment." Malthus advocated celibacy and delayed marriage as the means to cope with population pressures. As a reminder of the linkage of different themes, settings, and people in Austen's lifetime, he died in Bath and was buried in the abbey.

Population problems were accentuated by the benefits that others, such as farmers, drew from the economic strains of the period. Aside from serious food rioting caused by price rises, naval mutinies in 1797 owed much to anger over pay and conditions, as well as political radicalism. These mutinies threatened national security. Social stability appeared precarious, and radical societies were banned in 1799 for fear of the consequences in an increasingly difficult international and domestic situation.[36]

This sense of alarm was captured in *Northanger Abbey* but was also very much held at satirical bay by placing it alongside the fears created through reading novels:

> You, Miss Morland—my stupid sister has mistaken all your clearest expressions. You talked of expected horrors in London—and instead of instantly conceiving, as any rational creature would have done, that such words could relate only to a circulating library, she immediately pictured to herself a mob of three thousand men assembling in St George's Fields; the Bank [of England] attacked, the Tower [of London] threatened, the streets of London flowing with blood, a detachment of the 12th Light Dragoons, (the hopes of the nation,) called up from Northampton to quell the insurgents, and the gallant Capt. Frederick Tilney, in the moment of charging at the head of his troops, knocked off his horse by a brickbat from a upper window.[37]

Despite instability and a profound sense of alarm, the country (England, Wales, and Scotland; Ireland was different) nevertheless did not collapse into disorder. Nor was there famine or any eating of the seed corn. The greater popularity of George III in the 1790s helped. His popularity had already been apparent in the response to the Regency Crisis of 1788–89, the Whigs' attempt to use the king's unprecedented poor health to take over the government via George, Prince of Wales, with whom the Whigs were closely linked.

This popular response was very much seen in southern England during George's 1789 tour after his recovery, and the news of his enthusiastic reception would certainly have been heard in Steventon. Visiting Longleat, the seat of Viscount Weymouth, Queen Charlotte recorded: "His Majesty, the three Princesses and myself went in an open chaise [carriage] down the avenue and back again to satisfy the populace who were extremely desirous to see the King." George Huntingford, master of the school at Warminster, reported of this occasion: "At least twenty thousand persons were assembled to see them . . . every one present beheld them, and I believe nineteen out of the twenty were most highly gratified."[38]

George cultivated, with increasing success from the 1780s and even more 1800s, the image of being a father to all, and he did not inspire the large-scale negative feelings aimed at his French and Spanish counterparts. In the 1800s, the king was favorably contrasted with Napoleon, who was presented, with reason, as a violent bully and usurper. The patriotism of the war, and the king's virtual disengagement from day-to-day politics, combined fruitfully to facilitate the celebration less of the reality and more of the symbol of monarchy. The Jubilee celebrations of 1809 were a case in point. Thus, the precondition of the creation of a popular monarchy was the perceived decline in the Crown's political authority.

The association of radicalism with the French in the 1790s also helped damn it for most people, not least because of the anarchy, terror, and irreligion increasingly linked, in most English minds, to the French Revolution—notably so from 1792. In *Catherine, or the Bower* (1792), Austen refers to the "state of affairs in the political world . . . Mrs P, who was firmly of opinion that the whole race of mankind were degenerating, said that for her part, everything she believed was going to rack and ruin, all order was destroyed over the face of the world. The House of Commons she heard did not break up sometimes till five in the morning, and depravity never was so general before."[39]

As with much of Europe, patriotism in Britain, in this period and thereafter, was heavily, and increasingly, associated with anti-French sentiments and thus, from the early 1790s, to a considerable extent, conservative ones. Correspondingly, in Britain, although not only there, conservatism was increasingly nationalistic in tone and content. The experience of the Napoleonic Wars, in particular, underscored a patriotic discourse on British distinctiveness while simultaneously creating a new iconography of national military heroes. Thus, Robert Southey (1774–1843), who became poet laureate in 1813, developed the language of patriotism. War with France was justified on moral grounds. Southey also wrote patriotic accounts of Nelson, Wellington, and John, first Duke of Marlborough, the general of victory in the 1700s and the great-grandfather of Edward Nares's host at Blenheim, to again underline links. In the 1800s, "God Save the King," which had first been sung publicly during the acute Jacobite invasion crisis in 1745, became the national anthem. The Golden Jubilee of George III's reign, celebrated on October 25, 1809, provided a major opportunity for the display of respect and affection for the king as a central part of patriotism. Austen herself was no Southey, but she drew on the same attitudes.

The rallying to Church and Crown in response to the French Revolution played a potent role in the definition of nationhood, both British and English. The notion of objective national interests had developed rapidly during the eighteenth century, in large part as a product of the eighteenth-century Enlightenment proposition that humans live in a universe governed by natural laws that proclaim, among other things, the existence of nations, defined through a mixture of geography, language, culture, physical features, and even traits of personality, and that the interests of nations essentially are to be defined in terms of protecting their geographical, cultural, and physical (i.e., security) integrity.

Nationalism was not only a matter of long-term trends. The short-term crisis of the French Revolutionary period was also crucial, especially for Austen. In Britain, in November 1792, as a panic about pro-French radicalism rose toward a peak at a period of rapid French advance, Lord Auckland, who was never reluctant to give advice, called for a program of indoctrination in order to achieve an acceptable politicization of the country:

> Every possible form of Proclamations to the People, orders for Fast Days, Speeches from the Throne, Discourses from the Pulpit, Discussions in Parliament etc. I am sure that we should gain ground by this. The prosperity and opulence of England are such, that except the lowest and most destitute class, and men of undone fortunes and desperate pursuits, there are none who would not suffer essentially in their fortunes, occupations, comfort, in the glory, strength and well-being of their country, but above all in that sense of security which forms the sole happiness of life, by this new species of French disease which is spreading its contagion among us . . . the abandoning of religion is a certain step towards anarchy.[40]

This mixture of national identity, economic interest, religious conviction, and a "sense of security" proved potent. Loyalism was a genuine mass movement, especially in England, even if it proved difficult to sustain the level of individual engagement and the relationship between government and loyalism could be ambiguous.

There were many people not comprehended within loyalism, which underlines the problematic character of thinking in terms of a zeitgeist, or spirit of the age. Indeed, the 1770s onward saw an alternative model of political order that posed a substantial threat to the ideological confidence, even smugness, of both Whig and Tory elements in British politics. This alternative model was deployed with great effectiveness in the 1790s by the radicals, particularly Tom Paine,[41] in a way that potentially undercut the attempt to tar radicalism with the slur of advocating pro-French principles. Thus, the attempt to associate radicalism with Revolutionary France was, to a degree, a carefully orchestrated polemical move, rather than a wholly obvious and uncontentious one. Again, this served to underline the need for nuance in dealing with the clear-cut identification of certain assumptions and values as characterizing the apparently uniform abstraction known as British opinion.

A combination of the potential universal mission of the new republic, the real or feared aspirations of British radicals, and the response of British conservatives ensured that the French Revolution came to play a major role in British politics. Edmund Burke's determined insistence that what happened in France was of direct relevance to Britain appeared somewhat implausible when he published his *Reflection on the Revolution in France, and on the Proceedings in Certain Societies in London Relative to That Event* on November 1, 1790, for France was then very weak.[42]

Burke's views soon seemed vindicated by events because, as the French Revolution became more radical, it nevertheless continued to attract a measure of domestic British support, culminating in December 1792 in an insurrection that was feared by the government but never occurred.

The British radicals who appealed to the French National Convention for support—sending, for example, petitions and other messages—played into Burke's hands. At the same time, their activities reflected a perception they shared with Burke that events in France were of direct relevance to Britain and that Britain was necessarily involved in a wider European struggle between the supporters and opponents of revolution. Indeed, Catholics during the Reformation, and Communists and Fascists during the Nazi-Soviet Pact of 1939–41, are but instances of a wider process in which the opponents of the state aligned with hostile foreign powers, and very deliberately so.

Burke's analysis of direct relevance had been resisted by the Pitt ministry in the spring, summer, and early autumn of 1792, when the ministry had insisted on neutrality despite the outbreak of the French Revolutionary War that spring between France on one side and Austria and Prussia on the other. However, the entry of Britain into the conflict the following February, in response to a declaration of war by the French National Convention, transformed the situation. The French Revolutionary and Napoleonic Wars reshaped British patriotism, strengthening its association with conservatism in place of its earlier eighteenth-century identification with reforming traditions.

The Church played a major role in the equation. Thus, in 1797, the Reverend Edward Nares (1762–1841), fellow of Merton College Oxford (1788–97) and, later, Regius Professor of Modern History at Oxford (1813–41), preached a sermon on a day of public thanksgiving for a series of British naval victories. Published in 1798, it was dedicated to Elizabeth, Viscountess Bateman, the wife of one of his patrons. This combination of links reflected the nature of what has been termed the English church-state,[43] which indeed encompassed Austen. Just as Burke had stressed the moral lessons to be drawn from history, which he saw as involving the will of God, so Nares proclaimed the value of history because it displayed the providential plan. In terms that reflected his assessment of the current situation in Europe, Nares contrasted the historical perspective with the destructive secular philosophy of present-mindedness with its sense of the end of history:

> The enemy begin their operations on the pretended principle of giving perfect freedom to the mind of man. I call it a pretended principle, not only because their subsequent actions have been entirely in contradiction to it, but because, in fact no principle, as the world at present stands, could be found more inimical to the real interests of human nature. For it is plain, that the first step to be taken in vindication of such a principle, is to discard all ancient opinions as prejudices; every form of government, however matured by age, is to

be submitted afresh to the judgment and choice of the passing generation, and the Almighty to be worshipped (if at all) not according
to the light vouchsafed to our fore-fathers, but as every short-lived
inhabitant of the earth shall, in his wisdom, think proper and sufficient . . . when the calamities of war befall us, we are not irrational
in considering these also as under the direction of God. . . . The great
point is to discover the heavenly purposes.

Nares's sermon, which paralleled the idiom of Anglican sermons in the Seven Years' War (1756–63), as well as in other conflicts, came to the reassuring conclusion that British victories
proved the existence and role of divine support. The perception of
Britain's imperial destiny as having both a providential purpose
and providential endorsement was a central plank in the Church
of England's public theology. Moreover, the French Revolution
gave new energy to the defense of established Christianity. In
1805, Nares delivered the Bampton Lectures at Oxford, defending Christianity in his *A View of the Evidences of Christianity at
the End of the Pretended Age of Reason* against "modern infidels."
In 1808 and 1809, Nares was a select preacher at the university. As
he eloped with Lady Charlotte Spencer (the second daughter of
George, fourth Duke of Marlborough), whom he met at Blenheim
at amateur theatricals, Nares appears in a very different context
in chapter two.

In the face of the new challenge from Revolutionary France,
there was also much charity and sympathy for French refugees,
including Catholic clerics. The Jesuit school for English Catholics, originally founded abroad at St. Omer in 1593, moved to
Stonyhurst in Lancashire in 1794. Once atheistic France had been
identified with the Antichrist, Catholics could appear as allies.
However, as a reminder of the range of religious views, militant
millenarians took the view that the revolution would hasten the
fall of the papacy and, therefore, bring about the apocalypse.

The defense of what was presented as the British system took a
number of forms. The dedication of the *Supplement* to George III

in the third edition of the *Encyclopaedia Britannica,* which was published in 1801, declared that it was designed to counteract the *Encyclopédie.* The repository of wisdom and opinion of the enlightened French *philosophes,* the *Encyclopédie* came to be seen as a precipitant of revolution there. The king himself was in no doubt of the religious need to support the constitution. In 1793, he wrote to Pitt: "I most devoutly pray to Heaven that this constitution may remain unimpaired to the latest posterity as a proof of the wisdom of the nation and its knowledge of the superior blessings it enjoys."[44] Eight years later, referring to Catholic emancipation and architecture, George told Charles, eleventh Duke of Norfolk, "Take care not to meddle with the foundations,"[45] which was an example of his sense of humor: Norfolk, a Whig, was then carrying out building works at his seat at Arundel Castle.

The revolutionary and Napoleonic period witnessed both a renewal of the ideological themes of the British ancien régime and the birth of modern British conservatism, with its skepticism about the possibilities of secular improvement and its stress on historical continuity and national values, rather than present-mindedness and internationalism or the alternative modern impetus behind British conservatism, the furtherance of capitalism, and the concomitant defense of certain sectional interests. This Burkean conservatism was not necessarily restricted to Britain: Burke himself treated prerevolutionary Europe as a community and a commonwealth, was very concerned about the situation in France, and was averse to any peace with her that did not entail a counterrevolution. However, a stress on continuity and the value of specific constitutional and political inheritances did not readily lend itself to serving as the basis of an international ideology. The appeal to history against reason was inherently nationalist.

There was a broader pattern of stability in change, and change in stability, that helped, alongside governmental antirevolutionary measures, ensure that revolution was avoided in England, unlike in Ireland, despite multiple tensions.[46] Violence itself could serve as a release of tension: the nature of rioting, as a form of assertion of social norms, against what was seen as unfair disruption and innovation,[47] itself contributed to this essential cohesiveness around a "moral economy" that could align with loyalism, not least in terms of the defense of custom. Linked to this cohesion, the ideological dominance of a Christian moral "politeness" was significant.

As a consequence, political discussion, thought, and reflection were not divorced from their ethical context. There was little difference between upbraiding food hoarders as the cause of riots and declaiming against drunkenness or slavery. This morality drew on the major cultural themes of the middling orders in this period, especially Christian conduct, polite behavior, moral improvement, and the pursuit of a benign stability, and it was important to the shaping of that body of society and, by exclusion, the rest as well.

This shaping was not only from the pulpit. Thus, many items in the press served as secular sermons and were clearly intended as such. An admonitory tone characterized much of the discussion of politics and society, from the press to the pulpit. In *Persuasion*, Charles Hayter, the curate, takes up the newspaper to preempt conversation with Captain Wentworth while, very differently, the Bath paper offers news of arrivals there,[48] as was indeed its practice. Newspapers were part of the furniture in the sense of always being around. At a ball in *Persuasion*, Tom Bertram, who does not wish to dance, "took a newspaper from the table" and referred to news from America, probably a reference to the War of 1812 with Britain. Subsequently, Henry Crawford and Dr. Grant discuss politics at dinner at the latter's, and Henry soon after walks up with the newspaper in his hand. In Portsmouth, Mr. Price regularly borrows a newspaper from a neighbor, thus informing Fanny of Maria Bertram deserting her husband, and Mary Crawford assumes that Fanny Price gets political news via the press.

Sir John Middleton provides Mrs. Dashwood with his newspaper every day, and it is presumably one of those that Mr. Palmer reads when he calls on her.[49] In *Northanger Abbey*, General Tilney reads a newspaper at breakfast, probably a London one, but the family also has access to the Bath paper so Henry can note arrivals there.[50]

Moralizing, and therefore morality, were readily on offer from the newspapers as well as sermons. A complaint in the *General Advertiser and Morning Intelligencer* of August 16, 1777, about the drunkenness of a coach driver on the Brightelmstone [Brighton] stage coach, a service to and from London, began: "It is with the utmost pleasure that you give admittance, in your sensible and impartial paper, to every complaint that affects the public. It ought, and you have most judiciously made it the business of your paper, to hold up in exposure whatever is rendered obnoxious or hurtful by crime or malice." The *Middlesex Journal* of October 21, 1783, complained about the number of prostitutes on the streets of London and their shocking obscenities and proposed that they should be taxed and restricted to certain streets. No such restrictions, of course, were proposed for their clients. This aspect of the city did not feature in Austen's novels.

The shaping of the middling orders in terms of a set of practices and opinions required their agreement and thus entailed encouraging resonances to elicit group identification. An emphasis on the importance of the values of the middling orders for the entire community also helped focus attention on the press. A sense of what was appropriate, and thus respectable, was inculcated through print. In part, this reflected the success of creating a common code of behavior for what was termed "polite" society, which spanned town and countryside. However, the frequent attacks on popular superstitions, drunkenness, and activities thought to characterize a distressingly wide section of the population, such as profanity and cruelty to animals, do not suggest the press was asserting values shared by all.

Instead, the press offered a socially specific moral resonance appropriate for a medium with restricted circulation. This would not have disturbed writers calling for the moralizing of a supposedly dissolute population; subscribers to good causes wishing to see their names, causes, and prejudices recorded for posterity; or sellers offering high-value goods and services that required advertising in a world where advertising other than orally was uncommon. More broadly, the press reflected the interests and views of the middling orders. Thus, *Jackson's Oxford Journal* of July 3, 1790, reported:

> The riots so usual at contested elections have been uncommonly violent in many of the county boroughs, but none perhaps have been so dangerous as those at Leicester and Nottingham. The four candidates at the former town, imitating the example of greater men, on Wednesday last entered into a coalition to return one Member [MP] for each party. This junction was no sooner made public, than it became the signal for one of the most mischievous riots we ever heard of. The mob were so exasperated at being bilked of further extortion on the several candidates, that they broke open the town-hall, and completely gutted it. They made a bonfire of the Quarter Sessions Books, and the records of the town, burnt the public library, and would have murdered the Coalitionists, could they have got at them. Several persons have been most severely wounded, and one man is killed. It was not till after the military were called in, and the Riot Act read, that the mob was dispersed.

Criticism in this case, therefore, was directed not at the agreement among the elite to prevent a contest but rather at the popular response. This was an aspect of a political, social, economic, and moral paternalism that was, for example, against worker activism but contributed to the loyalism opposed to the French Revolution.

The frequent stress in the press on charitable acts by the fortunate was symptomatic of this "top-down" approach. Paternalism grounded in moral behavior and religious attitudes, rather than economic dominance, was the justification for the social policy required by the well-ordered society that was presented by the press as a necessary moral goal. Public opinion was not treated as an essentially democratic political phenomenon—understandably so given the nature of the constitution and the Christian-backed morality of the period.

Paternalism and loyalism were insufficient. Instead, the strain of the war, the anxieties arising from the defeat of Britain and its allies by France, and concerns stemming from domestic radicalism led to a major series of reform initiatives in the late 1790s and early 1800s in a pattern that was somewhat different from the active, but unambitious, state with a more modest agenda seen earlier in the century.[51] These reforms included the introduction of income tax in 1799, which helped make possible a shift from financing war by borrowing to financing it through taxation, thus tapping different revenue sources and types of wealth. In addition, Britain in 1797 came off the gold standard—the ready and fixed convertibility of the currency into gold.

Separately, parliamentary union with Ireland (1800–1) was regarded as a key way to reduce the vulnerability represented by Ireland as it was presented as making the link with Britain acceptable to Irish opinion. In part, this was an aspect of the attempt to reconcile Catholic opinion in Ireland that had been encouraged by the outbreak of the French Revolutionary War. There was also a stress on the acquisition of information as a way to strengthen government. The first British national census (1801) was an important instance, not least due to the significance of population numbers for recruitment, but more immediate value was gained by detailed mapping by the Board of Ordnance designed to help operationally in the event of a French invasion.

Thus, it was a significantly changing Britain that faced France. The extent to which this change is apparent in the culture of the period varies, and it is certainly not to the fore in Austen's novels or, more generally, those dealing with manners and those in the gothic genre. As yet, this was not a period of "Condition of England" novels.

So also with the coverage of politics. This was extensive in newspapers but not in novels. The latter did not offer an engagement with politics, secular or ecclesiastical, comparable to the Victorian novels of Anthony Trollope. Austen's life saw the breakup of apparently stable ministries, with the resignations of Frederick, Lord North, and William Pitt the Younger in 1782 and 1801 respectively, helping cause periods of ministerial instability in 1782–84 and 1801–12. Pitt resigned in 1801, principally as a result of George III's opposition to his support for Catholic emancipation and in response to ministerial disunity and the political problems posed by negotiating peace with France.[52] In April 1804, moreover, Pitt went into opposition to the Addington ministry that had been in power since he had resigned in 1801. The fictional Sir Thomas Bertram of Mansfield Park was an MP in this period. Moreover, Mr. Palmer in *Sense and Sensibility* is canvasing for a Somerset county seat in Parliament. He is sufficiently partisan not to be likely to visit Mr. Willoughby, an opposition supporter.[53]

Although George still supported Addington in 1804, the latter resigned, rather than being forced out by parliamentary action, which would have left George with fewer options. Thus, Addington protected the royal prerogative of choosing ministers. Pitt became first minister again but died young in 1806 while still in office.

A relatively consistent opponent of innovation,[54] George III had little time for the Ministry of All the Talents (1806–7), under William, Lord Grenville, formed after Pitt's death. He abhorred Grenville and his ministerial colleagues, especially Charles James Fox, the leader in the House of Commons of the Whigs, the reformist politicians who opposed Pitt. The ministry fell when it was unable to promise George not to raise anew the issue of Catholic emancipation, a cause very much supported by the Whigs.

The Portland administration (1807–9), which succeeded the Ministry of All the Talents, an administration led by Pittites, was properly mindful that it was the king's ministry and very much endorsed Tory views. Opposed to reform and respectful of royal authority, the administration looked to the parliamentary support of independent country gentlemen. William, third Duke of Portland, was a former home secretary (1794–1801), with responsibility in that role for the presentation of order.

The Portland administration, in turn, fell over the unsuccessful expedition sent against Antwerp in 1809—the Walcheren expedition, named after the nearby island where many of the troops died of disease. George played a major role in securing the reconstitution of the ministry when Spencer Perceval replaced Portland on October 4, 1809. George trusted Perceval, both as an individual and as an evangelical Protestant who had no truck with Catholic emancipation. Perceval had been chancellor of the exchequer and leader of the House of Commons.

George III's health finally broke down at the close of 1810. In an episode worthy of a novel, although not one by Austen, the shock of the fatal illness of his last born—his favorite daughter, Amelia—proved crucial to George's deterioration. It was initially thought that he would be all right despite her illness, but her prolonged death exacerbated the crisis, and both declined together. George frequently questioned the doctors on her progress and was popularly supposed to have been pushed over the edge when Amelia gave him a mourning ring containing a lock of her hair. Symptoms of insanity were obvious by October 25, the day of his last public appearance; on October 31, George was described as "silly"; and on November 1, "a state of debility and vacancy of mind" was reported. Amelia herself died on November 2.

On December 10, 1810, Perceval introduced a regency bill. The Regency Act was passed on February 5, 1811, and George, Prince of Wales, was sworn in as regent on February 6. For the first year, at the insistence of Perceval and against the wishes of the Whigs, his powers were limited in case his father recovered, as he had done in 1789. However, in February 1812, the prince gained the full prerogative powers of the Crown, although he was not to become king until his ill father, secluded throughout the regency in Windsor Castle, died of pneumonia on January 29, 1820.

In his youth, Prince George had been closely linked both politically and socially to the Whigs, but he changed his position from 1807. In part, this development reflected shifts in British politics, including the character of the Whigs after Fox's death in September 1806, but Prince George's changing attitudes as he got older were also important. He became more conservative—with a greater concern about the position of the Anglican church—and also sought closer relations with his father. Prince George's support for the war led him to oppose what he saw, for good reason, as the Whigs' appeasement of Napoleon. As prince regent, George followed his father in stressing his patriotism, duty, and wish for an inclusive ministry. In his first message to the Cabinet after he assumed his full powers in 1812, George stated his wish to pursue goals "common to the whole nation."

The continuation of the ministry led the Whigs to accuse George of being a turncoat. Convinced that he was ductile, they emphasized the Tory influence of his associates, not least Isabella, Marchioness of Hertford, with whom he was very close. However, critics (and others) underestimated George's capacity to make his own decisions. In 1812, George tried to bring the Whigs into what he hoped would be a widely inclusive ministry, but he refused to accept their liberal views on Catholic emancipation and the war. He had also, with familiarity, become satisfied with the ministers he had inherited. Furthermore, George did not appreciate the personal criticisms directed at him by Charles Grey and other Whigs.

The assassination of the prime minister, Perceval, in the lobby of the House of Commons on May 11, 1812, was the result of a private grudge against the government and was more dramatic than most episodes in the novels of the period. This assassination, so far the only one of a prime minister in British history, led to a renewed attempt to create an all-party ministry. However, the existing ministers were opposed to the plan, and the Whigs demanded too many places. The scheme failed, and the Whigs remained in the political wilderness. A new stable Tory ministry was established in June 1812 under Robert, second Earl of Liverpool, most recently secretary of state for war and the colonies. This ministry lasted until his stroke in 1827.

The Liverpool administration was strongly grounded within the political system. Thus, in April and May 1815, Parliament supported the government against opposition criticisms of its decision to oppose Napoleon. The opposition Whigs were seriously divided over the latter, and the government won substantial majorities in Parliament.

The prince regent, totally different in his personal life from George III, was a fan of Austen's novels, and his librarian, James Stanier Clarke, advised her in late 1815 on the subject for her next novel. Although he was a connoisseur in his artistic patronage, as he strove in his own fashion to compete with Napoleon, his artistic tastes were also not those of his father. He lacked the latter's strong sense of duty and moral concern and was lazy and self-indulgent.

Prince George, however, was able to respond to political developments. He had sense as well as sensibility. As ruler, George IV showed ability, more than is usually appreciated, and he took a constant interest in political affairs and government. Unlike his father, George IV was perceptive enough to understand that the monarch must be prepared to bend when necessary to the force of public opinion when that was reflected in the advice of his ministers or the majority in Parliament. George IV's years as ruler both as regent (1811–20) and king (1820–30) marked a vital stage in the transition to the rule of the Cabinet and Parliament.[55]

Radicalism in Austen's lifetime later attracted considerable attention, but it was not to the fore in the political system of her day. Indeed, the two political groups, the Tories and the Whigs, were each conservative from a radical perspective. This was clearly the case with the Tories but was also true of the Whigs. Their aristocratic liberalism sought to link reform with the sense that aristocrats were natural leaders—trustees of the people. The Whigs pressed for gradual reform that built on existing foundations, which they saw as organic reform.

Continuity on the part of the elite had political, social, and cultural consequences and contributed greatly to the exclusion by social status that was so important in politics, government, and society more generally. This was a hierarchical society with essentially oligarchic politics. Austen was not a critic of the latter and understood the former. At the same time, she offered a profound conservatism, as in *Emma* where she refers critically to schools' teaching "upon new principles and new systems."[56] Austen indeed could have echoed George III when, striking a characteristic note, he wrote in 1800: "I have no other view in life than to the best of my judgment to fulfil my duty."[57]

At the local level, elections offered much drama and excitement. They were an obvious topic for coverage, but Austen, like other novelists of the period, preferred to look elsewhere. More generally, the local press assumed that readers were more interested in news of the wider world than the particular locality, with the *Salisbury and Winchester Journal* (an important Hampshire newspaper and thus local to Austen) on March 29, 1790, noting: "We are sorry that the great overflow of advertisements this week will, of necessity, oblige us to postpone till next week, such as come late, and are not restricted to the present moment; and in this, we trust, we shall stand excused, as, in justice to our numerous readers, we deem it our indisputable duty to give every material article of general and provincial news that occurs."

That newspaper, like other papers, certainly offered much on the outside world. Louis XVI's unsuccessful attempt to flee France took up three and a half of the sixteen columns on July 4, 1791, with the paper commenting "on account of the extreme length of the late very important intelligence from France, we are under the necessity of omitting many advertisements this week." On February 21, 1791, the controversy in Britain about the French Revolution was regarded as sufficiently interesting to appear as a notice in the local news with the insertion, "for Dr Priestley's celebrated letter to Edmund Burke Esq see our last page." So also with the local news. The issue of the *Salisbury and Winchester Journal* on February 9, 1795, printed the petition and reported: "On Thursday, a general meeting of the inhabitants of this city, [cathedral] close, and neighbourhood was held at the Council Chamber, for the purpose of considering the propriety of petitioning Parliament for peace."

Austen's surviving correspondence referred to the war—understandable given the commitment of her family, which was not limited to her naval brothers. In 1796, her brother Henry, who had joined the militia in 1793, unsuccessfully sought a commission in a regiment he thought destined for Cape Town, which had been captured from the Dutch that year. Austen also followed the campaigning that did not directly involve her family. In April 1805, showing that she was reading the newspapers, Austen wrote to her sister: "The *Ambuscade* reached Gibraltar on the 9th of March and found all well; so say the papers."[58] In 1809, she was concerned about the fate of Sir John Moore's army in the Corunna campaign, although, in May 1811, she wrote of a battle: "What a blessing that one cares for none of them!" Waterloo stirred her more, and, in January 1817, she praised the *Poet's Pilgrimage to Waterloo* (1816) by Southey, the poet laureate.[59]

Two brothers in the navy—not the army, which was based mostly in Britain—meant there was even more need to follow the press. Thus, in April 1805, she wrote to Charles: "In consequence of my

Mother's having seen in the papers that the *Urania* was waiting at Portsmouth for the convoy for Halifax." Ann Barrett later recalled Austen's "enthusiasm for the Navy."[60] Charles distinguished himself in the defeat of the Dutch fleet at Camperdown in 1797, a major triumph. Francis did well in the successful action off St. Domingo in 1806 while, in *Persuasion*, significantly, Frederick Wentworth is made commander as a result of his role there. Charles and Francis eventually both became admirals, Francis adding a knighthood. Edmund Bertram refers to the navy as "a noble profession," but, in contrast, Sir Walter Elliot and Mary Crawford are placed as negative characters by their condescension toward naval officers.[61] Indeed, the navy was crucial to patriotic ideas of the nation,[62] and the response to it therefore fixed the nature of character.

Yet Sir Walter and Mary also captured the extent to which it was unclear how best to place naval officers socially. In practice, most officers were from the "middling orders,"[63] an aspect of the social complexities of professionalization also seen, as Austen repeatedly shows, with the clergy, the law, and medicine. Thus, naval lieutenants were expected to demonstrate a high level of technical training, which was very different to the purchase system employed in the army. The navy, therefore, did not require candidates to have money to gain appointment or promotion, and patronage, as with William Price in *Mansfield Park*, was largely a matter of recognizing and recommending talent. This was linked to the idea that talent justified the gentility of the status and not wealth. Thus, "politeness" had a particular echo in the Royal Navy, where there was not the great wealth of much of society unless through the merited means of prize money. This politeness required that naval officers behave as gentlemen. As Austen showed, they should also be treated as such. Martial values were increasingly part of both English masculinity and gentlemanlike behavior.[64] This behavior was more important than the ownership of land in the definition of gentlemen,[65] although clearly not to some of Austen's characters.

Austen's pride in her brothers' naval careers preceded the wars. Thus, in her *History of England*, written in 1791, she compared the seventeen-year-old Francis Austen to Sir Francis Drake: "I cannot help foreseeing that he will be equalled in this or the next century by one who though now but young, already promises to answer all the ardent and sanguine expectations of his relatives and friends."[66] So also with her pride in British naval achievements. In her marginalia on Goldsmith's *History of England*, Austen shows such pride in her comments on George Anson's attack on the Spaniards in the Pacific during the War of the Austrian Succession.[67] His wife appeared in a very different context in chapter 8.

Yet Captain Wentworth offers criticism of the Admiralty that presumably derived from Austen's brothers: "The admiralty entertain themselves now and then, with sending a few hundred men to sea, in a ship not fit to be employed. But they have a great many to provide for; and among the thousands that may just as well go to the bottom as not, it is impossible for them to distinguish the very set who may be least missed."[68]

The navy also provides Austen with a point of departure for a more extended critique of the whole process of socially constrained courtship that she repeatedly anatomizes. On leave visiting Fanny Price at Mansfield Park, William Price, faced by the undoubted challenges of being a midshipman,[69] admits that he has had enough of Portsmouth because "the Portsmouth girls turn up their noses at anybody who has not a commission. One might as well be nothing as a midshipman. One *is* nothing indeed. You remember the Gregorys; they are grown up amazing fine girls, but they will hardly speak to me because Lucy is courted by a lieutenant." This earns a heartfelt response from Fanny:

"Oh! shame, shame!—But never mind it, William" (her own cheeks in a glow of indignation as she spoke). "It is not worth minding. It is no reflection on you; it is no more than what the greatest admirals have all experienced, more or less, in their time. You must think of that; you must try to make up your mind to it as one of the hardships which fall to every sailor's share—like bad weather and hard living—only with this advantage, that there will be an end to it, that there will come a time when you will have nothing of that sort to endure. When you are a lieutenant!"

William responds that he doubts he will be,[70] and he is only proved wrong by the exercise of patronage. There is a different, unfair—indeed, ridiculous—criticism of the navy in Mary Crawford thinking that "vile sea-breezes are the ruin of beauty and health."[71] In this remark, there is a preference for surface and show over truth and integrity.

When William is promoted, this enables Austen to chart the process of patronage and show how ridiculous it is. Indeed, this portrayal is in line with the criticism of the Admiralty by Captain Wentworth and that of senior naval officers by Joseph Harris in his "Naval Characters" published in the *Morning Herald* from 1786 to 1788 and then republished as *The Naval Atlantis* (1788). In order to ingratiate himself with Fanny, Henry Crawford introduces William to his uncle, an admiral, and persuades the admiral to help him. This assistance leads to the letters Henry gives Fanny:

> The first was from the Admiral to inform his nephew, in a few words, of his having succeeded in the object he had undertaken, the promotion of young Price, and inclosing two more, one from the Secretary of the First Lord to a friend, whom the Admiral had set to work in the business, the other was from that friend to himself, by which it appeared that his Lordship had the very great happiness of attending to the recommendation of Sir Charles, that Sir Charles was much delighted in having such an opportunity of proving his regard for Admiral Crawford, and that the circumstance of Mr William Price's commission as second Lieutenant of H.M. sloop Thrush, being made out, was spreading general joy through a wide circle of great people.[72]

This satire, entirely apposite, prefigures Charles Dickens's powerful attack on government bureaucracy, in the shape of the Circumlocution Office, in his novel *Little Dorrit* (1855–57). Patronage indeed played a key role in naval life, notably because the navy contained far more officers than could be employed at sea,[73] although the ratio was not as ridiculous as in the modern British navy.

As an instance of a broader pattern of the significance of war in the formation of British Enlightenment and romantic culture,[74] Austen's novels were also affected by the wars, not least in their setting. Thus, written in 1796–97, *Pride and Prejudice* was set three years earlier, when the militia regiments were embodied. Many of her characters are in the military or related to those who are. While Elizabeth Bennet is visiting Hunsford, two nephews of Lady Catherine de Bourgh visit Rosings—not only Darcy, but also his cousin, Colonel Fitzwilliam, the younger son of "Lord ———."[75] In *Sense and Sensibility*, the thirty-five-year-old Colonel Brandon, who has served "in the East Indies"—in other words, India—is a positive character.[76] Service there was very much linked to talent and energy. Those of great social position preferred positions at home and did not tend to serve in distant and disease-ridden India unless they were true professionals. In *Mansfield Park*, Mary Crawford's friend Flora Ross jilted a "very nice young man in the Blues" for the ugly, stupid, and villainous Lord Stornaway. This is a comment on Mary. In *The Watsons*, there is a promise of many officers at a ball such that the daughters "will hardly want partners."[77]

Like *Emma*, *Persuasion* was set in 1814. It referred to a particular type of journey: the homecomings of sailors. Army officers are present, notably Colonel Wallis, but, in accordance with the general theme in the eighteenth century although not in the aftermath of Waterloo the following year, the navy dominates, and Austen presents the deleterious consequence of peace for individual prospects and income. There will be no more prize money. The novel closes with an affirmation of the "national importance" of the navy. Admiral Croft in *Persuasion* is far more benign than General Tilney in *Northanger Abbey*.[78]

Mansfield Park offers a very positive account of William Price when he meets his sister en route to going to sea while Edmund Bertram "tells her such charming things of what William was to do, and be hereafter, in consequence of his profession, as made her gradually admit that the separation might have some use."[79] It is possible to imagine Austen likewise being reassured about her brothers. Speaking of her brother, the generally quiet Fanny Price is unusually "animated in speaking of his profession, and the foreign stations he had been on, but she could not mention the number of years that he had been absent without tears in her eyes." On his return from sea seven years later, William is an impressive young man.[80] He was probably modeled on Charles Austen.

Alongside the settings of her novels were the periods of composition, as already mentioned for 1814. Thus, in 1810–12, when Austen had *Sense and Sensibility* finished and published, brings *Pride and Prejudice* to fruition, and begins work on *Mansfield Park*, Britain is isolated, as it had been in 1804 when Austen was writing *The Watsons*. The Fourth Coalition against France had collapsed in 1809 with Austria's defeat, and in 1808–12 successive British advances into Spain encountered major difficulties and led to the British forces withdrawing to Corunna and later into Portugal. War with the United States began in June 1812, and it was not until late that year that it became clear Russia had defeated Napoleon. Prior to that, Napoleon's success appeared inevitable, adding to Britain's parlous condition. This was a very different context from that of 1814–16, when first *Emma* and then *Persuasion* were written. *Emma* was set in 1814 as Frank Churchill talks of visiting Switzerland, a journey dependent on the peace that followed the abdication of Napoleon on April 11, 1814, and the restoration to the French throne of Louis XVIII. *Persuasion* is also a novel of the coming of peace.

Slavery was another context of Austen's novels, most explicitly but not only in *Mansfield Park*. "The slave of his designing friends," Elizabeth Bennet's description of the weak Bingley in the face of pressure from his sisters captures a very different form of slavery than rests behind *Northanger Abbey*. So also when Lady Catherine says to Elizabeth, "Five daughters brought up at home without a governess!—I never heard of such a thing. Your mother must have been quite a slave to your education,"[81] and with Mary Crawford not being "the slave of opportunity." In *Persuasion*, Mr. Smith's sequestrated property in the West Indies is not specified.[82] Moreover, the share ownership of slaves meant that even relatively modest families made money from slavery; nineteen people in Winchester were slave owners.

Yet slavery as understood today was increasingly to the fore as an issue in Britain from the late 1780s. Legislation for the abolition of the slave trade was discussed in Parliament every year from 1791 to 1799 and again in 1804 and 1805. Widespread opposition to populist reform that stemmed from hostility to the French Revolution had shadowed abolitionism in the 1790s, making the cause more difficult than at the start of the decade.

However, in the 1800s, the emphasis on reform that affected much opinion and government policy encompassed the slave trade. The reforming, liberal, middle-class culture that was becoming of growing importance in Britain, and that ably used the press to articulate its views, regarded the slave trade and slavery as abhorrent, anachronistic, and associated with everything it deplored. Abolitionists, indeed, were encouraged and assisted by a confidence in public support. This confidence, moreover, helped influence the debate amid the elite. Both confidence and debate were affected by the more general sense of reform, including concern over the treatment of animals. This provided a context within which the brutal conditions to which slaves were exposed seemed even more abhorrent.[83] Protestant/evangelicalism was an important aspect of the reform movement.

Abolitionism, moreover, offered the country, tired by the travails of a seemingly intractable war with Napoleon, the opportunity to sense itself playing a key role in the advance of true liberty. Abolitionist medals show how self-conscious this was.[84] This attitude was particularly valuable in 1806 as Britain's allies succumbed after crushing French victories at Ulm (1805), Austerlitz (1805), and Jena (1806), and the Third Coalition of powers against France collapsed as a result, with first Austria (1805) and then Prussia (1806) surrendering to France. Russia fought on only to make peace with France in 1807. Indeed, the parlous state of the war encouraged the idea that defeats were divine punishments for national sin and that the abolition of the slave trade was necessary for Britain to benefit from divine providence.[85]

This approach focused evangelical ideas and underlined the significance of British views. The transformation of God's work in order to build a new Jerusalem in accordance with divine providence was an attractive view that aligned human inventiveness with moral purpose. Thus, eighteenth-century Enlightenment ideas were transmitted in a new language, although still with the underlying idea of a benevolent God who had equipped humans with the means to serve his purposes. There was the powerful conviction that moral purpose was necessary in all endeavors to assuage divine wrath, as with the ending of the slave trade. Providentialism was probably a more significant factor in support for ending the slave trade than some of the secular calculations generally mentioned in modern discussion.[86]

The Abolition Act of 1807, which banned slave trading by British subjects, passed the Houses of Commons and Lords with substantial majorities. Moreover, in 1811, participation in the slave trade was made a felony. Slavery continued to be prominent in Austen's lifetime, as in 1816 when a large British fleet bombarded Algiers, the major slaving base on the Mediterranean, forcing it to free its slaves. The British presented themselves as acting on behalf of the civilized world, and the commander, Admiral Lord Exmouth, was made a viscount and voted the freedom of the City of London. This was a Britain that enjoyed its glory.

The social impact of the West Indies' settler class in Austen's novels varied. The Bertrams of *Mansfield Park*, who own a plantation in Antigua, are also respectable, long-established landowners in Britain, and Sir Thomas is an MP, of whom there are relatively few. Fanny Price asks him about the slave trade, and he responds with "information."[87] In contrast, the prospect of visitors from the settler class coming to Sanditon leads to a mixed response among its sponsors, bringing up not concerns about slavery but a lack of certainty over how the economy worked—a lack, moreover, that provides a focus for social anxieties and prejudices. The money the West Indian settlers offer is welcomed, but Lady Denham adds:

> "Because they have full purses, fancy themselves equal, may be, to your old country families. But then, they who scatter their money so freely, never think of whether they may not be doing mischief of raising the price of things—and I have heard that's very much the case with your West-injines—and if they come among us to raise the price of our necessaries of life, we shall not much thank them Mr Parker."
>
> "My dear madam, they can only raise the price of consumable articles, by such an extraordinary demand for them and such a diffusion of money among us, as must do us more good than harm.—Our butchers and bakers and traders in general cannot get rich without bringing prosperity to *us*.—If *they* do not gain, our rents must be insecure—and in proportion to their profit must be ours eventually in the increased value of our houses."
>
> "Oh!—well.—But I should not like to have butcher's meat raised, though—and I shall keep it down as long as I can."[88]

NOTES

1. M. Butler, *Jane Austen and the War of Ideas*, 2nd ed. (Oxford, 1987); C. Johnson, *Jane Austen: Women, Politics and the Novel* (Chicago, IL, 1988).
2. *Juvenilia*, 335.
3. *Juvenilia*, 332.
4. *Juvenilia*, 336.

5. *Juvenilia*, 338–39.

6. *Juvenilia*, 337–38.

7. *Juvenilia*, 339.

8. *Juvenilia*, 340.

9. This response is also seen in G. V. Bennett's scholarly account, *The Tory Crisis in Church and State, 1688–1730: The Career of Francis Atterbury, Bishop of Rochester* (Oxford, 1975).

10. *Juvenilia*, 342.

11. *Juvenilia*, 343.

12. *Juvenilia*, 343–44.

13. *Juvenilia*, 343–51.

14. *Juvenilia*, 351.

15. J. Black, *Charting the Past: The Historical Worlds of Eighteenth-Century England* (Bloomington, IN, 2019).

16. *Emma* I, 8.

17. *Emma* II, 11.

18. *Emma* II, 14.

19. *Persuasion* I, 5.

20. *Persuasion* II, 9.

21. *Sense* III, 5.

22. *Juvenilia*, 287–88.

23. Queen Charlotte's diary, September 16, 17, 1789, Windsor Castle, Royal Archives, GEO/Add. 43/1; Earl of Cardigan, *The Wardens of Savernake Forest* (London, 1949), 286–87.

24. A. Smith, *An Inquiry into the Nature and Causes of the Wealth of Nations* (London, 1776), book 5, chap. 3.

25. G. A. Starr, "Defoe and China," *Eighteenth-Century Studies* 43 (2010): 438–40; K. Bae, "The Historical Significance of Money in *Robinson Crusoe*," *Notes and Queries* 261 (2016): 585–87.

26. Auckland to Pitt, February 23, 1790, London, National Archives, 30/8/110 fol. 158.

27. *Juvenilia*, 196.

28. *Juvenilia*, 222–23.

29. *Emma* II, 1–2.

30. *Persuasion* I, 6.

31. D. Le Faye, "*Pride and Prejudice*: Chapman's Internal Dating Corrected," *Notes and Queries* 263 (2018): 351–57.

32. J. R. Western, "The Volunteer Movement as an Anti-Revolutionary Force, 1793–1801," *English Historical Review* LXXI, no. 281(1956): 606.

33. J. E. Cookson, *The British Armed Nation, 1793–1815* (Oxford, 1997).

34. *Letters*, 110.

35. R. Wells, *Wretched Faces: Famine in Wartime England, 1793–1801* (Gloucester, UK, 1988).

36. R. Wells, *Insurrection: The British Experience, 1795–1803* (Gloucester, UK, 1983).

37. *Northanger* I, 14.

38. Queen Charlotte's diary, September 15, 1789, Windsor Castle, Royal Archives, GEO/Add 43/1; Huntingford to Henry Addington, September 17, 1789, Exeter, Devon Record Office, 152 M/C 1789/F 12.

39. *Juvenilia*, 251.

40. Auckland to the Foreign Secretary, William, Lord Grenville, Foreign Secretary, November 26, 1792, BL. Add. 58920 fols. 178–79.

41. J. C. D. Clark, *Thomas Paine: Britain, America, and France in the Age of Enlightenment and Revolution* (Oxford, 2018).

42. J. C. D. Clark, ed., *Edmund Burke: Reflections on the Revolution in France: A Critical Edition* (Stanford, CA, 2001).

43. J. C. D. Clark, *English Society, 1688–1832* (Cambridge, 1985).

44. George to Pitt, May 8, 1793, NA. PRO. 30/8/103 fol. 494.

45. J. Black, *George III: America's Last King* (New Haven, CT, 2006), 450.

46. I. R. Christie, *Stress and Stability in Late Eighteenth-Century Britain: Reflections on the British Avoidance of Revolution* (Oxford, 1984).

47. J. Bohstedt, *Riots and Community Politics in England and Wales 1790–1810* (Cambridge, MA, 1983).

48. *Persuasion* I, 9; II, 4.

49. *MP* I, 12; II, 5–6; III, 7, 12, 15; *Sense* I, 6, 19.

50. *Northanger* II, 10.

51. J. Hoppit, *Britain's Political Economies: Parliament and Economic Life, 1660–1800* (Cambridge, 2017).

52. P. Mackesy, *War without Victory: The Downfall of Pitt, 1799–1802* (Oxford, 1984).

53. *Sense* I, 20.

54. J. M. Black, *George III* (New Haven, CT, 2006), 449–50, and *George III: Madness and Majesty* (2020).

55. E. A. Smith, *George IV* (New Haven, CT, 1999).

56. *Emma* I, 3.

57. George III to William Grenville, June 28, 1800, BL. Add. 58861.

58. *Letters*, 99.

59. *Letters*, 163, 171, 173; M. Burns, "Another Unexplained Reference in Jane Austen's Letters: 'no one in fact nearer to us than Sir John himself,'" *Notes and Queries* 263, no. 3 (September 2018): 324–26.

60. D. Le Faye, "Jane Austen's Friend Mrs Barrett Identified," *Notes and Queries* 244, no. 4 (December 1999): 452.

61. *Persuasion* II, 6; *MP* I, 6.

62. D. Leggett, "Navy, Nation and Identity in the Long Nineteenth Century," *Journal for Maritime Research* 13 (November 2011): 151–63.

63. E. Wilson, *A Social History of British Naval Officers, 1775–1815* (Woodbridge, UK, 2016).

64. L. Colley, *Britons: Forging the Nation, 1707–1837* (New Haven, CT, 1992).

65. P. Langford, *A Polite and Commercial People: England, 1727–1783* (Oxford, 1989), 65–66.

66. *Juvenilia*, 185.

67. *Juvenilia*, 345–46.

68. *Persuasion* I, 8.

69. S. A. Cavell, *Midshipmen and Quarterdeck Boys in the British Navy, 1771–1831* (Woodbridge, UK, 2012).

70. *MP* II, 7.

71. *MP* III, 12.

72. *MP* II, 13.

73. E. Gill, *Naval Families, War and Duty in Britain, 1740–1820* (Woodbridge, UK, 2016).

74. N. Ramsey and G. Russell, eds., *Tracing War in British Enlightenment and Romantic Culture* (Basingstoke, UK, 2015).

75. *PP* II, 7.

76. *Sense* II, 9.

77. *MP* III, 5; *Later Manuscripts*, 80.

78. *Persuasion* II, 12.

79. *MP* I, 2.

80. *MP* I, 6; II, 6.

81. *PP* II, 1, 6; *MP* III, 5.

82. *Persuasion* II, 9.

83. K. Jacoby, "Slaves by Nature? Domestic Animals and Human Slaves," *Slavery and Abolition* 15 (1994): 96–97.

84. S. Drescher, "Whose Abolition? Popular Pressure and the Ending of the British Slave Trade," *Past and Present* 143 (1994): 136–66, esp. 165–66.

85. J. Coffey, "'Tremble Britannia!': Fear, Providence and the Abolition of the Slave Trade, 1758–1807," *English Historical Review* 127 (2012): 844–81.

86. R. Anstey, *The Atlantic Slave Trade and British Abolition 1760–1810* (London, 1975); G. D. V. White, *Jane Austen in the Context of Abolition* (Basingstoke, UK, 2006).

87. *MP* II, 3.

88. *Sanditon* 6.

ELEVEN

—ﬡ—

THE ROMANTIC LANDSCAPE

I took up my Residence in a romantic Village in
the Highlands of Scotland, where I have ever since
continued, and where I can uninterrupted by
unmeaning visits, indulge in a melancholy solitude.

—*Love and Freindship*, in *Juvenilia*

THE ROMANTIC LANDSCAPE OF AUSTEN'S lifetime was
crowded and complex. As the possibilities of the novel developed
qualities and forms of imagination, the sentimental novel was
taken in a distinctive direction in the gothic novel. The latter put
sentimental characters and themes under particular strain and
largely omitted the explicit love intrigues of sentimental fiction,
instead sublimating them into more extreme desires and threats
that provided some of the classic themes of danger overcome with
a far more lurid course and setting.

The gothic novel, of which the most influential exemplar was
Horace Walpole's *The Castle of Otranto* (1764), the second edition
of which was subtitled *A Gothic Story*, departed from the existing conventions of the novel, not least, as he made explicit in his
preface to the second edition, by breaking with the emphasis
on realism. Indeed, Walpole deliberately emphasized the need

to employ "fancy," which included strangeness and uncertainty. Mystery was underlined by manifestations of the supernatural, and the reader, like the protagonist, was unclear about what was happening. This lack of clarity was heightened to a nightmarish character by menace, danger, pursuit, and assault.

As the plot lines amply demonstrated, these elements were repeatedly present in gothic novels, as in Clara Reeve's *The Old English Baron* (1778), which originally appeared in 1777 as *The Champion of Virtue*. That novel explicitly drew on *The Castle of Otranto*. The love between Emma and Edmund is a key element of the plot.

A painterly equivalent to the gothic novel was provided by Joshua Reynolds's *Ugolino and His Children in the Dungeon* (1773), a dramatic history painting in the fashion of the genre that closely configured with the gothic imagination. Based on an episode in Dante's *Inferno*, the painting depicted the imprisoned count having to decide to starve to death or eat his similarly imprisoned sons and grandsons when they die. This painting caused a stir when exhibited at the Royal Academy. Castles and dungeons were key sites for gothic fiction, focusing the menace and mystery that were more generally present in these novels and moving plots forward.

Walpole had visited Naples in 1740 as part of his Grand Tour but did not travel on to Otranto. In 1786, when Lady Craven, who had traveled there, gave Walpole a drawing of the castle, the delighted Walpole responded, "I did not even know that there was a castle of Otranto"; indeed, the book's descriptions of the castle and its environs are extremely sparse. This was in common with much fiction, including that of Austen. Alongside sometimes very specific urban settings, those outside towns tended to be far less particular.

The gothic drew on ideas of the sublime. Edmund Burke's aesthetic *Philosophical Enquiry into the Origin of Our Ideas of the Sublime and the Beautiful* (1759) underscored the extent to which "the sublime" could transform the reader and spectator and emphasized that terror was important in creating the sense of the sublime. The word *sublime* was used of Handel's music at the time but was defined by Burke as whatever led to ideas of danger, pain, or terror: he suggested obscurity, vastness, privation, and infinity. Burke argued that these could cause delight if their source was imaginary. Emotions and potent sensory experiences, rather than nobility, reason, and dignity, were crucial for Burke, whose work had great influence in the development of the idea of the sublime.[1]

That Burke has already appeared in chapter 10 of this book as an important figure in a political context serves as a reminder that individuals were of significance in various ways and also operated in different contexts. This was also true of Austen, of some of the characters in her novels, and, indeed, of other individuals mentioned in this text, including William Blake, Fanny Burney, George III, Dr. Samuel Johnson, Edward Nares, and Mary Wollstonecraft. So also with particular sites and years. The simultaneity of the past is its key feature, and the use of sequencing in the explanation inevitably involves distortion as well as prioritization. This is a problem for novelists as for historians.

Burke's argument was important in the gothic impulse—for example, in the six gothic novels of Ann Radcliffe (1764–1823), particularly in their popularity—and in early romanticism. The quest for picturesque mountain scenery that was designed to elicit "the sublime" was amply realized in the pages of gothic fiction. Radcliffe was a Londoner but was happy to write about what she had not seen, to a degree not seen with Austen. In Radcliffe's *The Mysteries of Udolpho* (1794), a work she sold for five hundred pounds and that was influential as a counterpoint in *Northanger Abbey*, Emily, crossing the Alps into Italy, "often as she travelled among the clouds, watched in silent awe their billowy surges rolling below; sometimes, wholly closing upon the scene, they appeared like a world of chaos, and, at others, spreading thinly, they opened and admitted partial catches of the landscape—the torrent, whose astounding roar had never failed, tumbling down the rocky chasm, huge cliffs white with snow, or the dark summits of the pine forests, that stretched mid-way down the mountains."[2]

In Radcliffe's *The Italian, or The Confessional of the Black Penitents* (1797), for which she was paid eight hundred pounds, the captured Ellena offered an appropriate response to the darkening forcefulness of the landscape that she was thrust into with all the attention of an enraptured spectator of an awesome painting. Indeed, as an instance of the movement between genres, there are references to illustrations:

> It was when the heat and the light were declining that the carriage entered a rocky defile, which shewed, as through a telescope reversed, distant plains, and mountains opening beyond, lighted up with all the purple splendor of the setting sun. Along this deep and shadowy perspective a river, which was seen descending among the cliffs of a mountain, rolled with impetuous force, fretting and foaming amidst the dark rocks in its descent, and then flowing in a limpid lapse to the brink of other precipices, whence again it fell with thundering strength to the abyss, throwing its misty clouds of spray high in the air, and seeming to claim the sole empire of this solitary wild. Its bed took up the whole breadth of the chasm, which some strong convulsion of the earth seemed to have formed, not leaving space even for a road along its margin. The road, therefore, was carried high among the cliffs, that impended over the river, and seemed as if suspended in air; while the gloom and vastness of the precipes, which towered above and sunk below it, together with the amazing force and uproar of the falling waters, combined to render the pass more terrific than the pencil could describe, or language can express. Ellena ascended it, not with indifference but with calmness; she experienced somewhat of a dreadful pleasure in looking down upon the irresistible flood; but this emotion was heightened into awe, when she perceived that the road led to a slight bridge, which, thrown across the chasm at an immense height, united two opposite

cliffs, between which the whole cataract of the river descended. The bridge, which was defended only by a slender railing, appeared as if hung amidst the clouds. Ellena, while she was crossing it, almost forgot her misfortunes.[3]

"The sublime" had earlier been thought of without reference to terror, and it is employed in that way by Fanny Price,[4] but, in Burke's sense, it did not have to wait for gothic novels. Indeed, it could be seen across a host of activities—for example, the acting of David Garrick, particularly his re-creation of Shakespeare's Macbeth from 1744, his depiction of Hamlet faced with the ghost of his father, and his Richard III.[5] Such acting matched support for the presentation of moments of strong emotion by painters that could link sensibility to romanticism. Painters presented scenes from drama, including by actors such as Garrick.

Radcliffe might seem very different from Austen, not least in being married, but there were instructive similarities, especially in their being very private individuals: less is known about Radcliffe's life. Moreover, both had strong female characters and were very much professionals in their writing, not least in carefully considering reviews and trying to develop their style. This point serves to underline the limitations of pushing genre as a classifying model and still more as the basis for judgment.[6]

For both Austen and Radcliffe, there was also the question of the relationship between experience and reality—an issue, probed in *Northanger Abbey*, that was of particular concern for novelists, seeking, as they did, to build on the capacity for imagination.[7] *Northanger Abbey* sees Austen writing about the gothic at length, but the gothic also features elsewhere in her works. In *Emma*, Harriet Smith tells Emma that Robert Martin, her suitor, had never heard of Radcliffe's highly popular *The Romance of the Forest* (1791), her third work, or Regina Maria Roche's *The Children of the Abbey* (1798), a Radcliffe imitation, before she had mentioned them. He at once determines to obtain copies of them.[8]

Austen's novels were praised for not being gothic by some, including the critic, editor, and satirist William Gifford (1756–1826). He was editor of the *Quarterly Review* from 1809 to 1824. Founded by the publisher John Murray (1778–1843), it was very much a Tory quarterly. Gifford recommended to Murray that the latter accept *Emma* precisely because they kept gothic excesses away or mocked them. Sir Walter Scott favored Austen's novels in the March 1816 issue of the *Quarterly Review* for the same reasons. Austen could do drama; in an arresting passage in *Sense and Sensibility*, on a "cold and stormy" night, with the wind roaring round the house, Elinor Dashwood sees the "flaring lamps of a carriage" drawn by four horses and therefore moving fast. Elinor starts "back with a look of horror . . . and the first impulse of her heart in turning instantly to quite the room," but the visitor turns out to be no more sinister than John Willoughby, who had jilted her sister but comes to offer explanation, express contrition, and show his concern for the sick Marianne.[9]

The idea of the soul as a seat of passion, and passion often as the cause of anguish, was most luridly expressed by the Swiss painter Johann Heinrich Füssli (he anglicised his name as Henry Fuseli) (1741–1825), who spent most of the period from 1764 in England, becoming a member of the Royal Academy in 1790. He offered visions of horrific fantasy comparable to some of the contemporary gothic novels. Influenced by reading Rousseau, Füssli was a precursor of romanticism. He argued that the individual and society, art and morality, were in conflict and that the arts were a divine gift that elevated man by their force, impact, and terror. Praised by George III and William Blake, Füssli's most famous painting, *Nightmare* (1781, exhibited 1782), was a gothic fantasy that offered a powerful vision of the mysterious and the subconscious.

Producing work designed to arouse the imagination—for example, *The Serpent Tempting Eve* (1802), Füssli painted visions that exposed both the limited sway of social order and psychological balance and harmony and the depths in human experience reason could not explain. His paintings looked toward the unfixed, metaphorical quality that would be so important to much romantic work and that was also pronounced in gothic literature, such as Radcliffe's novels. However, at the end of each novel, Radcliffe provided a rational explanation to what had seemed supernatural. So also, and far more, with Austen in *Northanger Abbey*. There, Henry Tilney, a cleric, reminds Catherine Morland that she is a "Christian."[10] This, more generally, is a critique of the willful imagination at play in gothic fantasies.

While the theme helps explain the link, Reynolds's massive *Macbeth and the Witches*, painted in the late 1780s, echoed aspects of Füssli's work. The grip of *Macbeth* on the imagination reflected interest in fantastical stories and the supernatural but was also in accord with the instinctive response by theater audiences that was then increasingly fashionable, in contrast to the earlier intellectual response. This was an aspect of a shift from text to a theatrical experience in which emotional atmosphere created by other means, such as scene painting, was increasingly important. The theatricality of the gothic was affected by the enlargement of Covent Garden in 1792 and Drury Lane in 1794, which increased the distance between actors/performers and audience and led to London theaters that were less intimate and, instead, more conducive to the drama of spectacle. These changes proved especially conducive to the fashion for gothic drama in the 1790s.

Drama that tested contemporary boundaries was provided in a different way by William Beckford's *Vathek: An Arabian Tale* (1786), a novel about the quest for deadly knowledge and legendary power in which the explicit defiance of established morality was in part expressed by a sexual adventurousness seen as an aspect of its subject's desire to fulfil his sensuality. The end note, however, was that of morality, with the protagonist becoming "a prey to grief without end."[11]

Vathek looked to the exoticism of some gothic fiction and to troubled villains, such as Ambrosio, the protagonist of Matthew Lewis's dramatic gothic novel *The Monk* (1796). Ambrosio is presented as a victim of his own irrational impulses, specifically lustful self-destructive drives, which at the end of the novel are attributed unconvincingly to diabolical forces. He was more frightening than the creations of Walpole and Radcliffe, and Radcliffe was troubled by the novel. Like the paintings of Füssli, the plots of gothic literature, with their deliberate embrace of instability,[12] tested conventional notions of probability, not least the established patterns of expressing and molding experience with reference to the interior and natural world.

Gothic fiction, meanwhile, reworked many of the images of landscape poetry. A changing appreciation of nature was important as a harbinger of the emphases that would be compounded in romanticism. James Thomson, in his preface to his poem *Winter* (1726), presented nature in reflective terms rather than with the emotional intensity seen toward the close of the century: "I know no subject more elevating, more amusing; more ready to awake the poetical enthusiasm, the philosophical reflection, and the moral sentiment, than the *Works of Nature*. Where can we meet with such variety, such beauty, such magnificence? All that enlarges, and transports, the soul? What more inspiring than a calm, wide, survey of them? In every dress *Nature* is greatly charming!" With landscape painting, there was new appreciation of the "sublime" qualities of savage landscape. Nature was increasingly seen as an elemental creative force, not as a pleasing and inconsequential landscape, and, as a related point, the human soul was considered a seat of passion rather than harmony. The changing nature of the emphasis on sensibility and its growing linkage with the notion of spiritual awareness were important in prefiguring romantic taste. Early anticipation can be seen in the poet Mark Akenside in his *The Pleasures of Imagination* (1744), a didactic poem that stressed the value of a well-formed imagination. The equivalent in portraiture was an attempt to give subjects natural and open expressions, as in Joshua Reynolds's *Mrs Levina Luther* (1763–66).

Toward the close of the century, the taste for picturesque landscape was widely diffused, and this taste served to direct popular interests toward what would be seen later as romantic values. Linked to this came a fascination with ruins that was pronounced from mid-century and sometimes pseudomelancholic; indeed, ruins were increasingly presented as an innate part of the landscape.[13] William Mason closed his paean to "Landscape" in *The English Garden* (1772):

> Most happy, if thy vale below
> Wash, with the crystal coolness of its rills,
> Some mouldring abbey's ivy-vested wall.

Similarly, from Thomas Warton's "The Solemn Noon of Night" in *The Pleasures of Melancholy* (1747) came the appeal of "yon ruin'd Abbey's moss-grown piles." *Berry Pomeroy Castle* by the Exeter-based landscape painter Francis Towne (1739–1816) showed trees growing up among the ruins. In 1770, Thomas Whately captured what was seen as the suggestive nature of the human imagination and, therefore, its openness to the arts: "At the sight of a ruin, reflections on the change, the decay, and the desolation before us, naturally occur; and they introduce a long succession of others, all tinctured with that melancholy which these have inspired."[14]

An interest in ruins—for example, the folly ruins seen in landscape gardening—was related to the focus on mortality by those later termed the "graveyard poets." Locating their meditations in nocturnal churchyards, writers such as Robert Blair and Edward Young sought sublime effects that meshed religious thoughts and fine sensibility, moving beyond melancholia to find a more active reflection.

Although not addicted to churchyards, the same was true of William Lisle Bowles's highly popular *Fourteen Sonnets Elegiac and Descriptive: Written during a Tour* (1789). Number Two was written at Bamburgh Castle, a medieval remnant on "the wave-worn rock sublime." Bowles (1762–1850), like Edward Young and James Hervey, author of *Meditations among the Tombs*, was a cleric. Descended from a line of clerics, Bowles was a vicar near the Austens in Chicklade (Wiltshire) from 1792 to 1797, Dumbleton (Gloucestershire) from 1797 to 1804, and Bremhill (Wiltshire), adding a prebendal stall in Salisbury Cathedral in 1804 and being made chaplain to the prince regent in 1818. Bowles preferred images drawn from nature to those drawn from art, arguing that the former were poetically finer.

At the same time, the theme of meditation on death could not always be readily comprehended within Christian belief, although there was little downright rejection of it. Aside from poetry on mortality, there was also prose fiction, although that was less common. "J.S." in *Swinney's Birmingham and Stafford Chronicle* of January 11, 1776, published an allusive dream essay on time, pleasure, and death, with time's inexorable triumph the major theme.

In gothic fiction, monastic stonework and trees became ruined abbeys and sinister woods that served as malign settings for the plot and also represented the psychological strains of the psyche. This was very different from the metropolitan settings that had dominated the culture of print at the start of the eighteenth century. Catherine Morland has a "passion for ancient edifices . . . and castles and abbies made usually the charm of those reveries which his image did not fill."[15] In contrast, Marianne Dashwood is able to propose to her sister that "we will often go to the old ruins of the Priory, and try to trace its foundations so far as we are told they once reached,"[16] without any sense of melodrama.

The focus on individual emotions became, in the romantic fascination with the ego, an emphasis on the willful protagonist. To be heroic, however, the romantic hero required a brooding quality, a dignified melancholy and mysterious introspection, that separated him from the more easily driven and readily explained villains of gothic novels, although Schedoni, the complex, troubled, austere monkish villain of Radcliffe's *The Italian* (1797), showed signs of being such a hero.

In contrast, Sir Edward Denham in *Sanditon* is a pretend seducer—or rather, a waffler-would-be version. The note of bathos is ably struck: "He felt a strong curiosity to ascertain whether the neighbourhood of Timbuctoo might not afford some solitary house adapted for Clara's reception;—but the expense alas! of measures in that masterly style was ill-suited to his purse, and prudence obliged him to prefer the quietest sort of ruin and disgrace for the object of his affections, to the more renowned."[17]

Dramatic accounts of character were offered by painters, as with Reynolds's 1784 portrait of *Mrs Siddons as the Tragic Muse* (1784). Siddons (Sarah Kemble, 1755–1831), the leading tragic actress of the age, was successful in showing that the gothic could be theatrical and, in this, that the potent psychology of the paranormal the gothic had come to express could be channeled to dramatic effect.[18] Reynolds's rich, dark painting, with its figures of Pity and Terror, looked forward to romanticism. The painting was a great success and was praised by James Barry as "the finest picture of the kind, perhaps in the world, indeed it is something more than a portrait." The last point reflects the shift in Reynolds's later portraits away from conversation pieces and toward a more otherworldly style, with more clouds and smoke.[19]

Romanticism, itself a retrospective concept (as are many concepts), has been variously defined, with an increased emphasis since the early 1980s on social and political elements, not least a greater awareness of the political and social interests of nearly all the major writers.[20] An older view of what would be seen as the romanticism of the 1790s also still has value. In this, romanticism is associated with the individual emotions of the artist, often at variance with social and cultural conventions and the Enlightenment ideas of earlier in the century, and inspired by the intoxicating power and wildness of elemental natural forces. Drawing on earlier ideas of the honesty of natural feelings, this association was contrasted with artifice. In *Lady Susan*, there is reference to "every honest, every natural feeling."[21]

Dr. Johnson claimed that novels showed "life in its true state."[22] In part, this reflected the extent to which the romantic focus on the exalting character of the imagination, and its ability to endow some literature (art, music, etc.) with great quality, had not been anticipated in any measure in the first half of the eighteenth century. Instead, although largely coming to fruition from the 1790s, the ideas and assumptions associated with romanticism were all largely innovations of the second half of the century and related to the eighteenth-century expression of "the sublime." The romantic focus on the imagination was to overturn the role of rules in establishing merit and to separate literature from other writings. This creates problems for modern readings of the eighteenth century as a whole, some of which overly reflect the focus and priorities of romanticism or, at least, adopt a teleological position.

Romanticism, itself a permeable category, was a tendency, not a program. Nevertheless, a central theme in this tendency was a reaction against earlier classical cultural themes, especially the emphasis on restraint and order and a literary tradition focused on the classical world. Romanticism, instead, embraced a diversity born of the individual experience of the artist and the artist's capacity as a result to engage with, and inspire, the imagination of the individual reader and spectator. In place of convention was an emphasis on the artist's individualism as a product of the integrity of innate vision, which also encouraged a rethinking of past quality. This vision was of the spirit, rather than the mind—indeed, of feeling unconfined by restraint, a tendency formerly ascribed in a pejorative fashion to women.[23]

From the late twentieth century, Austen was seen by many as part of the romantic canon.[24] This is a questionable approach as

Austen shows the willful defiance of convention as the prerogative of rogues, such as George Wickham, her commonplace version of Mozart and Lorenzo Da Ponte's existential hero-villain Don Giovanni from the 1787 opera. In romanticism, emphasis on the individual could lend itself not to the compromises and restraints of order but rather to a presentation of the vital soul of the individual and thus a critical view of social norms. This contrast is seen in *Sense and Sensibility* with the differing responses of Marianne Dashwood and her brother John to the news that Edward Ferrars does not intend to marry the wealthy Miss Morton, leading to his mother refusing to see him again or help him advance:

> Here Marianne, in an ecstasy of indignation, clapped her hands together and cried, "Gracious God! can this be possible!"
>
> "Well may you wonder, Marianne," replied her brother, "at the obstinacy which could resist such arguments as these. Your exclamation is very natural."[25]

The reference to what was "natural" reflected the profound differences of the period as to the characteristics inherent in humans as well as the appropriateness of behavior.

Breaking artistic boundaries was largely a matter of changes within individual genres but in some cases spanned genres, such as with William Blake. Blake also exemplified the romantic belief that the stress on the individual vision was "truer" and more "authentic" than that on learned artistic behavior.

In response to the radical drives of the period, a group of writers developed the novel as a means of social criticism. The most striking result was William Godwin's *Things As They Are; or The Adventures of Caleb Williams* (1794). In part, this was a literary vehicle for his *Enquiry Concerning Social Justice* (1793), and Godwin translated the problem of malignity from the depraved sin of gothic novels to the pain stemming from inequity.[26] Thomas Holcroft's *Anna St Ives* (1792); Charlotte Smith's *Desmond* (1792);

Mary Wollstonecraft's *The Wrongs of Woman: or Maria* (1798), which dealt with the heroine's detention in a madhouse at the behest of a dishonest husband; and Godwin's *St Leon* (1799) were other radical political novels. Earlier, in her *Vindication of the Rights of Woman* (1792), Wollstonecraft had criticized the condescending character of James Fordyce's *Sermons to Young Women* (1766), which Mr. Collins begins to read aloud to the Bennet women only to be interrupted by a bored Lydia.

The radical volatility of the period encouraged the probing of foreign perspectives in order to throw light on the situation in England. George Cumberland's *The Captive of the Castle of Senaar* (1798) introduces the utopian society of the Sophians. This society was different from contemporary England, without oppression, property, or marriage but, instead, with the rule of rational liberty. *Hermsprong: or Man As He Is Not* (1796) by Robert Bage (1728–1801), a novelist who ran a Staffordshire paper mill, offered a radical critique of the social system from the perspective of a Native American who personified the virtuous Noble Savage in a more modern setting but with the radicalism tempered by an appreciation of the constraints of society. As a result, the hero returns to his true role as part of the establishment, not a rejection of it. Austen owned a copy of the novel, and it influenced her work. Bage's earlier novel *Barham Downs* (1784) was a source for *Sense and Sensibility* and shared a critique of the cult of sensibility as artificial.[27] Austen drew inspiration for names, notably Bennet and Bingley in *Pride and Prejudice* and Dashwood in *Sense and Sensibility*, from Mary Hamilton's *Munster Village* (1778), which very much engaged with utopianism, notably in the form of equality in marriage.[28] Lady Mary, the youngest daughter of Alexander, fifth Earl of Leven, and estranged from her first husband, James Walker, a debt-encumbered physician, turned to writing to support her children and then lived with George Robinson Hamilton, the owner of a Jamaican sugar plantation.

Although these radical novels have enjoyed much attention, they were outweighed, at least in quantity, by the anti-Jacobin novels that appeared, especially after the French Revolution's Reign of Terror of 1793–94, works such as Isaac D'Israeli's *Vaurien; or Sketches of the Times* (1797). These novels depicted English radicals as dangerous allies of French Jacobins, with their secret intentions allegedly revealed by this connection, as well as personally immoral. In *Vaurien*, Wollstonecraft was Miss Million, a backer of sex outside marriage, and Godwin was Mr. Subtile, "the coldest blooded metaphysician of the age."[29] In contrast to the radicals, these novels contained a defense of existing social arrangements, not least through a presentation of the nobility as the traditional leaders of society.[30]

To a degree, Austen was part of this tendency, but the nobility were fairly problematic in her novels, notably her latter ones. Her approach can be presented as subversive, but it equally entailed a call for purpose and living up to responsibilities. The problematic members of the elite were those who did not live up to the responsibilities their status demanded—for example, the Hon. Mr. Yates in *Mansfield Park*. In contrast, Lady Catherine de Bourgh in *Pride and Prejudice*, although interfering and obnoxious, does concern herself with local affairs.

The anti-Jacobin literary offensive-defensive was matched in newspapers and periodicals and was the cultural counterpart of the powerful loyalist current of the period.[31] The general social context was an opposition to, or at least uneasiness about, social mobility, industrialization, and urbanization—in short, a repositioning of the earlier rural tradition in more clearly political terms. This opposition also drew on well-established notions of the value of restraint, as with Anna Maria Porter's novel *Walsh Colville: or, A Young Man's First Entrance into Life* (1797), with the dangers of indulgence and sin now in part interpreted in political as well as moral terms.

Separately, the picturesque had become more engaged with dramatic landscape as a result of the romantic impulse. In the dedication to his *Ode to the Sun* (1776), William Cumberland had called for an engagement with the English "sublime," which he located in the landscape. He claimed: "We penetrate the Glaciers, traverse the Rhone and the Rhine, whilst our own domestic lakes of Ulswater, Keswick, and Wyndermere exhibit scenes in so sublime a stile, with such beautiful colouring of rock, wood and water, backed with so tremendous a disposition of mountains, that if they do not fairly take the lead of all the views in Europe, yet they are indisputable such as no English traveler should leave behind." This ode and other early accounts of the Lakes, including John Dalton's *Descriptive Poem* of 1755, appeared in 1780 in the second edition of Thomas West's *A Guide to the Lakes: Dedicated to the Lovers of Landscape Studies, and to All Who Have Visited, or Intended to Visit, the Lakes in Cumberland, Westmorland and Lancashire*. West (1720–79), a Jesuit stationed in Cumbria, is a reminder of the great variety of types who contributed to cultural life. His book was the first major guide to picturesque mountain scenery.

The popularity of West's work ensured seven editions by 1799 and eleven by 1821. The collectable and display quality of these editions was enhanced first with maps and subsequently with aquatints. From the fifth edition (1793), the sixteen aquatint *Views of the Lakes* by Samuel Alken, after drawings by J. Smith and J. Emes, were advertised as of an appropriate size to bind with the guide. The more elegant nature of the production—the fifth edition having wider spaced type and broader margins—was an additional instance of the higher production values made possible and desirable by the profitability of this market.

Interest in the Lakes, the original hoped-for destination of the tour by Elizabeth Bennet and the Gardiners in *Pride and Prejudice*, was considerably further enhanced by William Gilpin's *Observations Relative Chiefly to Picturesque Beauty, Made in the Year 1772, on Several Parts of England: Particularly the Mountains, and Lakes of Cumberland and Westmoreland* (1786). Gilpin's work, which pleased Austen, lacked the precision seen in travel accounts earlier in the century but proved particularly successful in striking an impressionistic note that emphasized the personal response, a style matched with impressionistic aquatints. Popularity led to a second edition in 1788, with both text and plates revised in order to make the work more in accord with a market that wanted a sensibility focused on the sublime quality of landscape.

This approach had already been seen in Gilpin's *Observations on the River Wye and Several Parts of South Wales, etc. Relative Chiefly to Picturesque Beauty: Made in the Year 1770* (1782), which proclaimed the goal of examining the region described "by the rules of picturesque beauty . . . adapting the description of natural scenery to the principles of artificial landscape."[32] As a result, the illustrations were really of picturesque ideas and not of topographical drawings. Gilpin continued with accounts of the New Forest (1791) and the West of England (1798), each of which was more accessible to London than his earlier subjects. The linked emphasis on original virtue and the physical environment, at least in landscape, led to a stress on distinctive features and areas, such as the Lake District, rather than on the more general impact of civilization. This approach was intellectually matched by the definition of geology as an important and fashionable subject that underlined the distinctiveness of terrain.

Austen's *Love and Freindship*, finished in 1790, has Augusta prevail on her father to take a tour to Scotland as a result of reading Gilpin's *Observations, Relative Chiefly to Picturesque Beauty, Made in the Year 1766, On Several Parts of Great Britain; Particularly the High-Lands of Scotland* (1789). In her *History of England*, Austen names Gilpin as one of her three "first of Men," the others being Robert, Earl of Essex, a favorite who fell afoul of Elizabeth I, and Frederic Delamere, a fictional character. Austen's very brief *Tour through Wales* reflects the interest aroused by Gilpin.[33] His *Three Essays: on Picturesque Beauty; on Picturesque Travel; and on Sketching Landscape* (1792) influence Henry Tilney's discussion of landscape: "He talked of fore-grounds, distances, and second distances—side-screens and perspectives—lights and shades."[34]

Emphasizing a personal response to travel literature, Austen makes fun of the picturesque in *Pride and Prejudice*, when Elizabeth "laughingly" responds to the idea that the entire party walk together: "No, no; stay where you are.—You are charmingly group'd, and appear to uncommon advantage. The picturesque would be spoilt by admitting a fourth." Gilpin had argued that two or four would be an inappropriate combination in depicting cows, as three was the most picturesque. Later in the novel, there is a discussion of a proposed "tour of pleasure" with the Gardiners, possibly as far as the Lake District. Elizabeth Bennet's ecstatic response mocks the euphoria found in much of the literature: "'My dear, dear aunt,' she rapturously cried, 'what delight! What felicity! You give me fresh life and vigour. Adieu to disappointment and spleen. What are men to rocks and mountains?'"[35]

In *Northanger Abbey*, the power of the romantic landscape is such that "the General [Tilney] seemed to think an apology necessary for the flatness of the country, and the size of the village" of Woodston.[36] In *Sense and Sensibility*, Edward Ferrers describes to Marianne Dashwood a walk he has just taken in Devon, a county Austen had visited:

> Remember I have no knowledge in the picturesque, and I shall offend you by my ignorance and want of taste if we come to particulars. I shall call hills steep, which ought to be bold; surfaces strange and uncouth, which ought to be irregular and rugged; and distant objects out of sight, which ought only to be indistinct through the soft medium of a hazy atmosphere. You must be satisfied with such admiration as I can honestly give. I call it a very fine country—the hills are steep, the woods seem full of fine timber, and the valley looks comfortable and snug—with rich meadows and several neat farm houses scattered here and there. It exactly answers my idea of a fine country, because it unites beauty with utility—and I dare say it is a picturesque one too, because you admire it; I can easily believe it to be full of rocks and promontories, grey moss and brush wood,

but these are all lost on me. I know nothing of the picturesque.... I like a fine prospect, but not on picturesque principles. I do not like crooked, twisted, blasted trees. I admire them much more if they are tall, straight, and flourishing. I do not like ruined, tattered cottages. I am not fond of nettles or thistles, or heath blossoms. I have more pleasure in a snug farm-house than a watch-tower—and a troop of tidy, happy villages please me better than the finest banditti in the world.[37]

Yet Austen is more positive in *Persuasion*, writing of Lyme Regis, a town she had visited, just into Dorset from Devon:

The very beautiful line of cliffs stretching out to the east of the town, are what the stranger's eye will seek; and a very strange stranger it must be, who does not see charms in the immediate environs of Lyme, to make him wish to know it better. The scenes in its neighbourhood, Charmouth, with its high grounds and extensive sweeps of country, and still more its sweet retired bay, backed by dark cliffs, where fragments of low rock among the sands make it the happiest spot for watching the flow of the tide, for sitting in unwearied contemplation;—the woody varieties of the cheerful village of Up Lyme, and above all Pinny, with its green chasms between romantic rocks, where the scattered forest trees and orchards of luxuriant growth declare that many a generation must have passed away since the first partial falling of the cliff prepared the ground for such a state, where a scene so wonderful and so lovely is exhibited, as may more than equal any of the resembling scenes of the far-famed Isle of Wight.[38]

Love and Friendship shows how Austen could draw on a range of references when approaching landscape. Thus, her account of a Scottish landscape has been presented as a translation to Britain of the description of a Caribbean scene in Elizabeth Bromley's three-volume novel *Laura and Augustus, An Authentic Story* (1784).[39] Austen's father was to buy a copy of James Boswell's *Journal of a Tour to the Hebrides*. *Emma*, however, lacks this type of detail in the very brief account of the Campbells' trip to Ireland.[40]

Austen could engage with the gothic landscape and evoke a sense of place accordingly. Thus, Netley Abbey, a ruined

Cistercian abbey in Hampshire that Austen planned to visit in 1808, was a site for the rise of gothic tourism; indeed, in some respects it was a source of the gothic imagination. Some writers, such as Gilpin, were critical of supernatural accounts of such sites, but others sought more than the picturesque. The contrasting views of Netley provide a background to Austen's approach in *Northanger Abbey*.[41] A similar assessment is possible for other sites, including some mentioned by Austen. In her *History of England*, Austen mocks the gothic preference for ruins, as expressed by Catherine Morland in *Northanger Abbey*.[42] Austen observes of Henry VIII: "Nothing can be said in his vindication, but that his abolishing Religious Houses and leaving them to the ruinous depredations of time has been of infinite use to the landscape of England in general, which probably was a principal motive for his doing it, since otherwise why should a Man who was of no Religion himself be at so much trouble to abolish one which had for Ages been established in the Kingdom."[43]

Drawing on the description of Melrose Abbey in Walter Scott's *The Lay of the Last Minstrel* (1805), Austen has Fanny Price mistake what she will see with the chapel of Sotherton Court: "Fanny's imagination had prepared her for something grander than a mere, spacious, oblong room, fitted up for the purpose of devotion . . . 'This is not my idea of a chapel. There is nothing awful here, nothing melancholy, nothing grand. Here are no aisles, no arches, no inscriptions, no banners.'" This leads Edmund Bertram to reply: "You forget, Fanny, how lately all this has been built, and for how confined a purpose, compared with the old chapels of castles and monasteries."[44]

Austen mocks the taste for the sublime in her account of the conversation of the facile Sir Edward Denham in *Sanditon* as he seeks to interest Charlotte Heywood:

> He began, in a tone of great taste and feeling, to talk of the sea and the sea shore—and ran with energy through all the usual phrases employed in praise of their sublimity, and descriptive of the

undescribable emotions they excite in the mind of sensibility.—The terrific grandeur of the ocean in a storm, its glassy surface in a calm, its gulls and its samphire, and the deep fathoms of its abysses, its quick vicissitudes, its direful deceptions, its mariners tempting it in sunshine and overwhelmed by the sudden tempest, all were eagerly and fluently touched;—rather commonplace perhaps—but doing very well from the lips of a handsome Sir Edward,—and she could not but think him a man of feeling—till he began to stagger her with the number of his quotations, and the bewilderment of some of his sentences.[45]

Austen is very good on both unnecessary quotations and bewildering sentences, as with Denham and others. She doubts Denham's sincerity. Indeed, the latter is revealed as arrogant and condescending to women: "It were hypercriticism, it were pseudo-philosophy to expect from the soul of high-toned genius, the grovellings of a common mind. The coruscations of talent, elicited by impassioned feeling in the breast of man, are perhaps incompatible with some of the prosaic decencies of life . . . nor can any woman be a fair judge of what a man may be propelled to say, write or do, by the sovereign impulses of illimitable ardour."[46]

The market for an engagement with landscape, in turn, encouraged writers and artists to travel, write, and paint, although they did not have to do so, as evidenced by Austen and Joshua Reynolds, neither of whom traveled much. Experience could be acquired indirectly and, indeed, through the imagination. Landscape painting unrelated to the parkland of country houses developed, with early examples including Thomas Gainsborough's *Extensive River Landscape* (*c.* 1748–50) and George Lambert's *Moorland Landscape with Rainstorm* (1751). George Lambert's *The Great Falls of the Tees* (1746) depicted rustics, but when he returned to the subject in 1761, in a most impressive work, they were replaced by tourists dwarfed by the monumental rocks and clouds. John Inigo Richards (1731–1810) was the earliest prominent painter to visit the Dartmoor region. Francis Towne (1739–1816), who studied in London but was based for much of his life in Exeter, showed the interaction of metropolitan and provincial artistic circles. In Devon, he taught drawing at country houses and also painted and sketched local landscapes. By exhibiting works in London—such as his *View on the Exe* at the Royal Academy in 1779—Towne encouraged metropolitan interest in Devon landscapes. Travelers found not only subjects but also inspiration. Thomas Girtin (1775–1802), a watercolor painter who was a master of depicting light and shade, was much influenced by a visit to the North of England in 1796.[47] Artistic views were widely diffused. Thus, in *Mansfield Park*, Fanny Price has transparencies of Tintern Abbey and "a moonlight lake in Cumberland" in her room.[48]

Travel accounts, whether printed or not, were regarded as incomplete without illustrations. William Maton's *Tour in the Western Counties* (1797) was illustrated with views sketched by Rackett that were engraved by Aiken. Among those in the manuscript version, but not reproduced, were picturesque sketches of Ivy Bridge and Pendennis Castle.[49] John Swete, an affluent cleric whose illustrated journals were not published until recently, entitled them "Picturesque Sketches of Devon"; employed the term *picturesque* 125 times in his first four surviving journals; wrote of the sublime, the romantic, and the beautiful; and referred to Gilpin. Swete's values were seen in his description of a view near Torquay that he described in 1793, "a greater variety of pleasing and romantic scenery will rarely be met with—rocks, woods, houses, a villa and the sea, are seen intermingled in the happiest manner, altogether forming a landscape of uncommon beauty."[50]

Many traveled with journals, sketchbooks, and portable drawing aids, such as the Claude glass, a convex mirror that reflected the landscape tinted in miniature. Moreover, drawing manuals sought to aid travelers. Walking with Catherine Morland around Beechen Cliff near Bath in *Northanger Abbey*, the younger Tilneys view "the country with the eyes of persons accustomed to drawing, and decided on its capability of being formed into pictures, with all the eagerness of real taste," only for Austen to undercut this by remarking, with reference to fashionable views, "It seemed as if a good view were no longer to be taken from the top of an high hill, and that a clear blue sky was no longer a proof of a fine day."[51] This was typical of her style in offering criticism in a light and accessible fashion. Similarly, William Combe poked fun at Gilpin with his *Dr Syntax in Search of the Picturesque*, which was illustrated by Thomas Rowlandson.

Nevertheless, the perception of the country had changed. The literature on rural aesthetics helped shape travelogues and became prominent toward the close of the century, with Richard Payne Knight's *The Landscape: A Didactic Poem* (1794) and Uvedale Price's *An Essay on the Picturesque* (1794). Picturesque tourism also affected and shaped the response to travel abroad. Whereas the painter James Barry went to Italy in 1766–71 to look at ancient sculpture to equip himself to be a history painter, John Robert Cozens went there in 1776–79, and again in 1782–83, to look for dramatic scenery. Meanwhile, Switzerland became of interest because of the Alps, which very much provided an experience of the sublime, as Italy did for the neogothic.

Unlike Radcliffe, Austen does not take her characters abroad, but she liked to get them into the outdoors. The young Catherine Morland, "fond of all boys' plays," enjoys cricket.[52] As discussed in chapter 9, walking is a key aspect of the robust independence of Austen's characters. There is a clear match with their unwillingness to be socially confined and manipulated for matrimonial and other reasons—as happens, for example, to Anne Elliot.

Interest in the grandeur of untouched landscape was linked to a less sympathetic account of the appeal of urban life. The latter had always, in the classical manner, been seen as lacking integrity,[53] but the world of urban order and gentility was an attempt to share in civilized values—indeed, to disseminate them. These values were frequently seen as conspicuously lacking in rural fastnesses.

The romantic movement transposed this approach, with the city as the culmination of a false consciousness—indeed, corruption and decadence—that was opposed not to rural order but to an untrammeled naturalness seen in "sublime" landscape. Wordsworth and Samuel Taylor Coleridge in *Lyrical Ballads* (1798), and Wordsworth in "Tintern Abbey" (1798), were the poets of this attitude. Wordsworth believed a writer could only be true to himself if he lived in such areas.

Separately, Wordsworth and Coleridge sought to display a "prosaic" poetry to show how far the language used by the bulk of the population could serve the ends of poetry. Wordsworth, in fact, did not live up to this idea because, although sometimes simple, his language remained refined. Instead, the Scottish poet Robert Burns was the innovator in this quarter, melding folk song and "higher" forms in a language of an acutely varying register. If Wordsworth's idea of a prosaic poetry was far less influential on contemporaries than it became subsequently, it nevertheless reflected the sense of cultural and political flux.

While looking to the contemporary context of lasting issues, and very aware of current writers, Austen also drew heavily on the models of the past, notably Samuel Richardson's novel *Sir Charles Grandison*. Austen was a great reader and keen critic of the work of other writers, as can be seen in her correspondence and her novels. Thus, in 1807, she observed to Cassandra: "'Alphonsine' did not do. We were disgusted in twenty pages, as, independent of a bad translation, it has indelicacies which disgrace a pen hitherto so pure; and we changed it for the 'Female Quixote,' which now makes our evening amusement; to me a very high one."[54]

Her protagonists, who provided the tone of each novel, were characters lived from within in a different fashion than some of the more striking displays of individualism among romantic writers—for example, in Caroline Lamb's Byronic novel *Glenarvon* (1816), a rapidly written and deliberately shocking work by Lord Byron's former lover. Austen emphasized the consistency of a character, which in part meant writing in the tone of that character. Thus, the revision of the two chapters of *Persuasion*, the original chapters 10 and 11 from the second volume, indicate the need to bring the writing into line with Anne Elliot's character.[55] This life from within, carefully crafted by Austen, provided a depth that aided the understanding of motivation. Whether that depth should be seen as novel, modern, romantic, and/or subversive is in part a matter of definitions and preferences, but great literature is not dependent on exegesis and analysis.

NOTES

1. F. P. Lock, *Edmund Burke I, 1730–1784* (Oxford, 1998), 91–124.

2. A. Radcliffe, *The Mysteries of Udolpho* (London, 1794), chapter 1.

3. A. Radcliffe, *The Italian, or The Confessional of the Black Penitents* (London, 1797), 155–57.

4. *MP* I, 11.

5. E. J. Clery, *The Rise of Supernatural Fiction, 1762–1800* (Cambridge, 1995).

6. D. Townshend and A. Wright, eds., *Ann Radcliffe, Romanticism and the Gothic* (Cambridge, 2014).

7. J. Lamb, "Imagination, Conjecture, and Disorder," *Eighteenth-Century Studies* 45 (2011): 53–69.

8. *Emma* I, 4.

9. *Sense* III, 7–8.

10. *Northanger* II, 9.

11. W. Beckford, *Vathek*, ed. R. Lonsdale (Oxford, 1980), 120.

12. E. R. Napier, *The Failure of Gothic: Problems of Disjunction in an Eighteenth-Century Literary Form* (Oxford, 1987).

13. A. Janowitz, *England's Ruins: Poetic Purpose and the National Landscape* (Oxford, 1990).

14. T. Whately, *Observations on Modern Gardening* (London, 1770), 155.

15. *Northanger* II, 2.

16. *Sense* III, 10.

17. *Sanditon* 8.

18. B. Sutcliffe, ed., *Plays by George Colman the Younger and Thomas Morton* (Cambridge, 1983), 10.

19. N. Penny, "An Ambitious Man: The Career and Achievement of Sir Joshua Reynolds," in *Reynolds*, ed. N. Penny (London, 1986), 39.

20. M. Butler, *Romantics, Rebels and Reactionaries: English Literature and Its Background, 1760–1830* (Oxford, 1981).

21. *Lady Susan* 24; *Later Manuscripts*, 52.

22. S. Johnson, *The Rambler*, no. 4, March 31, 1750.

23. M. B. Ross, *The Contours of Masculine Desire: Romanticism and the Rise of Women's Poetry* (Oxford, 1990).

24. C. Tuite, *Romantic Austen: Sexual Politics and the Literary Canon* (Cambridge, 2002).

25. *Sense* III, 1.

26. K. W. Graham, *The Politics of Narrative: Ideology and Social Change in William Godwin's Caleb Williams* (New York, 1990).

27. S. Derry, "Robert Bage's *Barham Downs* and *Sense and Sensibility*," *Notes and Queries* 239, no. 3 (September 1994): 325–26.

28. A. K. Mellor, *Romanticism and Gender* (London, 1993), 53; A. Johns, *Women's Utopias of the Eighteenth Century* (Champaign, IL, 2003).

29. *The Monthly Epitome*, vol. 1 (London, 1797), 180.

30. M. O. Grenby, *The Anti-Jacobin Novel: British Conservatism and the French Revolution* (Cambridge, 2001).

31. *Poetry of the Anti-Jacobin* (London, 1799); J. J. Sack, *From Jacobite to Conservative: Reaction and Orthodoxy in Britain, c. 1760–1832* (Cambridge, 1993).

32. William Gilpin, *Observations on the River Wye and Several Parts of South Wales, etc. Relative Chiefly to Picturesque Beauty: Made in the Year 1770* (1782), 1.

33. *Juvenilia*, 224.

34. *Northanger* I, 14.

35. *PP* I, 10; II, 4.

36. *Northanger* II, 11.

37. *MP* I, 18.

38. *Persuasion* I, 11.

39. S. Derry, "Sources of Jane Austen's *Love and Freindship*: A Note," *Notes and Queries* 235, no. 1 (March 1990): 18–19.

40. *Emma* II, 1.

41. D. Townshend, "Ruins, Romance and the Rise of Gothic Tourism: The Case of Netley Abbey, 1750–1830," *Journal for Eighteenth-Century Studies* 37 (2014): 377–94.

42. *Northanger* II, 8.

43. *Juvenilia*, 181.

44. *MP* I, 9.

45. *Sanditon* 7.

46. *Sanditon* 7.

47. M. Andrews, *The Search for the Picturesque: Landscape, Aesthetics and Tourism in Britain, 1760–1800* (Aldershot, UK, 1989).

48. *MP* I, 16.

49. Exeter, Devon Record Office, Z19/2/10a.

50. T. Gray, ed., *Travels in Georgian Devon: The Illustrated Journals of the Reverend John Swete, 1789–1800* (Exeter, UK, 1997), xiv, 161.

51. *Northanger* I, 14.

52. *Northanger* I, 1.

53. M. Mack, *The Garden and the City: Retirement and Politics in the Later Poetry of Pope, 1731–1743* (Toronto, 1969).

54. *Letters*, 115–16. A preference for Charlotte Lennox's *The Female Quixote* (1752) over Mme de Genlis's *Alphonsine* (1806).

55. R. W. Chapman, ed., *Jane Austen: The Manuscript Chapters of Persuasion* (London, 1985).

—ꝏ—

CONCLUSIONS

It was a sweet view—sweet to the eye and the mind.
English verdure, English culture, English comfort,
seen under a sun bright, without being oppressive.

—*Emma* III, 6

Like *Pride and Prejudice*, who knew that
the film was originally a book

—Kate Fox, discussing *Jaws*, BBC Radio 4

A STRONG FEELING OF ENGLISHNESS,[1] or, rather, an Englishness, emerges from Austen's novels. Kipling indeed called her
"England's Jane." It is an Englishness of place and people, of a
rural society that was part of a broader pattern of spatial relationships focused on London. Behavior was important to this Englishness. In *Emma*, where landscape is praised, Austen refers to
the meeting of the Knightley brothers "in the true English style,
burying under a calmness that seemed all but indifference, the
real attachment which would have led either of them, if requisite,
to do every thing for the good of the other."[2]

At the same time, there is a well-grounded sense of a nation under threat, one that leads Henry Tilney to discuss politics.[3] This sense draws on a patriotism that connects with Austen's life, beliefs, and work, even more so because this sense is presented with decorum. Austen's novels scarcely appear particularly nationalist or patriotic today. They are not perceived as counterparts to more recent treatments of those years, such as Bernard Cornwell's *Sharpe* novels, which appeared from 1981. However, struggle was a central theme in national identity and was crucial to the life of three of Austen's siblings.

This struggle had a moral character difficult to capture today. There was struggle against vice—international and domestic, political and religious—a theme that linked moralists who had very different political prospectuses but that also captured the moral obligations of statehood. Liberty and religion seemed dependent upon the moral caliber of the people; in a long-standing Tory theme, this caliber was threatened by subversion encouraged by poor governance and a lack of adequate leadership by the social elite.

Furthermore, the achievements of the past that had led to the present situation were no more than stages upon the road; nationhood had to be defended, not least if the country wished to be ensured of the support of providence. This defensiveness accorded with the belief that Anglo-Saxon liberties had been overthrown by the Norman Conquest of 1066. Thus, nationalism was cumulative, a matter of past as well as present and structures as well as events. The Handel celebrations held in 1784–91, and strongly supported by George III, showed the continuing popularity of the idea of Britain (in practice England) as an "elect nation" and a second Israel chosen by God. Nationalism was identified with divine support. It was also cumulative. Thus, Toryism, from the late 1740s increasingly shorn of its earlier Jacobitism, had been integrated into the national political culture and language under George. National cultural interests, rather than cosmopolitan alternatives, were to the fore, and the past was interpreted to emphasize Englishness. In addition, the sense and stability of the locality were building blocks for the nation, and the security of the nation guaranteed stability in the locality. The role of religion was crucial in these equations.

The cultural approach to nationalism is echoed in *Mansfield Park* with the reading aloud of Shakespeare, first by Fanny Price and then by Henry Crawford, which is followed by Henry's affirmation of Shakespeare: "Shakespeare one gets acquainted with without knowing how. It is a part of an Englishman's constitution. His thoughts and beauties are so spread abroad that one touches them every where, one is intimate with him by instinct." Edmund Bertram adds a characteristic caveat: "No doubt, one is familiar with Shakespeare in a degree from one's earliest years. His celebrated passages are quoted by every body; they are in half the books we open, and we all talk Shakespeare, use his similies, and describe with his descriptions; but this is totally distinct from giving his sense as you gave it. To know him in bits and scraps, is common enough, to know him pretty thoroughly, is perhaps, not uncommon, but to read him well aloud, is no everyday talent."[4] Ann Radcliffe and Frances Burney quoted Shakespeare frequently in their works.

During the French Revolutionary and Napoleonic Wars (1793–1815), Church and Crown ideology became stronger while Toryism was re-created as a politics of patriotism and nationalism. There was also a renewed interest in revealed theology—revelation, providentialism, and biblicalism—rather than apparent natural religious truths. Politics and religion are backgrounded in Austen's novels—notably so for many modern readers—but both are present. At the party at the Coles' house in *Emma*, "politics and Mr Elton" were talked over,[5] but the former is not described. That helped make the book less specific to contemporaries as well as subsequently, which increased its general and lasting appeal.

The politics outlined by Austen are broad. Thus, the social hierarchy can be amusingly challenged, as in the discussion of whose advice to seek on the Weston ball. Mrs. Weston wishes for popularity: "I wish one could know which arrangement our guests in general would like best. To do what would be most generally pleasing must be our object—if one could but tell what that would be." Frank Churchill responds "very true" twice, adding: "You want your neighbours' opinions. I do not wonder at you. If one could ascertain what the chief of them—the Coles, for instance. They are not far off. Shall I call upon them? Or Miss Bates? She is still nearer.—And I do not know whether Miss Bates is not as likely to understand the inclinations of the rest of the people as any body. I think we do want a larger council."[6]

Emma comments uncharitably on Miss Bates, but, as Austen notes, Emma is also correct about Miss Bates being an "approver" and not a "counsellor." The balance of judgment on consultation is finely poised, as so often in her novels. This is an aspect of Austen's Englishness.

A sense of Englishness, specifically mentioned, was captured by Austen in *Persuasion*, and it was intentionally presented in a rural light. Moreover, the reference to the long-established authority of squire and parson captured the joined themes of continuity and legitimacy. Even the change that had occurred was scarcely disruptive: "Uppercross was a moderate-sized village, which a few years back had been completely in the old English style; containing only two houses superior in appearance to those of the yeomen and labourers,—the mansion of the 'squire, with its high walls, great gates, and old trees, substantial and unmodernised—and the compact, tight parsonage, enclosed in its own neat garden, with a vine and a pear-tree trained round its casements; but upon the marriage of the young 'squire, it had received the improvement of a farm-house elevated into a cottage for his residence."[7]

The hypocritical Mr. Elliot sought to reassure Sir Walter that his feelings, as to connections, were strict—indeed, "too strict to suit the unfeudal tone of the present day!"[8] In practice, Austen, like many other conservative writers across the ages, had to adjust not just to social change but, more specifically, to the end of feudalism and its social sway. An emphasis on Englishness offers a means to do so, with the social values of the past diffused into the landscape, both in general and in particular, and most particularly so with the end of the medieval sway of castles and abbeys.

Far more than landscape is involved in Englishness, as is made clear in *Northanger Abbey*. The sensible Henry Tilney offers a justified correction to Catherine Morland's suspicion that his father was a murderer: "What have you been judging from? Remember the country and the age in which we live. Remember that we are English, that we are Christians. . . . Does our education prepare us for such atrocities? Do our laws connive at them? Could they be perpetrated without being known, in a country, like this, where social and literary intercourse is on such a footing; where every man is surrounded by a neighbourhood of voluntary spies, and where roads and newspapers lay every thing open?"[9]

Englishness is a theme when Catherine, rebuked by Henry, comes to appreciate that she has been misled by her reading:

> Charming as were all Mrs Radcliffe's works, and charming even as were the works of all her imitators, it was not in them perhaps that human nature, at least in the midland counties of England, was to be looked for . . . there was surely some security for the existence even of a wife not beloved, in the laws of the land, and the manners of the age. Murder was not tolerated, servants were not slaves. . . . Among the Alps and Pyrenees, perhaps, there were no mixed characters. . . . But in England it was not so; among the English, she believed, in their hearts and habits, there was a general though unequal mixture of good and bad.[10]

Austen brought this mixture into clear view without probing Catherine's unintentionally amusing suggestion that the situation might be less benign in the further reaches of England. The idea that abroad individuals are virtuous or evil, whereas in

England they are mixed, offers an interesting insight on Austen's presentation of her characters. Certainly, the unalloyed good of sentimental novels and the bad of their gothic counterparts thus emerge not only as implausible but also as un-English.

At the same time, Austen's novels came to be seen as quintessentially English, both in what they depicted and in her response to the characters she created. The nuance of her characters is not just an aspect of her Englishness but also of her genius, in contrast with the cardboard characters of the gothic romance—or, indeed, Netflix romances. Austen's understanding of human nature is both light-hearted and deeply felt and observed. In addition, when Abbey Mill Farm is depicted in *Emma* as English and "seen under a sun bright, without being oppressive,"[11] the implied contrast is with the oppression of Continental countries, notably, but not only, France. This is a pointed contrast, given the long conflict with that country, that underlines the role of that conflict in the development and expression of English patriotism and culture.

Hated by Mark Twain but read by Winston Churchill, Austen has had varied fortunes but has grown to what at present appears to be an enduring popularity. Twain was to the point: "I haven't any right to criticise books, and I don't do it except when I hate them. I often want to criticise Jane Austen, but her books madden me so that I can't conceal my frenzy from the reader; and therefore I have to stop every time I begin. Every time I read *Pride and Prejudice* I want to dig her up and beat her over the skull with her own shin-bone."

Speaking of Edgar Allen Poe, Twain remarked: "To me his prose is unreadable—like Jane Austen's. No there is a difference. I could read his prose on salary, but not Jane's. Jane is entirely impossible. It seems a great pity that they allowed her to die a natural death."[12] Churchill, in contrast, read Austen during difficult wartime moments. In December 1943, when he had pneumonia and a heart attack in North Africa, Sarah Churchill read him

Pride and Prejudice. On the voyage back from the second Quebec conference, in September 1944, Churchill read *Emma* and commented on the difference between her age and the present.[13]

Today, is Austen on the wrong side of the historical moment in Britain? She appears most frequently in modern Britain on the ten-pound note, the banknote most commonly distributed from ATMs and most frequent in people's purses. She has taken this role since September 2017, replacing—in part in response to the need for a woman other than the queen on bank notes—the image introduced in 1993 featuring Charles Dickens and an illustration of the village cricket match from *The Pickwick Papers*. For Dickens, this was nostalgia rather than realism, as scenes of urban life, notably in London, were far more frequent in his novels. The 2017 replacement, although presenting a misleading image of Austen that is heavily airbrushed, depicted her novels accurately in an illustration of Godmersham Park, a country house owned by her brother Edward, and not one of her urban scenes in Bath or London. However, this apparently puts Austen on the wrong side. More positively, there is a quotation on the banknote: "I declare after all there is no enjoyment like reading!" However, this line is stated ironically in *Pride and Prejudice* by Caroline Bingley, who does not mean it.[14]

"A profoundly reactionary vision" was the view of David Marquand in 2017 when seeking to explain Brexit in terms of "myths, memories and rhetoric" that "for centuries" had "transmitted a vision of Englishness of extraordinary power." This vision had Shakespeare to the fore as Marquand's target and not "a second England, sustained by a second vision of Englishness"—that of the Peasants' Revolt, John Milton, Tom Paine, the Chartists, and the suffragettes. The 2016 EU referendum was seen as a defeat for this second England because the "leavers had the better tunes. They allegedly spoke to the heart."[15]

Austen apparently fits in with this narrative—but in the first, not the second, England. The view of Shakespeare offered by

Marquand is certainly misleading. He is presented as the exponent of a misconceived and anachronistic "hymn to England as a 'precious stone set in the silver sea'"[16] and not, for example, as the pointed critic of the harshness of the social system, as in *King Lear*, or the misuse of power, as in *Measure for Measure*. Austen herself praised Shakespeare in *Mansfield Park* as "part of an Englishman's constitution. His thoughts and beauties are so spread abroad that one touches them everywhere; one is intimate with him by instinct." The Bertram boys acted Shakespeare as children in order to be able to speak with propriety.[17]

So, again, Austen appears on the wrong side, certainly as judged by Marquand and, indeed, as part of a culture that was successively rejected after she died. This rejection took a number of forms that occurred in a series of stages. Secularization, socioeconomic change, political transformation, and the changing position of women all made Austen's world appear redundant and worse. Moreover, doing so made modern presentations of Austen appear dangerously nostalgic and part of the world Marquand attacked. Austen, however, avoided much of the criticism, in part due to the role of feminism and the argument that her work included feminist themes and had similarities with that of Mary Wollstonecraft. In practice, Austen's novels were centrally comedies, with her comic means focused on irony, and the feminism was more moderate.[18]

Austen's world appears more comprehensible in terms of aspects of the society that came to a close in the 1960s. At the same time, there had been many earlier indications of change. Moreover, looking both to today and to longer shifts in society, there are more lasting themes that Austen would have understood, including social ambition. Thus, if Austen comments on social ambition that is a lasting theme. One of the characters in E. C. R. Lorac's *Murder on the Oxford Road* (1933) "wants his son to marry a title."[19] In that novel, as in those of Austen, there is the question of a new family being received into the neighborhood and the linked issue of visits. Marquand and others are mistaken if they see questions of status and issues of courtship as somehow redundant or not applicable today. Moreover, there is a clear need to distinguish between whether Austen herself is nostalgic or whether modern presentations of her world are nostalgic. Obviously, anyone writing just over two centuries ago is writing about a very different world. But especially in *Persuasion*, Austen is very aware that things are changing and is not clinging to the past.

Austen, who died in 1817, was not one of the literary lions of the age. That feat was achieved by Byron and Scott. Austen, however, had acquired a clear commercial value by the close of her life and was judged worthy of compliment by the prince regent. At the same time, her early death hit hard in terms of sales, which for most authors tended to be limited to the first year or two of publication. Indeed, a presentness was characteristic of Austen's writing as the novels were grounded in particular moments.

Reprints of Austen's novels were infrequent. Thus, although reprinted in the United States in 1816, *Emma* was not reprinted in Britain until 1833 when the Bentley "Standard Novels" began to appear. In part, this was characteristic of the fiction of the period, as much as any comment on Austen's work, then or subsequently, as not matching interest in the "Condition of England." The latter was certainly to the fore in much fiction from the mid-nineteenth century. Elizabeth Gaskell (1810–65) wrote about industrial strife, working-class living standards, and the role of entrepreneurs in *Mary Barton* (1848) and entrepreneurs in *North and South* (1855). George Eliot, the pseudonym of Mary Anne Evans (1819–80), depicted a seducing squire in *Adam Bede* (1859), social ostracism in *The Mill on the Floss* (1860), the cruel selfishness of the two sons of the squire in *Silas Marner* (1861), corrupt electioneering in *Felix Holt* (1866), a hypocritical banker in *Middlemarch* (1871–72), and the decadent mores of society in *Daniel Deronda* (1878). Social rank is seen as divisive in *Middlemarch*.

However, such novels were but part of a more varied fictional world that covered a range of genres, including historical novels, the forte of Bulwer Lytton, notably in *The Last Days of Pompeii* (1834); Charles Kingsley; and many others.

An explanation of an event that does not occur is always difficult, but Austen's relative lack of popularity (by today's standards) can best be located in this context, notably in a focus on new works. The reprinting of old novels was well established in the nineteenth century, but interest in new novels was far more significant than later discussion of a literary canon might suggestion. Moreover, that remained the case into the twentieth century.

Austen herself was seen as somewhat cold and her characters as short of commitment and fire. Yet, she helped make female intellectual life readily compatible with Victorian respectability. Austen was also commercially attractive, as Henry James noted in his 1905 essay "The Lesson of Balzac": "so amenable to pretty reproduction in every variety of what is called tasteful, and in what seemingly proves to be saleable."[20]

At the same time, praise for Austen was countered in some circles—for example, by Mark Twain. Certain critics perceived a sense of a hardness in Austen's writing.[21] In his "Letter to Lord Byron," published as part of his *Letters from Iceland* (1937), W. H. Auden commented:

> Beside her Joyce seems innocent as grass.
> It makes me most uncomfortable to see
> An English spinster of the middle class
> Describe the amorous effect of "brass,"
> Reveal so frankly and with so much sobriety
> The economic basis of society.

Meanwhile, more Austen works had appeared, including *Lady Susan*, *The Watsons* and juvenilia from 1871, surviving correspondence from 1884, and a full version of *Sanditon* in 1925. These works, notably the tone of *Lady Susan*, caused controversy.

The literary canon has changed repeatedly, and here Austen came into her own in the late twentieth century. This reflected a range of factors. It would be easy to emphasize academic ones, but others drew on social assumptions, notably of the role of women. In March 2019, arriving at the Villiers Hotel in Buckingham, my room contained a card advertising on one side a series of presents, including "a spa break with Classic British Hotels," and, on the other side, "The Sisterhood Collection" from Penguin. It carried illustrations of new book covers for six classics: *The Railway Children*, *Anne of Green Gables*, *Heidi*, *Pride and Prejudice*, *Little Women*, and *A Little Princess*. *Pride and Prejudice* thus added some adult heft to a collection of stories classically for girls—a juxtaposition that might have surprised Austen.

Austen is potent in academic terms in part because she could be variously located, including within the romantic canon as the result of development from earlier preromantic texts. The latter, *Northanger Abbey*, *Pride and Prejudice*, and *Emma*, were thus succeeded by *Sense and Sensibility*, *Persuasion*, *Mansfield Park*, and *Sanditon*. There was certainly no unchanging style on Austen's part, and thus Austen responded to her rapidly developing culture.

As far as the public was concerned, name recognition was important to Austen's ability to act as a key figure in the rapidly developing field of heritage culture. Indeed, she joined this to an account of gender politics in terms of a witty assertiveness. This helps account for the present-day popularity of Elizabeth Bennet, as in *Pride and Prejudice and Zombies* (2016), a film where the existential challenge is expressed thus: "It is a truth universally acknowledged that a zombie in possession of a brain must be in want of more brains."

Austen's novels have been filmed from 1940, when *Pride and Prejudice* appeared to great commercial success. However, no other film adaptation appeared until 1995. In 1995–96, five film adaptations appeared: *Clueless*, *Persuasion*, *Sense and Sensibility*, and two versions of *Emma*. *Clueless* was a loosely based version of *Emma* set in a modern Los Angeles school but with some significant differences, not least a homosexual Frank Churchill. Television versions were frequent, including *Emma* in 1948, 1954, 1960, and 1972; *Persuasion* in 1960 and 1971; *Mansfield Park* in 1983; *Pride and Prejudice* in 1949, 1952, 1958, 1967, and 1980; and *Sense and Sensibility* in 1950, 1971, and 1981. The 1995 BBC television series of *Pride and Prejudice* had a major impact. Superbly acted, it was most noted at the time for Colin Firth, who played Darcy, meeting Elizabeth outside Pemberley wearing a wet shirt after a swim in the lake.[22]

This television series was closer to the novel than the 2005 film, which was more akin to romanticism, not least in the characterization and a scene with Elizabeth Bennet poised precariously on a cliff in the Peak District. The film was commercially successful, both in the UK and the United States.[23] The 1999 film of *Mansfield Park* was even more distant from the novel, notably in the engagement with slavery as an issue.

There is a division among the novels, with certain ones, notably *Pride and Prejudice* and *Emma*, receiving more film attention than others, especially *Mansfield Park* and *Northanger Abbey*. The latter did not reach the screen until 1986 and then only as a ninety-minute television film. A two-hour television film followed in 2007.

"The Jane Austen boom"[24] has extended to other works linked to Austen and across a range. Thus, there have been many and varied adaptations of *Pride and Prejudice*, including *Bride and Prejudice* (2004), *Pride and Prejudice: A Latter Day Comedy* (2003), and to a degree, although with important differences, *Bridget Jones's Diary* (2001). *Becoming Jane* (2007) provided a fictional account of a relationship between Austen and Tom Lefroy that suggested, on the basis of scant evidence, that the latter was the love of her life.

Death Comes to Pemberley (2011), a murder story written by the very prominent British mystery writer P. D. James as a sequel to *Pride and Prejudice*, became a television series broadcast on BBC1 in 2013 and on PBS in 2014. With a different content and tone, the episode of the popular British detective series *Midsomer Murders* broadcast on ITV on July 29, 2017, was set in an Austen revival weekend. More specifically, detective fiction's interest in Austen was taken up by Stephanie Barron beginning in 1996 in a series of novels entitled the *Jane Austen Mysteries*. "Detection"[25] is certainly a key theme in Austen's novels. Critics have taken up this interest, not least in the puzzles of Austen's plots and the challenges of reading character. The problems of the latter, notably in the face of confusion caused by sentimentality and misplaced sensibility, have been probed in terms of the exposition of puzzles.[26]

In terms of place, Chawton House and Library have become an Austen shrine, as has the Jane Austen Centre in Bath. Austen serves as an indicator of a certain character as well as quality of writing, as in the description of Elena Ferrante as "the Jane Austen of contemporary Italy."[27]

At the same time, Austen's characters and plots can risk appearing out-of-place as sentimental, class ridden, and nostalgic. In the (London) *Times* of May 27, 2019, Stephen Graham, a Merseysider seeking to define his gritty acting style, ended the interview: "The more strait-laced costume dramas are not for him. 'I'm probably not Mr Darcy, am I? Someone who smashes the window and gets in through the back door—that's more me.'" Attacking sentimentality in the (London) *Times* on January 3, 2019, Max Hastings found it "hard to believe that a girl as self-willed as Emma Woodhouse would much enjoy marriage to Mr Knightly, twice her age, forever subjecting her to pompous homilies... what of Elizabeth Bennet and Darcy? Cleverclogs say that her family's awfulness would not matter, because Pemberley lies far from Longbourn. Come off it. Mrs Bennet... would never be out of her daughter's Chatsworth-lookalike. Darcy would surely have taken the Grand Tour rather than endure the plaguey Bennets."[28]

Hastings captured the willingness of readers to react to Austen's characters, which is a product of her skill and sensitivity. They have lasted to the present and have become a part of Englishness.

NOTES

1. J. Sutherland, *The Good Brexiteer's Guide to English Lit* (London, 2018), 104–7.

2. *Emma* I, 12.

3. *Northanger* I, 14.

4. *MP* III, 3.

5. *Emma* II, 8.

6. *Emma* II, 11.

7. *Persuasion* I, 5.

8. *Persuasion* II, 3.

9. *Northanger* II, 9.

10. *Northanger* II, 10.

11. *Emma* III, 6.

12. *Who Is Mark Twain?* (New York, 2009), 47–51.

13. J. Rose, *The Literary Churchill* (New Haven, CT, 2014), 369.

14. *PP* I, 11.

15. D. Marquand, "Britain's Problem Is Not with Europe, but with England," *Guardian*, December 19, 2017.

16. D. Aaronovitch, "Our Island Must Stop Living in the Tudor Past," *Times*, January 24, 2013.

17. M. Weedon, "Jane Austen and William Enfield's *The Speaker*," *British Journal for Eighteenth-Century Studies* 11 (1988): 159.

18. L. W. Smith, *Jane Austen and the Drama of Woman* (London, 1983); M. Evans, *Jane Austen and the State* (London, 1987); A. Sulloway, *Jane Austen and the Province of Womanhood* (Philadelphia, PA, 1989).

19. E. C. R. Lorac [pseudonym for Edith Caroline Rivett], *Death on the Oxford Road* (London, 1933), 30, 83.

20. L. Edel, ed., *The House of Fiction: Essays on the Novel* (London, 1962), 62–63.

21. B. C. Southam, ed., *Jane Austen: The Critical Heritage*, vol. 2, *1870–1940* (London, 1987).

22. L. Troost and S. Greenfield, eds., *Jane Austen in Hollywood*, 2nd ed. (Lexington, KY, 2001); S. Parrill, *Jane Austen on Film and Television:*

A Critical Study of the Adaptations (Jefferson, NC, 2002); D. Cartmell, *Screen Adaptations: Jane Austen's Pride and Prejudice: A Close Study of the Relationship between Text and Film* (2010); N. F. Stovel, "From Page to Screen: Emma Thompson's Film Adaptation of *Sense and Sensibility*," *Persuasions On-Line* 32, no. 1 (winter 2011), http://www.jasna.org/persuasions/on-line/vol32no1/stovel.html.

23. Cartmell, *Screen Adaptations*; P. Demory, "Jane Austen and the Chick Flick in the Twenty-First Century," in *Adaptation Studies: New Approaches*, ed. C. Albrecht-Crane and D. Cutchins (Madison, NJ, 2010), 121–49.

24. B. Allen, "An Elusive Acquaintance," *New Criterion* (February 1998): 74–77, quote 74.

25. *PP* II, 12.

26. E. R. Belton, "Mystery Without Murder: The Detective Plots of Jane Austen," *Nineteenth-Century Literature* 31, no. 1 (1988): 42–59; P. D. James, "Emma Considered as a Detective Story," in *A Time to Be in Earnest* (New York, 1999), 243–59; L. B. Faucon, "Unravelling Mysteries: Developing a 'Method of Understanding' in Austen's and Ang Lee's *Sense and Sensibility*," *Revue de la Société d'Études Anglo-Américaines des XVIIe et XVIIIe siècles* 72 (2015): 287–312.

27. P. d'Acierno, "Naples as Chaosmos or, The City That Makes You Repeat Its Discourse," in *Delirious Naples: A Cultural History of the City of the Sun*, ed. P. Acierno and S. G. Pugliese (New York, 2019), 13.

28. M. Hastings, "We Can't Get Enough of 'Happy Ever After,'" *Times*, January 3, 2019.

SELECTED FURTHER READING

The Cambridge edition of the *Works of Jane Austen* is the best. In this series, *Jane Austen in Context* (Cambridge, 2005), edited by Janet Todd, is especially valuable for the purposes of this book. A full bibliography can be found there. The following is a selection.

Babb, Howard. *Jane Austen's Novels: The Fabric of Dialogue*. Columbus: Ohio State University Press, 1962.
Barchas, Janine. *Matters of Fact in Jane Austen: History, Location, Celebrity*. Baltimore, 2012.
Batchelor, Jennie, and Cora Kaplan, eds. *British Women's Writing in the Long Eighteenth Century: Authorship, Politics and History*. Basingstoke, UK, 2005.
Brown, Lloyd. *Bits of Ivory: Narrative Techniques in Jane Austen's Fiction*. Baton Rouge, LA, 1973.
Butler, Marilyn. *Jane Austen and the War of Ideas*. 2nd ed. Oxford, 1987.
Byrne, Paula. *The Real Jane Austen: A Life in Small Things*. London, 2013.
Carlile, Susan. *Charlotte Lennox: An Independent Mind c. 1729–1804*. Toronto, 2018.
Copeland, Edward. *Women Writing about Money: Women's Fiction in England, 1790–1820*. Cambridge, 1995.
Craig, Sheryl. *Jane Austen and the State of the Nation*. Basingstoke, UK, 2015.
Deresiewicz, William. *Jane Austen and the Romantic Poets*. New York, 2004.
Doody, Margaret. *Jane Austen's Names: Riddles, Persons, Places*. Chicago, 2015.

Duckworth, Alistair. *The Improvement of the Estate: A Study of Jane Austen's Novels*. Baltimore, MD, 1971.

Fergus, Jan. *Jane Austen: A Literary Life*. Basingstoke, UK, 1991.

Galperin, William. *The Historical Austen*. Philadelphia, 2003.

Garside, Peter, James Raven, and Rainer Schöwerling, eds. *The English Novel, 1770–1829*. Oxford, 2000.

Gay, Penny. *Jane Austen and the Theatre*. Cambridge, 2002.

Grey, J. David. *Jane Austen's Beginnings: The Juvenilia and Lady Susan*. Ann Arbor, MI, 1989.

Harris, Jocelyn. *Jane Austen's Art of Memory*. Cambridge, 1989.

Harris, Jocelyn. *Satire, Celebrity, and Politics in Jane Austen*. Lewisburg, PA, 2017.

Johnson, Claudia. *Jane Austen: Women, Politics and the Novel*. Chicago, 1988.

Kaplan, Deborah. *Jane Austen among Women*. Baltimore, MD, 1992.

Kelly, Helena. *Jane Austen, the Secret Radical*. London, 2016.

Keymer, Tom. *Jane Austen: Writing, Society, Politics*. Oxford 2020.

Knox-Shaw, Peter. *Jane Austen and the Enlightenment*. Cambridge, 2004.

Lascelles, Mary. *Jane Austen and Her Art*. London, 1939.

Le Faye, Deirdre. *Jane Austen's Country Life*. London: Francis Lincoln, 2014.

Litz, A. Walton. *Jane Austen: A Study of Her Artistic Development*. London, 1965.

McMaster, Juliet. *Jane Austen the Novelist: Past and Present*. Basingstoke, UK, 1996.

Miller, D. A. *Jane Austen, or the Secret of Style*. Princeton, NJ, 2003.

Mooneyham, Laura. *Romance, Language and Education in Jane Austen's Novels*. Basingstoke, UK, 1988.

Moore, Roger. *Jane Austen and the Reformation: Remembering the Sacred Landscape*. Farnham, UK, 2016.

Mudrick, Marvin. *Jane Austen: Irony as Defense and Discovery*. Princeton, NJ, 1952.

Nardin, Jane. *Those Elegant Decorums: The Concept of Propriety in Jane Austen's Novels*. Albany, NY, 1973.

Nash, Julie, ed. *New Essays on Maria Edgeworth*. Aldershot, UK, 2006.

Nokes, David. *Jane Austen: A Life*. London, 1997.

Poovey, Mary. *The Proper Lady and the Woman Writer: Ideology as Style in the Works of Mary Wollstonecraft, Mary Shelley and Jane Austen*. Chicago, 1984.

Sale, Roger. *Closer to Home: Writers and Places in England, 1780–1830.* Cambridge, MA, 1986.

Selwyn, David. *Jane Austen and Leisure.* London, 1999.

Smith, LeRoy. *Jane Austen and the Drama of Woman.* London: Palgrave Macmillan, 1983.

Spencer, Jane. *The Rise of the Woman Novelist: From Aphra Behn to Jane Austen.* Oxford, 1986.

Sulloway, Alison. *Jane Austen and the Province of Womanhood.* Philadelphia, 1989.

Sutherland, Kathryn, ed. *Jane Austen: Writer in the World.* Cambridge, 2017.

Tandon, Bharat. *Jane Austen and the Morality of Conversation.* London, 2003.

Tanner, Tony. *Jane Austen.* London, 1986.

Tave, Stuart. *Some Words of Jane Austen.* Chicago, 1973.

Todd, Janet, ed. *The Cambridge Companion to "Pride and Prejudice."* Cambridge, 2013.

Tomalin, Claire. *Jane Austen: A Life.* London, 1997.

Townshend, Dale, and Angela Wright, eds. *Ann Radcliffe, Romanticism and the Gothic.* Cambridge, 2014.

Waldron, Mary. *Jane Austen and the Fiction of Her Time.* Cambridge, 2001.

Wallace, Tara. *Jane Austen and Narrative Authority.* Basingstoke, UK, 1995.

Wiesenfarth, Joseph. *The Errand of Form: An Assay of Jane Austen's Art.* New York, 1967.

Wilt, Judith. *Ghosts of the Gothic: Austen, Eliot, and Lawrence.* Princeton, NJ, 1980.

INDEX

JEREMY BLACK is Emeritus Professor of History at the University of Exeter and a Senior Fellow both of Policy Exchange and of the Foreign Policy Research Institute. He is the author of many books, including *A Subject for Taste: Culture in Eighteenth-Century England, George III: America's Last King, England in the Age of Shakespeare,* and *Charting the Past: The Historical Worlds of Eighteenth-Century England.* Black is a recipient of the Samuel Eliot Morison Prize from the Society for Military History.